DOING THE RIGHT THING
Twelve Portraits in Moral Courage

By
Tom Cooper, Ph.D.

Published 2020 by Abramis academic publishing

www.abramis.co.uk

ISBN 978 1 84549 766 8

Typeset in Garamond

Abramis is an imprint of arima publishing.

arima publishing
ASK House, Northgate Avenue
Bury St Edmunds, Suffolk IP32 6BB
t: (+44) 01284 700321

www.arimapublishing.com

FOR MY OUTSTANDING …

WIFE, EILEEN FLANAGAN

DAUGHTER, ANGELICA COOPER

MENTOR, DAVID KARCHERE

PRESIDENT, LEE PELTON

lying - page 94

TABLE OF CONTENTS

Foreword   by Richard Keeble v

Preface   by Clifford Christians...vii

Acknowledgments...xii

Introduction...1

Chapters

  1. John F. Kennedy: Drawing a Line in the Sand.................................17

  2. Queen Esther: Anti-Semitism, Female Leadership and High Risk.........35

  3. Socrates: Death as a Teaching Moment 53

  4. John Adams: Peace at All Costs?..69

  5. William Wilberforce: Cheating with Integrity? 89

  6. Marie Curie: Radiant and at Risk 107

  7. Mohandas Gandhi: Fighting Fire Without Fire 127

  8. Harry Truman: The Most Important Ethical Decision Ever?.............147

  9. Rachel Carson: Against the Tide?...169

  10. Edward R. Murrow: The Camera Is Mightier than the Sword.............197

  11. Nelson Mandela: Speaking Truth to Power..................................221

  12. Malala Yousafzai: From Twilight to Dawn..................................241

  13. Ethical Decision Making: What it Takes 261

For Further Reading...281

FOREWORD

I have known Tom Cooper for many years and worked on a number of academic projects with him—particularly in connection with the UK-based *Ethical Space: The International Journal of Communication Ethics*, of which I have been the joint editor since its launch in 2003. He gave a very well-received talk to my students at the University of Lincoln when he was visiting the UK one year—and I regard him as one of the world's leading contemporary communication ethics specialists.

This, his latest book, carries all the passion, theoretical richness, and original insights which I associate with his work overall. Focusing in detail (and in always accessible ways) on how twelve individuals grapple with some extraordinary ethical dilemmas helps open new avenues for moral and political inquiry. The historical span is vast: from Queen Esther of Babylon (462-430 B.C.E.) to Malala Yousafzai, the young Pakistani educational activist who stood up to Taliban oppression and became the youngest recipient of the Nobel Peace Prize in 2014.

Moreover, as Cooper points out, the case studies cover eight national and ethnic groups; multiple political, philosophical, scientific, and religious perspectives; all major classes, and more than a dozen professions since some had two or more careers. Significantly, Mohandas Gandhi (1869–1948), the pacifist campaigner for Indian independence, and Nelson Mandela (1918–2013), the South African, anti-apartheid revolutionary leader who became President of his country after spending twenty-seven years in prison, are considered. And Marie Curie (1867–1934), the Nobel Prize-winning chemist and physicist, and Rachel Carson (1907–1964), the American marine biologist whose book *Silent Spring* (1962) and her other writings helped inspire global environmental campaigns, are two of the four featured women.

Cooper suggests in his "Introduction" that we can all learn from the examples set by "leaders who encountered some of the toughest ethical decisions of all time. Many key figures in history, and in the current news, have had to decide whether to sacrifice their health, lives, or reputation, on the one hand, or on the other, to undermine their consciences, commitments to integrity, country, and family." Thus, American President John Adams (1735–1826), William Wilberforce (1759–1833), leader of the UK movement to abolish the slave trade, and Edward R. Murrow (1908–1965), the American broadcaster and war reporter, as well as Queen Esther, "had to decide whether to take death threats seriously enough to end their quests to prevent further war, genocide, bullying, and slavery. Their decisions wrote history, a history which would be vastly different had any one of them taken a different path."

He is also careful to highlight surprising backstories to the ethical case studies. Few, for instance, are aware of the cost that testifying before Congress and even making a television appearance had upon Rachel Carson's life.

Moreover, Cooper (always systematic in his presentation) offers ten crucial ethical factors and then goes on to examine each of the case studies with these in mind. These factors include notions of fairness and justice, the importance of impact or consequences, the debate over ends and means, the significance of tone and atmosphere, issues relating to allegiance and loyalty—and so on.

Tom Cooper is clearly a super teacher: here he invites his readers (and students in general) to delve into the complexities of ethical decision-making because—as he stresses—it can be challenging, fascinating, engaging, and fun. Above all, he highlights the critical approach, the constant questioning and creative listening that lie at the heart of ethics. He invites us to question whether these twelve are exemplars for us (I personally, for instance, would debate the inclusion of some of those chosen). In addition, the text encourages us to draw up our own list of twelve moral heroes. I wonder who would feature in yours.

Richard Lance Keeble
University of Lincoln and Liverpool Hope University

PREFACE

This profound book teaches moral philosophy with ingenuity. Tom Cooper reimagines moral philosophy and demonstrates its reconstruction. Under the aegis of the theorizing few, moral philosophy is arid and marginal. But in this literary masterpiece, morality belongs to the human race across history and geography. Its stunning transformation of moral philosophy into public discourse is historic. *Doing the Right Thing* has the promise of becoming a twenty-first century classic.

Moral philosophy, in its descriptive aspect, accounts for the moral practices and traditions of particular persons or groups. It analyzes the way values function in decision-making. Its normative dimension studies what classes of conduct are worthy of praise or blame. And the critics are largely correct. Descriptive ethics isolated from theory does not enable the choice of ethically distinctive practices outside of the description. Normative strategies have tended to engage narrow issues in functional terms rather than generate sustainable concepts. With centripetal tightness in moral philosophy's various domains and stifling ambiguities about moral agency, Cooper's new model is welcome scholarship.

While this book does not aim to amend specific deficiencies in the status quo, it opens a visionary pathway where theory is a dynamic organism and moral heroism is the coherence modality. Cooper's new model reflects the ethicist Stephen Ward's call in 2019 for "radical conceptual reform" in which "new ideas are brought together into a comprehensive perspective;" ethical problems "can no longer be addressed properly by minor formulations of existing precepts. We need to dig deep intellectually. It is time to be philosophically radical."

Already in 1991, Hans Küng called for the moral philosophy this book represents. For Küng, today's complex and fragile world requires moral standards to survive, "It does not need a unitary religion and a unitary ideology, but it does need norms, values, and goals to bring it together." I welcome this "Preface" to elaborate on how *Doing the Right Thing* reconstructs moral philosophy as a response to what Küng calls the "current lack of certitude that marks the extraordinary age in which we live."

One notable transformation in Cooper's theory is a redefinition of virtue. Confucius (551–479 BC) was the first known person in history to create a morality of virtue. More than a century later, Aristotle (384–322 BC) developed virtue ethics systematically in the West. For the ages, they established the idea that excellence in character and not social position determines human status. When human beings develop their virtues to the fullest, they achieve what

Confucius called "harmony" and Aristotle *eudaemonia*. Virtue ethics is a profound idea in moral philosophy, and it attracts premier scholars yet today; though in its superficial forms, virtues such as tolerance become excuses for moral indifference.

Virtue ethics presumes that organizations and social systems can be morally revitalized by enabling virtuous people until their numbers reach a critical mass and organizations are transformed. However, depending on personal motivation while ignoring structural constraints is insubstantial.

Cooper moves creatively in and out of the personal and structural. His account of decision-makers to emulate does not isolate well-meaning persons from seemingly intractable institutions and entrenched structures. John Kennedy, John Adams, Edward R. Murrow, Rachel Carson, and Harry Truman, for example, are positioned at the ethical crossroads of personal obligation and political systems. For Mohandas Gandhi and Nelson Mandela, there was obviously a justice higher than the governing states in which they lived. Cooper's moral philosophy is coherent because he recognizes that normed phenomena are embedded in culture and history. He demonstrates what we know from cultural anthropology, that humans establish moral codes along the boundaries of their existence, without which no discursive meaning is possible.

The moral philosophy of *Doing the Right Thing* not only resolves the virtue-institution dilemma, but is over-the-horizon in understanding transnational and intercultural morality. UNESCO published its landmark *Many Voices, One World* in 1980 on the possibilities for democratic governance under "the new world information and communication order." The challenge theoretically and methodologically since MacBride is to replace the Eurocentric axis of moral philosophy with a decisively cosmopolitan model.

In shifting to a world matrix, moral philosophy has made advances in internationalizing such concepts as justice, equality, and reciprocity, and on the "one vs. many" problem inherent in globalization and multiculturalism. However, controversies persist that require a fundamental restructuring of moral philosophy as an intellectual enterprise: its nation-state bias, abstractionism, and relativism. Scholarly initiatives have been developed that distinguish cultural relativity and epistemological relativism, and that demonstrate the world mind in other problematics. But Cooper's moral philosophy is distinctively at the leadership edge of the field, international in letter and spirit, with none of the besetting limitations and without patchwork on the incongruities. Though these internationalizing issues are complex, let me summarize two of them in order to communicate the revolutionary character of this book's thirteen chapters as a unitary whole.

In Martha Nussbaum's pathbreaking *Frontiers of Justice* (2006), the future of ethics depends on overcoming its country-by-country orientation, "because all the major Western theories of social justice begin from the nation-state as their basic unit." The "world" in moral philosophy has typically invoked the political networks among the 96 countries and 61 territories of the world, each with sovereign rights and enforcement institutions. The concepts and policies of advanced Western democracies tend to create hierarchies, criticized as the industrial North's subjugation of the global South.

In contrast, Cooper's global imaginary is not statist but communal. The world's population is understood as a mosaic of people groups, a diverse composite of identities that intersect to form social bonds. The idea is that people groups have obligations beyond their lifeworld acquaintances and beyond the formalities of citizenship. Cooper does not merely account for generic human life but for particular persons in their communities across geography and history.

The dominant view in moral philosophy, as it has worked from a world mind, is that ethical principles are prescriptivist; they are absolutes in the sense of holding true for all rational beings over time and space. In this mathematical version of context-free rationality, linear abstractions replicate the globe's coordinate system of longitude and latitude. But rationalist absolutes belong to Western intellectual history and are legitimately critiqued as unsuitable for transnational and intercultural ethics.

Cooper advocates cross-cultural norms that are categorically distinct from the abstractions of rationalist ethics. His humanistic universals are derived from and conditioned by people's everyday existence, with variety in cultures emphasized rather than homogenized by theorems. Cooper restructures moral theory so that transnational values, such as esteem and recognition, restrain the range of normative decision-making. In his perspective, the moral domain is particular and universal at the same time. For Wilberforce, his choices were loyalty to himself and his family or to the oppressed generations of the human race. For Queen Esther, her own death or exile were at odds with the survival of the Jewish nation. Malala Yousafzai's personal tragedy speaks to the world. In interactive universals, value discourse grounded in everyday experience refers concurrently to our common humanity. The worthiness intrinsic to the human species represents a combination of individual uniqueness and the simultaneous dignity of our mutual humanity. As Cooper develops the idea of inner and outer authorities for his global theory, and schools us in the ten factors that distinguish conflicting values and principles, he forms overriding conceptions of the world with himself and his readers in it. In *My Father's House*, Kwame Appiah is correct about human identity, here inflected to Africa: "We will only solve our problems if we see them as problems arising out of a special situation."

Tom Cooper advances our thinking on virtue and internationalism, and his moral philosophy is also distinctive in its definition of the human. Humans as autonomous, rational individuals has been the prevailing view, with holistic human beings retheorizing moral philosophy in *Doing the Right Thing*. Challenging reductionist definitions, "humans as a complex whole" is the core idea in understanding the decision-making of its twelve portraits in moral courage.

In Western moral philosophy since the eighteenth-century Enlightenment, human beings have been considered sovereign as ends in themselves, and self-determination is the highest good. Rational choice becomes the foundation of deontological and utilitarian ethics when Kant assimilates ethics to logic. In John Stuart Mill's self-and-society dualism, individual liberty has priority over the moral order. Ethical systems that depend on these approaches are formalistic, grounding reason in an apparatus of neutral standards.

Cooper starts over intellectually with human existence rather than individual autonomy. He eschews the rational-choice tradition and represents a humanistic theory of language instead. His moral philosophy operates from a linguistic foundation that enables him to develop normative discourse instead of rules and abstract principles. From his perspective, "humans in lingual relation" is the key to understanding the purpose and meaning of human existence. The symbolic realm is a primal competence through which humanity discloses the fundamental conditions of its humanness. Therefore, natural language, rather than the artificial language of mathematical logic, is the mode of human understanding. Cooper develops his discursive moral philosophy from the natural languages of those struggling with life-changing dilemmas.

According to Cooper's portrayal of moral decision-making, the human conceptual framework is a composite of beings presently living, and of civilizations past, that continue to exist in art, music, literature, and ideas. In the philosophy of language that this book illustrates, understanding expands our existential horizon and deepens our humanity, not only to see more but to see differently. Cooper's moral philosophy engages enduring issues on the human agenda, even as he gives value-based depth to an alternative consciousness.

In this book's transformative moral philosophy, humans are seen as an organic unity in which the body, mind, and spirit live together in concert. He defines ethics as "the process of making difficult moral choices," and each mini-drama is not, first of all, an intellectual comprehension of propositions, but moral judgments which congeal the desire and willingness that belong to our unitary wholeness. Rational calculation and impartial reflection are replaced by the risk-takers' experience with moral issues in their day-to-day interactions with what they had learned as the good.

Our symbolic, linguistic humanness means that interpretation is the key to understanding humans, their capacities, the meaning of life, promises, and obligations. Beyond the human need to survive is the need for meaningfulness in human interaction. Therefore, as this book makes compelling, we are able to form a conception of the world of the good and to engage in critical reflection about its meaning for us. Since symbols with multiple meanings are the material basis for Cooper's moral philosophy, he overcomes a bias toward the essence of the self as thinking substance.

Zygmunt Bauman calls our mobile age one of "liquid modernity," and in response, *Doing the Right Thing* proposes contemplation as the basis for action. Nancy Fraser in 1992 pleaded for spaces of withdrawal and regrouping. Morally astute narratives are created in and implemented through these discursive arenas. As Cooper explains it, they are alternative lifeworlds where value-based practices are given "reflective equilibrium" and a plurality of virtues are integrated into a moral way of life.

As the provocative narratives in *Doing the Right Thing* indicate, the meaning of such ethical concepts as goodness and duty are multidimensional. The lives of groups of people in the global imaginary are loaded with multiple interpretations and grounded in cultural intricacy and paradox. The agency of holistic humans is existentially intersubjective. In dwellings where language, symbols, and poetics illuminate the mystery of being and create counter-narratives, human existence is given stability.

Czechoslovakia's playwright and president Vaclàv Havel (1936–2011) understood the issues at stake at this historic juncture in terms that parallel *Doing the Right Thing.* "We are rightly preoccupied with finding the key to ensure the survival of a civilization that is global and at the same time clearly multicultural," he said in *Vital Speeches of the Day* (1994). But mechanisms for peaceful coexistence "are doomed to fail if they do not grow out of something deeper, out of generally held values." The twelve decision-making visionaries of this book live out what Havel calls the "miracle of our existence." Cooper presents in harmony these prophets for this contentious age where, as Havel puts it, "everything appears possible, but nothing is certain." In its elaborations of conscientious difference-makers in their various histories, *Doing the Right Thing* establishes the agenda for twenty-first century moral philosophy. This book's invigorating ideas and perceptive applications enable us to flourish on a high-road journey, its theory motivated by the conviction that human beings are living good lives when they do the right thing.

Clifford G. Christians
University of Illinois

ACKNOWLEDGMENTS

No one could have a more kind and supportive President (Lee Pelton), Provost (Michaele Whelan), ensemble of Deans (Rob Sabal, Jan Roberts-Breslin, Jim Hoppe, Raul Reis, and Amy Ansell), and Chair (Brooke Knight) than I have had throughout the writing and editing of *DOING THE RIGHT THING*. Ethics colleagues at Emerson such as Pablo, David, Betsy, Greg, Manny, Jerry, and others have also always been there with great ideas and support when it was time to think ethics.

A wide array of other ethics colleagues—Cliff at Illinois, Ted at Stanford, Tamar at MIT, Anantha in Texas, Ed at Berkeley, Jeff at Harvard, Deni at USF, and so many others, including those no longer active (e.g. Jay and Ralph in Utah; Mike, Don, and Lou, who have passed on), have done so much to keep our standards high. I also wish to thank those beyond academe such as Sigall at the United Nations; and Andrea, Greg, Merel, and Jochen with their special initiatives, with whom I have had the privilege to work on ethics in other ways. In one way or another, all have wisely informed and supported this book.

And there are so many colleagues in other fields who would not call themselves ethicists but who have nourished my thinking and been close friends—Bob and Scott in Emerson's performing arts; Tom, Jan, Cher, John, Shujen, and Shaun in the visual arts; Sharon, Jason, and their team guiding our students; Sylvia, Jabari, Tamera, Tamia, and friends in our Center for Social Justice who always hold the light high.

In a sense this book was inspired by all of them and by my marvelous students over thirty-eight years at Emerson College and briefly at Harvard, the University of Hawaii, the University of Maryland, Middle Tennessee State University, and Temple University. They have taught me more than most of the books I have readily ingested.

I have always been blessed with wise mentors not only in academe but in life itself. A very close friend, David at Sunrise Ranch in Colorado, has not only been a constant source of inspiration but also a wise guide to my daughter as well. Many others at Sunrise—Dorian, Jerry, Shareen, Bob, Keahi, Ruud, Jane, Uma, Gary, and on and on, are part of a family of spirited friends I greatly value including associates worldwide such as Howard, Anne-Lise, Andrew, Ruth, Hugh, Barb, Marilyn, Patricia, and many others.

My great English colleague, Richard Keeble, referred me to Richard Franklin and his excellent press called Abramis. I am most thankful for the partnership with both wise Richards. Elizabeth Heijkoop and Zoe Kopp-Webber, my outstanding editors, have been brilliant word sculptors and masters in the strong improvement of my manuscript. And my publicist, Lissa Warren, has been a terrific leader in her field (who literally wrote the book about publicizing one's books), wise advisor, and strong friend.

If you find a mug stating, "world's best partner," please send it to my wife, Eileen, who has supported this book and my life like none other. She is a tremendous best friend and kindly, wise advisor to all my work.

If you find the matching mug labelled "world's best daughter," mail it directly to Angelica, for whom I am most grateful and of whom I am most proud. I am so thankful for her love and commitment to brightly shine her light.

And there are so many friends who defy classification—the extra-talented and radiant Kristin, the life-long Sundance musical clan (Arnie, Steve, Geoff, Rebecca, Dan, and sometimes Jerome), spiritual partners like Rabbi Al, Rev. Dockery, director Julie, and Spirit of Emerson leaders Sharon, Jaqi, Eiki, Raz, Gabby, Rebecca, and Brandon. We have such truly gracious Massachusetts neighbors and neighbors-to-be in "aloha land," where my great PTC friends— Sharon, Grace, Kate, and many others—reside.

Speaking of PTC, I also acknowledge so many other great friends including Tara, Bruce, Tim, Paul, Lynn, Joe, Heather, Liz, and a great tribe of leaders worldwide.

My parents were exceptional teachers and supporters. Their Cooper and Pardue families have always been wonderful kin, allies, and friends.

Beyond these many friends and family, this volume could not have ever been written without a pre-existing ethical condition—the one created by the twelve who inspired this book, from Esther to Malala. And there are so many other ethics exemplars, many of whom inspired me, that several sequels could be written about them.

Finally, there have also been great "ethicists" who expressed themselves via electronic media who have engrossed me over the years—David Smith, who started the World Good News Network; Rod Serling and Norman Lear, who cleverly asked us to be more open-minded about social justice; Jean-Luc Godard, who led a revolution in thought and cinematic vision; and the many who raised consciousness about economic, gender, and racial justice such as Spike Lee who inspired the name for this book.

Virtually all of these exemplars acknowledged something higher than themselves such as the focal point of their faith (e.g. God, Allah, or Krishna) or, if they were more secular, they called it "integrity," "justice," or "a better world." By whatever name they knew it, and you or I know it, the ultimate acknowledgement must go to that "something higher" from whence comes the all-important impulse to do the right thing.

Dr. Tom Cooper, February 2020,
Boston, Massachusetts

INTRODUCTION

For years I have asked my students, "How many of you believe in torture?" Very few hands are ever raised. I then follow this question with another one: "What if we knew that there is a terrorist in this classroom who is about to kill all of us with a bomb?" And then I ask: "What if we knew that this terrorist would succumb to torture and defuse the bomb? How many of you would recommend torture in that case?" Far more hands are raised.

These and similar questions force us to consider what actions are "unethical" and what conditions might lead us to change our minds. Is ethics only about who is impacted? For example, in the case above, torture often seems more justified to many when it is used to save our own lives. But is it ethical for us to put our lives above the lives of others? Is it ethical to deliberately create and sustain horrendous pain for a fellow member of humanity?

Sometimes I ask students, "If you had to choose between saving one or two lives, would you save the life of one bright young high school student who has her entire life ahead of her, or would you save two seventy-five-year-old grandparents who have four loving children and eleven grandchildren?" No matter how much sympathetic detail I provide about the elderly couple or the youth, my students are never unanimous in their vote nor in their justifications.

Sometimes I ask: "If you were the captain of the lifeboats on the Titanic, and had only one seat remaining in the last lifeboat, to whom would you give the seat if two people approached you at exactly the same time? The first is a black woman with a second-class ticket and an infant in her arms who insists that her other children are already on the lifeboat. The second is a white man with a first-class ticket who claims to be Jonas Salk. He says he has found a cure for polio, which only he can explain and implement to save thousands if not millions of lives."

All of these questions force us to think and also to feel. Being ethical is not just about mouthing platitudes such as "everyone should be moral," or "the world needs good people." In at least some of these cases it is not initially clear what is meant by "ethical" or "good." When our choices are not between clear-cut good and evil but are instead between two goods, two evils, or two (or more) unknowns, what do we do?

This book is about substantial leaders like Gandhi, Mandela, Adams, Curie, and Malala, each of whom faced vexing choices about the lesser of two evils, the greater of two goods, and between hazardous unknowns. How did they make such challenging decisions, and how do we do so?

We may claim that few people must make such extreme choices involving torture, saving lives, and filling one last seat on a lifeboat. And yet, while we may not face such extremes, we all do routinely make moral choices every month, if not every week or day.

For example, depending upon our roles in life, we may need to decide whether to oppose or support capital punishment; if and when to move our parents to nursing homes; whom to hire, promote, and fire; whether to oppose or ignore workplace injustices; which civic causes and candidates to promote, ignore, or oppose; whether to pass or fail borderline students; what to screen and permit our children to screen via on-line and traditional media; when to protect or report loved ones or friends who are breaking the law; whether to own and use a gun; what substances to put into our bodies, including when we are pregnant; which submissions, applicants, and bids to accept and reject; what behavioral, social, and sexual boundaries to impose upon our children; whether to have, advocate for, or oppose abortions; whether and when to enlist in the military; if, how, and when to intervene when there are problems with addiction or abuse within our families or offices; and how and when to end our lives and those of people in severe pain or comas. This list of ethical choices seems endless.

There are no universal rules for handling such dilemmas. Our parents, advisors, religion, philosophy, government, colleagues, educators, lawyers, friends, and culture may be key vectors in determining what we decide. However, some of them may be ambivalent about such decisions or in the aggregate they may provide conflicting guidance. Moreover, for some of us, our inner voice is as important—if not more important—than these outer ones. What to do?

LEARNING FROM MORAL EXEMPLARS

One answer to this question is that we can learn from "the greats"— philosophers, spiritual leaders, and other thinkers—such as Aristotle, Lao-Tzu, the Buddha, Kant, Mill, Jesus, Moses, Mohammed, Rawls, Gilligan, Chief Seattle, and a host of others. And indeed, one dimension of this book is the provision of exposure to such thought leaders as we examine twelve dynamic case studies involving well-known world leaders, scientists, advocates, spiritual exemplars, etc. You'll learn about some of these moral thought leaders and their approaches to ethical decision-making in each chapter.

But this book goes much further by also asking "what may we learn from those who actually faced difficult, often life-and-death dilemmas themselves?" No doubt all of us can learn from leaders who encountered some of the toughest ethical decisions of all time. Many key figures in history, and in the news, have had to decide whether, on the one hand, to sacrifice their health, lives, or reputations—or on the other, to undermine their consciences, commitment to integrity, their countries, and families.

President Harry Truman faced what may have been the greatest ethical dilemma of all. Upon becoming president of the United States, he soon had to decide whether to drop "the bomb" upon innocent civilians, and thus irreversibly unleash the nuclear age, or to allow nations ruled by dictators to develop their own nuclear weapons first while they were concurrently torturing and killing thousands of "his boys"—young American soldiers.

Seventy years later, a Pakistani girl named Malala had to decide whether or not to stand up to brutal Taliban assassins who were bombing dozens of girls' schools and beheading the local police. Half a century earlier, despite terminal illness, biologist Rachel Carson had to determine if she should testify before Congress and engage in national media interviews in order to limit the use of toxic pesticides. Doing so could prematurely terminate her award-winning work, her hidden, long-time same-sex romance, her care for her beloved son, and undoubtedly her life.

President John Adams, Queen Esther, Edward R. Murrow, and William Wilberforce were among those who had to decide whether or not to take death threats seriously enough to end their quests to prevent war, genocide, bullying, or slavery. Their decisions wrote history, a history which would be vastly changed had any one of them taken a different path.

Vexing ethical dilemmas have come to people of all ages and stages. Many have stared death in the face—be it death to career, health, reputation, body, family, democracy, an entire species, or humanity. Key decisions made by others have determined whether you and I would now be alive.

In 1967 my own father, a U.S. naval officer, was suddenly forced to make instant decisions that had bearing upon which sailors would live and die during a sea emergency. An aircraft carrier, the USS *Forrestal*, had exploded into fire. Not everyone who was dying could be saved. Some sailors might be spared by being rushed to over-crowded medical facilities, while others continued to be burned alive.

My father's decisions, although possibly the right ones, changed his life, thinking, memories, and relationships for years to come. He was later tasked with reliving the incident again and again when visiting and comforting dozens of families who had lost their young sons, fathers, and husbands.

Such visits meant that he frequently asked himself: "Did I make the right decisions that day? Am I responsible for premature and horrible deaths?"

One life that was spared that day, although not by my father, was that of a young officer on the USS *Forrestal* named John McCain—the very same John

McCain who became a U.S. senator who cast deciding votes in serious congressional debates. Some of these votes changed and saved lives. Earlier, McCain had refused to give into immense pressure when held as a prisoner of war. Such action may have saved other lives.

How would U.S. public affairs, laws, and congressional priorities be different if another life had been spared instead of McCain's? Who else would have perished or been saved years later if McCain had died on the *Forrestal?* For example, his daughter Meghan McCain, the television commentator, would never have been born, and his wife, Cindy, would still be Cindy Hensley, or would have married someone else.

We might all be speaking another language, or never have been born, had history been sculpted by different human choices. This book, a story of stories, is about perplexing ethical choices that carved the human narrative and reshaped millions of lives.

These stories also reveal the tools and factors that many leaders and thinkers have used and considered when encountering what was seemingly a moral "dead end"—tools and factors which many citizens might wish our own leaders would employ. Some of these are tools for our own workshop, since we are all likely to face serious ethical decisions at some points in our lives.

In that sense this is also a handbook for all of us. An overview of how we might make vexing decisions will be outlined in the final chapter. We will review a variety of factors, with analysis and inspiration about how great hearts and minds resolved taxing dilemmas. Specific patterns appear when you look at case after case.

THE TWELVE

I have selected twelve "ethics exemplars" from the past and present. With the exception of the introductory case, I have presented them in chronological order. The twelve are Queen Esther, Socrates, John Adams, William Wilberforce, Marie Curie, Mohandas Gandhi, Harry Truman, Rachel Carson, Edward R. Murrow, John F. Kennedy (presented first), Nelson Mandela, and Malala Yousafzai.

These are stories of high drama with important impact not only upon each of these individual's lives, but also upon the generations that followed and those yet to come. Each involved a moral dilemma that pressured the profiled player to feel torn between allegiances and to be fearful of the outcome.

Overall, these twelve stories cover twenty-five centuries; eight national and ethnic groups; multiple political, philosophical, scientific, and religious perspectives; all major classes; and more than a dozen professions, since some of these twelve had two or more careers. The cases are sufficiently diverse to suggest that no group, gender, or people hold a monopoly on ethical decision-making or upon integrity.

Each case is unique and intriguing. Each has a hidden backstory. The first and last (Esther and Malala) were the youngest to encounter life-and-death moral choices. Esther was a teenage queen, and Malala won the Nobel Peace Prize at the age of seventeen. When encountering his first major ethical dilemma, Nelson Mandela was only twenty-one.

Historically, most of these exemplars were seen as controversial or even anti-social. Therefore, no attempt to canonize any of them as saints has been made. I wish instead to make their human lives and decisions accessible, if not admirable or exemplary. Each reader may choose whether each character is saint or sinner, real or paper hero.

WHY THESE TWELVE?

In times of flawed leadership, economic adversity, increasing violence, and government deception, we humans often look for heroes to overcome a pocked environment and consistently dark news. Never have so many heroes been marketable and popular—the Avengers, Wonder Woman, Batman, Supergirl, Antman, Superman, Harry Potter, Iron Man, the Lord of the Rings, Spiderman, and far too many others to name. In the aggregate such characters and stories dominate the electronic and print media. So too have real-world heroes such as the "hit squad" in Zero Dark Thirty; first responders to hurricanes, floods, 9/11, and mass shootings; Navy Seals, and many more. Both epic superheroes and real-life heroes embody our eternal search for role models.

Ultimately, superheroes are justice beacons who protect a virtuous world order and save underdog victims. So too are the heroes of history from Mandela to Malala, from Esther to Carson. They championed the abused and marginalized. No matter how different and shaded each of their biographies, all twelve held in common an over-arching sense of ethical purpose driven by personal conscience.

That does not mean they were perfect people, nor that their bedroom, boardroom, or back-room behavior was virtuous. Another book could be written about the personal blind spots, and often unresolved and sometimes failed relationships several faced.

One reason why some of the best-known candidates (names like Lincoln, Jesus, Muhammad, Washington, Keller, Buddha, Dubois, Gore, Frankl, Obama, Mother Theresa, and others come to mind) were not included is precisely because their stories are so well known. I have chosen both lesser-known moral leaders and well-known historical figures whose hidden "backstory" surprises us.

In my research I have sought to discover submerged contexts and facts that have long been obscured. For example, although many know much about Abraham Lincoln's fight to end slavery, fewer know the almost unbelievable story of William Wilberforce, who was the greatest single force ending the slave trade in England. While some may know the name Rachel Carson, few know the cost that testifying before Congress and even making a television appearance had upon her life.

While every schoolboy and girl has heard that Socrates drank the hemlock, few understand his reasons for consuming poison when he had a clear path of escape, not to mention a family and many students in his care. The other *dramatis personae* selected had unusual or latent factors influencing them, and were forced to make agonizing decisions that transformed their narratives into mystery, not just biography.

WHY ETHICS AND MORAL COURAGE?

Some have called recent decades the "Age of Enron," or the "9/11 Apocalypse," or the "#MeToo Era." We also hear much about the epoch in which we are trumped by "alternative facts" and "fake news." The media are constantly targeted, if not scapegoated. In turn, the media have far more to say about unethical, criminal, or morally immature behavior today than ever before—and not just about Trump and his colleagues and rivals. As I write this, much more is reported about Kim Jong-Un, Felicity Huffman, Rupert Murdoch, Whitey Bulger, Jeffrey Epstein, the Boston Marathon bombers, terrorists in London, Vladimir Putin, the "Hollywood Madam" Heidi Fleiss, R. Kelly, Kevin Spacey, Lori Loughlin, and Equifax executives—than about the integrity of those at the opposite end of the spectrum.

After all, it is an age in which even those most identified with the lighter world of comedy such as Robin Williams, Louis C.K., and Bill Cosby, point toward tragedy. Not to mention that the spotlight has also been upon another supposed source of light: religion. The Catholic priesthood and some cult spiritual leaders have been pocked with a narrative of abuse and pedophilia worldwide.

Business is not off the hook either. Enron leaders Ken Lay and Jeffrey Skilling faced moral decisions and entirely ignored their own corporate ethics code. Executives at Hewlett-Packard, Goldman Sachs, Equifax, Wells Fargo, and many other corporations have also made headlines for questionable behavior.

But what about those who struggled long into the night facing similar decisions, who took one for the team and faced the music?

It is important to identify and acknowledge people of character so that there are visible role models available not only to our youth, but for all of us who face moral pressure. Václav Havel, Juan Manuel Santos, Cesar Chavez, Liu Xiaobo, Ellen Johnson Sirleaf, Leymah Gbowee, and Tawakkol Karman are examples. Yet the fact that these people, five of whom are recent Nobel Peace Prize winners, are hardly household names, is a case in point about who steals the spotlight. Whose behind-the-scenes and between-the-sheets deeds do we know more about—Kim Kardashian, Pete Rose, Caitlyn Jenner, Kendra Wilkinson, Tiger Woods, Paris Hilton, and Antonio Brown—or the civic leaders portrayed in Caroline Kennedy's *Profiles in Courage for our Time*? Can you name even two of them?

Somehow, we know more about Mel Gibson's use of racial slurs and Pamela Anderson's sex tapes than about those who may well be saving lives and preventing wars. Mass killers in schools and public venues, whether in France, England, the Middle East, Texas, Connecticut, Washington, Florida, Virginia, or Colorado, are usually a sustained lead story. Yet those who all but miraculously nurse and doctor some of the victims back to health, whether in Boston, Las Vegas, Virginia Beach, or Ethiopia, often remain unknown.

Understandably stories about Ferguson, Charlottesville, El Paso, Baltimore's Freddy Gray, the Confederate flag and statues, shootings inside of churches, malls, and mosques captivate the public attention. And yet reportedly far more acts of terror and murder have been prevented in recent years, many of which remain widely unknown. So why not provide a book that counterbalances our global tragedy with the precedents of victory?

ETHICS IN THE CLASSROOM AND IN REAL LIFE

In the classroom we can acquaint students with a wide spectrum of possible solutions to arresting ethical questions. Teachers have typically presented options such as how Aristotle, Kant, Mill, Rawls, and other "ethics experts" would have made such decisions. In this age of diversity, many of us teachers also present ethical options from multiple cultures and from multiple genders.

One teacher might ask students how Confucius, Chief Luther Standing Bear, or feminist Carol Gilligan might have handled a vexing decision. And another ethicist might ask how leaders from primary world philosophies—perhaps Hindu, Islamic, or Judeo-Christian; socialist or capitalist—might have acted.

Being aware of this menu of options helps the student learn to engage in moral reasoning from multiple perspectives. Such training also opens the mind to numerous modes of thinking. Ultimately, when we face ethical decisions in the real world, whether we are students, professionals, or unemployed, we may have to make snap judgments without any time to consult the texts of Kant or Gilligan. Or if we do have more time, and we can consult others, we often discover that even the great ethicists and our own trusted confidants might disagree about how to handle the same situation. What do we do?

BEYOND HYPOTHETICALS

Over the years I have received calls and e-mails from dozens of former students and colleagues facing stressful and sometimes complex ethical decisions on the job and in their private lives. Their ethical dilemmas are no longer classroom, hypothetical cases.

For example, a former student was asked by his employer to "creatively round off" various numbers on the company income tax report, and to delete a few incidentals because "everyone else does it." Should she risk losing her job over such a widespread practice?

Some years ago, I heard from a foreign student that he had been drafted into the military and would be facing combat within a week. He had been trained to kill others, but he did not see how he could actually do so when the moment of combat arrived. Indeed, there are innumerable stories of soldiers in combat who faced agonizing decisions about when and whether to kill. And many officers have faced similar dilemmas in which they struggled to determine the extent to which they should endanger their troops. Many of these precisely followed orders, but others hesitated, deliberately missed their targets, chose a different path, or briefly delayed their missions to save lives. Some felt that, although they were wrong within a military context, they were right according to humane, universal ethics.

One of my students from an African country explained to me that he must receive an "A" grade in my class. He said that he had no choice whatsoever. When I asked him why, he answered that without top grades, he would lose his scholarship. And without his scholarship, he would be deported back to his home country, where his people were being slaughtered. He feared that he faced certain death unless I rewarded him with an "A" on his final exam. What to do?

Without identifying this international student, whom I have not seen in years, I tell his story to the class. I ask my other students: "What grade would you give this African student, if we assume that he is telling the truth? If you were the teacher, and he had earned a 'C' on his final exam, what grade should he receive?"

I then explain that ethics is not simply something they will face later in the real world, but it is something I and others face in the classroom and other parts of campus every week when we are grading, writing letters of recommendation, making personnel decisions about whom we promote and terminate, and other issues. Professors and students perpetually face issues of plagiarism, academic fraud, and cheating on exams. No profession, classroom, or person is exempt from ethical questions.

PERSONAL DECISION-MAKING

At a certain point the question is no longer "what would Aristotle (or Lao-Tzu or Nel Noddings) have done?" The question becomes "what will I do?" In writing this book, I felt it might be helpful not only for students, but for all those who face ethical decisions, to know how people we greatly revere have handled difficult dilemmas. Some of their decisions involved millions of lives and turned thousands of hairs gray.

DECONSTRUCTING AN ETHICAL DILEMMA

Sometimes it is helpful, both in the classroom and in life, to break down an ethical decision into some of the key factors that lie beneath, to see what is really involved. Throughout this book I will provide a list of ten important factors that often inform ethical decision-making. In each chapter I will explain how these factors figured into the important cases of Queen Esther, Socrates, Adams, Gandhi, Curie, Murrow, Kennedy, Wilberforce, Carson, Truman, Malala, and Mandela.

Discovering and considering these ten underlying factors can be helpful to all of us. For example, I ask not only my students, but also myself the following questions when faced with a vexing conundrum: Who might be helped or hurt, and to what degree? What precedent might I be setting if others replicate my actions? Are there unintended consequences I might discover if I think further about the impact of this action? Will my decision be perceived as fair and transparent by all? Do my desired ends truly justify the means I am choosing? When taking a stand, what values and principles am I advocating? Am I appropriately employing, or am I abusing, the power others trust me to use for the welfare of all? No matter what the short-term outcome of my decision is, will the long-term consequences be of service to my community and to humanity?

These and other related questions often take me deeper into the case such that I can make a wiser, more informed choice. I also often consult with other ethicists and those involved in the situation. I feel better about cogitating in this way and conclude that I can live with myself, since I did my best to consider as many pertinent questions, factors, principles, and points of view as possible.

These are the ten important factors as listed below. Many of them were considered by the decision-makers in this book, so I will list and discuss their relevance toward the end of each chapter.

1. **Notions of fairness and justice:** Many members of the cast of this book were driven by a sense of what seemed just or fair, whether within or beyond their own cultures. Gandhi, Mandela, Esther, Malala, and Wilberforce, for example, all felt that there was a justice higher than that of the government of the state in which they lived. Many ideas about fairness and justice, some of which seem to conflict with one another, will be introduced throughout the twelve cases.

2. **Impact or consequences:** Some philosophers, such as the notable English thinker John Stuart Mill (1806-1873), articulated that outcomes, or consequences, are important. "All's well that ends well" is one desired goal of a dilemma for such utilitarians. Of course, "well" can have different meanings, and we must all ask about costs when we look at outcomes. We will do so in the chapters to come.

3. **Ends and means:** Some famous ethicists have argued that the consequences are not as important as the way they come about. The German philosopher Immanuel Kant (1724-1804) proffered that one ought never lie, even if it might save a life. In a similar manner, he felt human beings should never be used as only a means, but rather each person has intrinsic importance as an end of himself. Thus, no matter how great the potential outcome, Kant insisted that we cannot use people as stepping stones, nor employ deception to obtain a positive consequence. The means to an end greatly matters. Many others have disagreed to varying degrees. In each case we will evaluate whether the key historical figure felt that the ends were more important than the means.

4. **Tone and atmosphere:** Some moralists reason that it is ultimately the tone that one models or demonstrates that matters most in an ethical decision. Thus, for some the objectionable tone of human torture is unacceptable no matter what the outcome. If a father is smoking a cigarette while telling his children not to smoke, he has no credibility. He is literally creating a cloudy atmosphere while advocating a clear one. Emerson put it this way: "Stop talking. Who you are thunders over you so loudly, I can't hear a word you are saying." We will consider to what extent tone and atmosphere mattered in each decision, and to what degree it should also matter to us when we make decisions.

5. **Motivation and higher law:** In murder trials, the verdicts and penalties are quite different if the murder is shown to be in self-defense rather than pre-meditated. Depending on the motivation, the same person pulling the same trigger may be seen either as a criminal, victim, or hero. Thus, a person's reason for making an (im-)moral decision matters. In most ethical systems, but not all, making a moral choice which is self-serving is seen as less virtuous than if the same choice is motivated by service to others, or to a higher law or greater good.

6. **Allegiance and loyalty:** In the second chapter, Esther has conflicting allegiances to her husband and mentor, to state and religion, and to her people and royal court. Many ethical decisions involve two or even multiple opposing allegiances to people who matter to the actor. Consider a judge who must sentence his best friend's son to death; should the matter of loyalty cause him to reduce the sentence if he would not do the same for any other offender? All humans face potentially conflicting loyalties and sometimes must make agonizing choices.

   Many have claimed that their highest loyalty is to what, for others, is an abstraction: an ultimate allegiance to a higher power such as God or Buddha or Allah, or the truth, or humanity, or conscience. But because belief systems differ, two groups may claim to give highest allegiance to the truth or to their god(s) or another ultimate belief, and still be at war with each other. To what extent should loyalties be a basis for ethical decision-making, and which loyalties, if any, should be prioritized?

7. **Values and principles:** Behind every ethical dilemma there are values and principles that compete for the upper hand. For example, if I value both individual freedom and parental protection, it becomes harder for me to determine what type of curfew to impose upon my thirteen-year-old daughter than if I prefer or value only one of these. Since legendary

journalist Edward R. Murrow (chapter 10) equally valued truth and reputation, it made it harder for him to broadcast a news story that told the truth about—and thus destroyed the reputation of—an American hero.

Values and principles may come into conflict when one considers that they are as different as "women and children first" and "all men (cf. people) are created equal." We will consider others in conflict in forthcoming chapters.

8. **Cultural context:** Obviously different cultures give different emphasis and validity to specific values and principles. In what might be called the "Vatican culture" of Rome, divine value is given to embryonic life such that human abortion is unthinkable. Yet an atheistic culture might value embryonic life far less. In China, baby boys have traditionally been more valued than infant girls, as was also the case during the reign of Persian King Xerxes in the culture known to Queen Esther (see chapter 2). Within John Adams' 18th century U.S. culture (chapter 4), free men were more highly valued than slaves, a value which William Wilberforce challenged a century later in England (chapter 5).

The host context is always at play as a factor in ethical decisions. For example, in Esther's story (chapter 2), the King was supremely valued as both the penultimate human leader and a deity on earth. But by the era of William Wilberforce (chapter 5), the divine right of kings was no longer accepted, and thus parliament was valued as much or even more than royalty. Cultural context substantially contributes to an understanding of what is considered to be moral and of value.

9. **Implications:** Immanuel Kant suggested a neat formula for making ethical decisions. Roughly stated, his first "categorical imperative" asked that a person should imagine a world in which everyone follows his or her example when making a moral decision. For example, if I am going to stay home from work whenever I feel mild discomfort, then I am asked to envision a world in which everyone who feels slightly unpleasant stays home from work. Before I decide whether or not to phone in "sick," I might ask: "What if all police, doctors, soldiers, nurses, bankers, ambulance drivers, garbage collectors, and firefighters stayed home from work whenever they felt slightly uncomfortable?" Although we can't foresee all long-term implications, asking questions of this sort helps us realize that there may be unforeseen ripples and outcomes with almost all decisions.

10. **Proportion and balance:** When multiple loyalties, principles, values, risks, consequences, notions of fairness, ends, means, motivations, contexts, and implications compete for attention, how does a decision-maker know how much weight to give each one? Complexity and confusion could drown the decision-making process. Aristotle's notion of finding a midpoint between excess and deficiency suggests that one might find the point of balance—but where is that point, and does it vary for each case? Ultimately, upon which of the other nine factors above does the final decision rest? What does a wise and balanced decision look like? Can it be truly justified?

These ten factors will be expanded and applied to all of the cases to help us better understand the anatomy of decision-making. Ideally, we will become better decision-makers ourselves.

Many groups employ professional ethics codes, ethicists, policies, trainings, and guidelines. These too may be studied, compared, refined, and discussed as part of classroom ethics education. However, Enron used a 62-page code of ethics that was ignored—and Enron is regarded as a tragedy within both the history of business and social ethics.

It has been demonstrated repeatedly that codes and trainings are only as effective as those who model and implement them. So, ethics education and decision-making are not only about classroom training and company policies, but also about what is modeled at the top and consistently practiced. Similarly, it is demonstrated in the case studies within this book that while training, vision, and background are important, it is ultimately how that vision was implemented during a perturbing crisis that mattered.

SITUATIONAL ETHICS

To my view I have wonderful students whom I greatly admire. They ask important questions such as "but isn't ethics relative?" or, phrased differently, "doesn't ethics depend upon the situation?" or "doesn't ethics depend upon your profession or your nationality and, if relevant, your religion?" All of these are important variations on a time-honored debate among ethicists about this question: "Are there ethical universals which transcend time, culture, and space?" In other words: "If it's the right thing to do, isn't it *always* the right thing to do?"

Naturally I honor these questions, and the chapters that follow illustrate the importance of the cultural background, role, and situation of each person involved. And yet I answer my students who feel that all ethics are relative in this way: "Despite the importance of situations, culture, and role, I cannot imagine a situation which, for example, morally justifies genocide, or rape, or child abuse. Can you?" Usually the room falls silent.

Nor can I imagine other ethicists I have worked with worldwide voicing moral arguments that defend genocide, rape, or child abuse. So, one tension within the forthcoming personal dilemmas to be discussed is the one between those universal moral laws that virtually all ethicists support, and the situational and cultural factors that argue for exceptions to those laws.

It has often been claimed that one valuable tenet of a liberal arts education is that it accommodates and acquaints us with numerous points of view. One learns to see the world from multiple perspectives and disciplines. Thus, a lesson that students in many ethics classes learn is that, at least in some situations, there may be no single right answer.

For example, the answer might be very different for a Marxist than, say, for a First Nations thinker who honors spirituality. A political scientist may value aspects of a case differently than an economist or a professor of law. A liberal arts university welcomes and is earmarked by the interplay of such diverse perspectives.

THE REAL WORLD

However, the world is not populated only with such pluralists who can mix and choose from a wide menu of ethical approaches. For example, there are those at the military academies who do not debate whether killing is right or wrong. Instead, they are taught an ethic which names the conditions, candidates, boundaries, and protocol for killing. Similarly, those within certain fundamentalist religious colleges may not debate questions about whether abortion and infidelity (cf. adultery) are ever morally justified. In many such institutions there is no prevailing passion to fully honor and entertain all points of view.

As students join the workforce they enter a population with mixed ethical training—some of those they meet are trained by religious leaders and by teachers in religious colleges; others are trained by higher-ups in their profession, including military, medical, business, and legal professionals; others are primarily trained by their parents and caregivers; still others are trained in liberal arts settings. And then there are those who are trained within all or none of the above.

To further complicate the matter, many of these ethical training patterns are contradictory. A person's religion may teach him "thou shalt not kill," while his training as a professional policeman or soldier may teach him precisely those situations in which killing is justified. There are multiple other examples in which an individual's personal ethic may be contradicted by her professional or cultural ethic.

Ethical dilemmas are not always, or even often, straightforward. Indeed, in some classrooms students might spend an entire week or month on a single case study. Whether we all agree about which ethical approach to use, we often agree that more and better ethical thinking is needed.

Great ethics instruction, whatever else it does, gives new thinking tools to us so we may make more considered, and ideally more humane, decisions no matter what pressures we face. Learning about how others faced even more stressful moral decisions than we do often provides us with fresh insights and approaches.

AN OPEN DOOR AND AN OPEN MIND

So, welcome to my classroom. I often ask students: "Are you an ethical person?" By the end of the class the answer is often different than the reply at the beginning. When students decide to justify torture or the death of one victim in order to save the lives of two others, I jokingly warn them that I will be informing their parents that their children endorse cruelty and homicide. And yet in real life, the questions of whose health, welfare, and life to save are no laughing matter.

In the chapters that follow, we can all be students discovering where we might draw the line, and also learn how "the greats" made their own decisions. We may also be thinkers who learn from the overall patterns.

Ethical decision-making may be challenging, but it can also be fascinating, engaging, and fun. To my view, what is most important is to keep an open door, an open heart, and an open mind.

We are about to encounter many decisions that have drastically altered history. The ones that we will personally make will also greatly impact our own history and often that of others. How we write history is about how we utilize our own moral courage and create our own profiles day by day. As such, we are always simultaneously in the classroom of life and at the next fork in the road. Whether or not we take the road less travelled may make all the difference.

CHAPTER 1

JOHN F. KENNEDY
(1917–1963)

DRAWING A LINE IN THE SAND

Trying in vain to sleep, John F. Kennedy winced and repeatedly repositioned his body. The endless knives seeming to pierce his back would not let him forget either the war injury or the spinal surgery. Then there was the added stress from non-stop scheduling. Only that day he had faced consecutive events with a crown prince, U.S. ambassador, multiple advisors, members of the Panel on Mental Retardation, press secretary, Middle East diplomats, and congressmen. Some of these people were also pains in the back.

He also hadn't forgotten the mix of drugs that felt so good, then so bad, and the inner emotional bursts and nausea that came and went. But the mix was essential. There were days he could not tie his shoes nor reach the pen on his desk due to the pain. He tried to grasp the source of his agony, if only to massage it. He could not.

Still, the physical torment paled in comparison to the mental. Memories of a meeting earlier that morning, and others later in the day, were constantly recycled. They prevented, then haunted, his sleep.

At 8:45 that morning, Tuesday, October 16, 1962, while Kennedy was still in his bathrobe, National Security Advisor McGeorge Bundy had alerted him to a new and extremely serious international crisis. CIA agents laboring round the clock had analyzed aerial photographs and determined that a nuclear missile site near San Cristobal, Cuba, only ninety miles from Florida, already harbored lethal, long-distance missiles. The photos revealed cigar-shaped contours far too large to smoke.

As president of the United States, the sleep-deprived John F. Kennedy faced a new and agonizing challenge. Russia and Cuba would now have the capacity to quickly eliminate major cities and military targets throughout the United States. And there were other implications, too—he thought of the imminent elections, the spin that the press and Republicans would give this foreign threat, the pending international reaction to any decision he would make.

Kennedy had known about Cuba's so-called "defensive" build-up of protective weapons from Russia for weeks. But now he had proof of an offensive threat that could ignite World War III. These new mega-warheads were no longer just protective weapons for self-defense.

And then there was Jackie. Earlier that day she and the children had left him for their vacation home, Glen Ora, in Virginia. He had humiliated her the night before by leaving a White House social function early to be with another woman. Would she forgive him and return? What about the children?

Even more ominous was the thought of possible evacuation. Kennedy had been shown an envelope, which staffers and their families would receive in the event of a nuclear emergency. The envelope explained how to reach a protected safe haven after evacuation from Washington D.C. Each person who would stay with the president would have to find a way to tell extended family "... and now you're on your own." Would Jack have to give an envelope to Jackie, or would she bring the children to stay with him in the bunker? The answer was painfully unclear.

He could no longer lie upon the hard floor to which he had sometimes sentenced himself to relieve back spasms. He was still uncomfortably digesting the emergency national security meetings of the day. Shifting feet reflected a racing mind. But the severe spike of back pain whenever he stood did not make the prospect of walking appealing.

The horrible image reappeared. New York and Washington could quickly be vaporized like Hiroshima and Nagasaki. Where would Jackie and the children be? What of his closest friends, administrative colleagues, Congress, and the women he desired? Would he be the president who failed to protect those closest to him and brought nuclear war to the world?

Sneaking out of the bedroom, Kennedy limped quietly downstairs to review the report and photos again. Another knife to the back. As he entered, the pitch-black office no longer seemed oval. Reviewing the photos under a single, haunting desk light, Kennedy knew this would mean a stand-off with an irrational and dangerous arch-rival, Soviet Premier Nikita Khrushchev, who had publicly proclaimed: "We will bury you!"

To be sure, the president had already asked both Bundy and his brother Bobby to assemble his team of advisors to study their alternatives. And he himself had already attended the first meeting ... although he had kept other parts of his schedule untouched, so as not to arouse suspicion among the press and those who spoke to Moscow.

Struggling with the decision was quite intense. If he agitated Khrushchev, world peace was at stake. Indeed, Khrushchev was known for rudeness, one-upmanship, and bursts of anger. An irate or cornered Khrushchev could mean unprecedented nuclear war. It was not just Khrushchev, but the military hawks both Kennedy and Khrushchev faced within their own staffs who would pressure both of them to be aggressive. If Kennedy did not stand up to the

Soviets, the entire free world and America's place in the world order were at risk. Suddenly, it was high noon in a cold war growing hot.

How to respond to Khrushchev became John F. Kennedy's obsession and most stressful decision. He broke into a mid-July sweat in mid-October. The president had already scheduled more meetings with his advisors from the Executive Committee of the National Security Council (EXCOMM) for tomorrow. Yet the decision would ultimately be his. And history, like his constituents, would ultimately blame or praise him for the outcome.

Another knife to the back ... Then another glance at Jackie's photo and a different type of pain. She had not answered the phone all day.

THE IMMEDIATE ISSUES

Over the next thirteen days, the president faced multiple ethical issues:

1) Whether, when, and to what degree the American public should be informed or deceived about the crisis and why he was not observing part of his planned schedule.

2) Whether to "play softball" and only communicate warnings to Soviet and Cuban leaders, or

3) whether to "play hardball" and take stronger military actions, which would endanger if not forfeit lives.

4) Whom to tell which parts of the secret he was carrying.

Crowded around a seemingly shrinking table in the White House situation room, foreign policy, military, and cabinet leaders grimaced and sometimes jockeyed for dominance. Some advisors urged diplomacy. Others recommended a limited air strike. Still others, raising their voices, wished to mount a full invasion of Cuba.

Each option invited other ethical questions about the relative loss of life and possibility of nuclear war. While the debate was about national security, no one seemed secure. Although they wore increasingly crumpled suits and ties, some seemed naked in their expressed fears and uncertainty.

The advisors were aware that the situation was further complicated by the presence of U.S. missiles in Turkey. The Soviets would point to these nuclear next-door neighbors to justify their own defensive arming of Cuba. Within the Cold War, the Soviet Union and United States each wished to reign supreme in the arms race and global influence, so arming Turkey had seemed expedient to the president as part of the global balance of powers.

FACING THE DECISION

It was hard to separate the pain in his back from that in his head and heart. No one decision would please a majority of his advisors, let alone be guaranteed to deter Khrushchev. Neither the sweat nor the pain subsided.

One object looked larger than all the others on his desk—the telephone. The problem loomed so large that Kennedy would eventually call three former presidents—Hoover, Truman, and Eisenhower—and the prime minister of Great Britain—among others.

All of those consulted knew that the greatest ethical dilemma was whether to wage peace through diplomacy against a charging bull—which was an unlikely victory—or to risk nuclear holocaust. The dilemma was complex. On the one hand, when he assumed his presidential role, Kennedy had taken an oath to protect the United States against all enemies and aggressors. On the other hand, any invasive naval action he might take could be seen as a hostile and illegal violation of international shipping rights, and a cause for retaliation.

A more aggressive air strike or land invasion of Cuba would risk the lives of thousands of military personnel and innocent civilians. Moreover, the missile operators in Cuba were probably Russians. Killing Russians would ignite not only the Cuban powder keg, but also the one owned by Khrushchev. Finally, any incident that could trigger nuclear response could also escalate the number of endangered lives from thousands to millions.

As he reflected in greater depth, Kennedy had no doubt that the Soviet missiles in Cuba could strike most, if not all, major cities on the east coast and indeed throughout most of South and North America. Bundy had requested that the photos be enlarged so the president could study missile shapes large enough to seem menacing.

There was little doubt that there could be no winner of a nuclear war—major portions of the world's population and species would either be quickly annihilated or eventually poisoned by lingering radiation. He recalled the photos of Hiroshima—faceless bodies, fleshless bones, homeless "zombie survivors," thousands of children's corpses, and ashen silhouettes.

So, the president was "playing for all the marbles," as they say. If his decisions, or those by Nikita Khrushchev, were off target, the entire world could be collateral. Second-hand smoke of a nuclear kind would have a colossal and tragic impact. His choice could have irreversible consequences for humanity. What could he do? What should he do?

THE LARGER PICTURE

Like President Kennedy, many leaders have faced unprecedented decisions which would change the course of history. This book is about not only Kennedy, but also about eleven other historical dilemmas and the often-hidden background factors that made the ethical choice vexing for vastly different individuals.

In the case of President Kennedy, he wrestled with the anxiety of intense confrontation for thirteen days. Other leaders facing ethical conundrums had only seconds to make substantial decisions, while still others took months or even struggled for a lifetime.

THE NATURE OF ETHICAL TENSION

A substantial ethical dilemma pulls an individual in two or more directions. Like the owner of two leashed greyhounds who jerk him toward opposite paths, a person in the ethics hot seat feels tugged by at least two contrary forces. Because there are likely to be moral costs no matter which choice he makes, the hot-seater may feel that she or others are "damned if I do" and "damned if I don't." So he or she may struggle to determine if there is a lesser of two evils, a greater of two goods, or a safer of two unknowns.

In John Kennedy's case, he had to weigh the possible loss of national security against a serious threat to world peace. Kennedy also had to juxtapose the lesser possibility of massive global casualties against a higher probability of losing the support of key members of his cabinet, re-election, public stability, and many American lives. When he decided to cancel part of his travel schedule in order to make crisis decisions in Washington DC, he also had to weigh the cost of public deception against the risk of national safety. Ultimately, Kennedy and his doctor chose to deceive the public by saying he was ill to explain his return to Washington, where he could secretly convene with key advisors. The tension and the secrecy were all but overpowering.

PROFILES IN COURAGE

Six years earlier, John Kennedy's own best-selling book, *Profiles in Courage* (1956), which won the 1957 Pulitzer Prize, had showcased nine of his own American political heroes. Each had taken strong stands despite possible loss of election, career, reputation, family, and even life. Choosing statesmen such as John Quincy Adams, Daniel Webster, and Sam Houston, Kennedy demonstrated how their iconoclasm, whether by breaking with their party, or casting a decisive but unpopular vote from a death bed, had made a heroic difference.

Both ironically and appropriately, Kennedy himself has now become my first example in a book inspired by his. This is also a book in which profiles in courage are important. But was Kennedy's own decision that courageous? Could he face a bully as formidable and trigger-happy as Khrushchev?

LIKE FATHER, LIKE DAUGHTER

John Kennedy's daughter, Caroline, expanded her father's acknowledgment of courageous political leadership under fire in her sequel entitled *Profiles in Courage for Our Time* (2002), published forty-six years after the original. By assembling a team of talented authors who each wrote one profile, Caroline was able to update her father's approach.

Ultimately, each player had to decide whether to compromise integrity under pressure. Each had to choose which tugging greyhound to follow or whether to rein in both. What would Kennedy do? If he did not act quickly, Russia could stockpile more missiles just ninety miles from Florida, and who could tell if they would be launched?

ETHICAL CONSIDERATIONS

Embedded within the Cuban nuclear crisis and each case to follow are serious ethical dilemmas. However, most people involved in ethical quandaries do not stop to consult the writings of Aristotle, Confucius, Kant, or other philosophers. Nevertheless, since wise thinkers have been contemplating moral dilemmas for millennia, it is helpful to consider their likely advice. So, in these cases some of their formulas or principles for ethical success will be briefly entertained.

Although many ethical decisions are made by intuition, or an inner sense of what is moral, practical, or wise, individuals often draw upon their own cultural training—if not programming— to determine right and wrong, or the closest approximation thereof. Frequently, that training has become unconscious, so that those on the hot seat are not thinking "my parents taught me to..." or "Mill believed that..." or "my socialist country advocated" or "my religious training prescribes..." or the like. And yet such cultural programming always lurks in the background. When we make an ethical decision, we may be echoing a process or endorsing principles chosen by our parents, teachers, religion, mentors, or government. But we may also be on entirely new ground and seeking an option that is outside the box.

In President Kennedy's case, he was known as a Harvard thinker, if not scholar, who would have read the classic philosophers. And he had grappled with the decisions of some of his role models when writing *Profiles in Courage* (although Theodore Sorensen is generally credited with having ghostwritten much of the book for Kennedy).

So, it is entirely possible that Kennedy consulted some of his favorite thinkers or poets—like Robert Frost, who to Kennedy's view, would have encouraged him to choose "the road less travelled." But it is more likely that these thinkers surfaced only briefly in his mind. He had no time to grab them off the bookshelf. For at every turn there were flesh and blood thinkers lobbying him to accept more political than philosophical solutions.

MAKING THE DECISION

Many pros and cons pulled at the president's consciousness as he explored each option with his team. Neither the view out the window nor the portraits of previous presidents distracted his attention as before. Only one agonizing headache loomed large—to strike, or not to strike.

Ultimately, Kennedy was convinced that there was a way to avoid both extremes. To handle this dilemma, JFK would have to choose a middle path, or what Aristotle would have called "the mean between deficiency and excess." By choosing a naval blockade of Cuba's waters, a plan championed by Secretary of Defense Robert McNamara, Kennedy could shut down a pipeline for further Soviet aggression and thus avoid the more violent and extreme paths of air strikes and armed invasion. He could also make a quid pro quo diplomatic agreement with the Soviet Union: "We will not invade Cuba—if you will remove your missiles."

But would his cabinet and advisors accept compromise? He had quickly lost sleep, weight, and calm searching for a wise answer the majority would endorse.

After listening to one perspective after another for days, and after searching his own soul, Kennedy, in concert with McNamara and selected cabinet members, chose the naval blockade. A second, secret tit-for-tat reciprocity agreement was made as well. In a hush-hush sidebar that remained undisclosed for decades, the U.S. agreed that it would slowly remove missiles from Turkey if the Soviet Union would, more quickly, remove theirs from Cuba.

Aristotle's ancient "golden mean" or middle path, when applied to this situation, meant that neither the extreme of rhetorical diplomacy (all talk and no action), nor of hawkish aggression (bombing or invading Cuba and risking world war) would be acceptable. So, Kennedy chose a middle and double path—he both verbally warned and physically roadblocked Khrushchev without violence. The blockade coupled with the negotiated deal succeeded, but only after almost two weeks of ethical quandaries—including severe angst about possible retaliation—and several more daggers to the back.

THE TEN FACTORS

It is important to consider some of the hidden assumptions and principles which inform, and the key thinkers who epitomize, ethical decision-making central to these historical studies. As mentioned in the introduction, here are some of the crucial factors in ethical decision-making which will be referred to as the "ten factors" henceforth.

Because they are so important, I am repeating a small portion of what was said about them in the introduction. Then I will examine each within the Kennedy case so you can see how to apply these tools to each dilemma, including your own:

1. **Notions of fairness and justice:** The Cold War justice in which Kennedy and Khrushchev participated called for a punitive, tit-for-tat reciprocity— or "eye for an eye" mentality—such that if missiles were aimed on one side, the same path would be adopted by the other. If visiting diplomats were expelled from one country, the same would soon occur on the other side.

   Many rival political states still adhere to this ancient justice system. Yet Gandhi observed "an eye for an eye and the whole world goes blind." Similarly, Kennedy and Khrushchev, despite the reciprocity–fairness paradigm they inherited, realized that "a missile for a missile and the whole world burns." So, the question of fairness may be expanded to become "fairness to whom?" What seems fair to a super-power may be unfair to humanity and other species.

   The great contemporary Harvard philosopher John Rawls (1921-2002) argued that justice must ignore social distinctions such that race, gender, age, nationality, and so forth cannot be reasons for disadvantage. Queen Esther, Wilberforce, Gandhi, and Mandela found their own ways to make similar pleas for social justice by overcoming racial distinctions. Malala Yousafzai extended fairness to include young girls deprived of education, and Carson went even further to include fairness to plants and animals.

   In most justice paradigms, "fairness" implies the right use, rather than the abuse, of power—a theme which Murrow and Mandela, among others,

24

championed. The time-honored Biblical narrative about King Solomon's court illustrates the responsible use of power. When two women appeared before Solomon, each claiming to be the mother of the same baby, King Solomon was asked to make a ruling about who was the true mother.

Solomon suggested that the fair way to solve the matter was to cut the child in half and give one half to each woman. Immediately, one woman cried out, "let her take the baby!" pointing to the other woman so that the infant would be spared. Solomon immediately discerned the real mother to be the one who wished to save the infant despite the personal loss of her child. So, what was ostensibly or mathematically fair was in no sense fair to the baby or its family.

The tit-for-tat, eye-for-an-eye justice system which Kennedy and Khrushchev inherited from their predecessors does not seem to penetrate the underlying moral problems at the core of adversarial relations. Deeper approaches to fairness and justice are required. Moreover, we must also consider the other nine factors.

2 **Impact or consequences:** In the story above, involving Solomon, despite the threat to the baby's life, the outcome was ethically perfect—the child lived, and the family members were reunited. Similarly, in the Cuban Missile Crisis, except for the death of one spy plane pilot, all tragedy was averted.

As mentioned in the introduction, some philosophers, such as the notable English thinker John Stuart Mill (1806-1873), articulated that such harmonious outcomes or consequences are what matter. "All's well that end's well" is one desired summary goal of an ethical dilemma for such utilitarians.

Kennedy and Khrushchev had many possible outcomes to consider: World peace vs. world war? Life vs. the deaths of many innocent people in three or more countries? The security of their own countries and the people who counted on them? Outcomes cannot always be predicted, but they must always be considered.

In his debates about tactics with colleagues, Nelson Mandela would often oppose an approach that, although well-intentioned, ultimately would prove ineffective in its outcome. Others, such as Mahatma Gandhi's son, argued with Mandela that unless the outcomes were obtained legitimately and without violence, the results were compromised. Thus, decision-makers not only consider consequences but also…

3 **Ends and means:** For Kennedy and Khrushchev, the end of obtaining national security did not justify the threat of nuclear annihilation. But, in the matter of deceiving the public, Kennedy did argue that preventing

paranoia in the U.S. required dishonest means. Ultimately, he decided to hide the Cuban Missile Crisis from American citizens in order to prevent a national panic. Are such deceptive means acceptable when one realizes that citizens expect their leaders to be transparent and trustworthy?

For the German philosopher Immanuel Kant (1724-1804), deception is never tolerated no matter what ends might be obtained. As noted in the introduction, Kant proffered that one ought never lie, even if it might save a life. In a similar manner he felt that human beings should never be used as only means, but rather each person has intrinsic importance as an end of himself. Thus, no matter how great the potential outcome, Kant insisted that we cannot use people as steppingstones, nor employ deception to obtain a positive consequence.

Many others have disagreed that honorable means carry the highest priority. Indeed, for Mill, if the lives of a few people are at risk to save thousands—assuming all other factors are equal—then the ends do justify the means and the few are less important than the many. All things considered, despite other subtleties that Mill introduced, more happiness or pleasure for more people is the objective of Mill's "greatest good for the greatest number" dictum.

But does quantity matter more than all else? Would the sustained, intense torturing of two young people in order to prolong the lives of six elderly people who are already dying truly be ethical? Such a scenario evokes serious concerns about...

4 **Tone and atmosphere:** It is hard to advocate an eco-friendly ethic while drinking from a Styrofoam cup. And it is hard for a great lecturer to call for peace while violently pounding on a lectern while surrounded by armed bodyguards. Tone matters.

For many indigenous nations or tribes, a tone of respect for all life was essential. A tree could not be cut down until there was a need and use for every part, including the bark and leaves. The pastures and water could not be spoiled, as such a tone showed disrespect for future generations, for relevant spirits (cf. gods), and for Mother Earth. For many world religions, this ultimate respect is for that which is highest, such as Allah for Muslims, ancestors for Shintoists, God for Jews and Christians, or the Tao (the Way of Life) for Taoists.

Feminist ethicists Carol Gilligan (born 1936) and Nel Noddings (born 1929) have advocated that the feminine voice and tone should be more central to ethical decision-making. Noddings argues for an ethics of care in which compassion and the quality of human relationships are at least as important as fulfilling more abstract notions of justice.

For Kennedy it was important that his public demeanor was of a higher tone than Khrushchev's. Through mass media Kennedy was often able to create a high-tone image of being civilized and humane, an image in sharp contrast to that of Khrushchev, who was portrayed as a brutish barbarian. On the other hand, behind the scenes, Kennedy was frequently betraying his wife and bedding other women, so one must question whether public tone matters at all if a person is unethical outside of public view.

One rationale for tone being foremost is the sense that it is the primary cause or essence of all action. Many world religions observe that one may not create a peaceful world if one is not personally at peace. Indeed, those who debated with Lenin, Robespierre, Bolivar, and Washington, who all advocated violence, asked them how they could possibly create peace with the brutal slaughter of revolution. So, to perform an ethical action, one must be ethical in spirit as well as deed. This is why some ethicists claim that what is most important is …

5 **Motivation and higher law:** For Kennedy and Khrushchev, although saving their own jobs or lives was not inconsequential, their ethics capital seemed to rise when they appeared to be motivated to save an entire nation. Saving the world creates a heroic and often legendary ethics status.

In chapter three, Socrates offers a variety of reasons for accepting his own death by drinking the hemlock juice. One rationale involved protecting free thinking and the independence of his perspective. Similarly, in chapter two, Esther risks instant death to protect her people and honor their God. The motivation to serve a higher law or greater good, divine purpose, virtuous principle, or humanitarian cause often seems ethically preferable.

But what if a person is delusional, and the higher good he serves is a cult ideology? In the Jim Jones' Jonestown case, hundreds of people drank lethal Kool-Aid and perished together. History suggests they did not serve a higher purpose, and many left behind orphans and heartbroken relatives. What if the greater state one serves is an empire made in the image of its dictator? Is this truly a higher good? Moreover, fully determining a person's sole or mixed motivations may prove challenging. The higher or highest good is not always clear cut.

6 **Allegiance and loyalty:** Many military chaplains are assigned to an army battle squad. A chaplain's loyalty to his faith or deity means that he or she cannot kill or carry a weapon. But his loyalty to his country and sworn allegiance to the army make him accountable to protect his comrades. So,

what does he do when enemies are invading his foxhole and killing his sleeping army brothers? Does the chaplain grab a weapon nearby and shoot the attackers to save the lives of his comrades, or does he pray? Does he run away to possibly save his own life? His allegiance to patriotically protect his fellow soldiers is clearly at odds with his allegiance to his god and a non-violent faith.

To whom does a mother owe her allegiance when she is secretly harboring her seventeen-year-old son in her attic so he will not be drafted into an army at war—a war she does not believe in? Is her allegiance to her country, which protects her own family against invaders by drafting young men such as her son—or is her loyalty first to her son? Or is it to her own conscience and moral beliefs? Should her son be exempt from conscription if other sons are not? What about the first factor considered earlier—fairness and justice? To whom is her primary allegiance? And by what notion of justice does she rationalize her decision?

All humans face potentially conflicting loyalties and sometimes must make agonizing choices. Many have claimed that their highest loyalty is to what for others is an abstraction. An ultimate allegiance to a higher power such as God or Buddha or Allah or the truth or humanity seems noblest to many. But because belief systems differ, two groups may claim to give highest allegiance to the truth or their god(s) or another ultimate belief, and still be at war with each other.

Kennedy and Khrushchev each had conflicting loyalties determined by their cultural contexts. As will be spelled out in more detail below, to varying degrees Kennedy felt he owed allegiance to his office and country, to his domineering father, to Roman Catholicism, to humanistic liberal arts values, and even (in hidden ways) to forces seeking to pressure him such as the FBI, mafia, lobbyists, and clandestine lovers. Khrushchev, alternatively, owed a primary allegiance to the Communist Party, although he also felt lesser loyalties to friends, favorites, and family.

In many case studies, the question of allegiance or loyalty is crucial. Indeed, one famous tool that prioritizes loyalties is often used by ethicists when evaluating a case study. Named the "Potter Box" after Harvard theologian/philosopher Ralph Potter (born 1934), the method requires one to identify the loyalties that tug at the central character. As with a dog walker exercising two greyhounds on leashes, loyalties to differing people can pull an ethics actor in opposing directions. Potter's Box also calls for an evaluation of the case's underlying…

7 **Values and Principles:** For Potter there were not only values but also corresponding principles behind moral decisions. If I am asked to work overtime throughout an entire weekend to protect a sick colleague who might lose his job, I could well consider the Golden Rule principle: "Do unto others as you would have them do unto you." But what if I am approaching illness myself or likely to lose family morale by working the entire weekend? Suppose I then determine that I really must stay at home. Then I would be honoring a different principle, "to thine own self be true," and I would decline the request to cover work for my colleague.

If I make this latter choice, I might then be applying "do unto others…" in a different way. I might be thinking of the "others" as my wife and child, not my colleague at work. So, principles and values are not always easily ranked nor unambiguous.

Moreover, as noted in the introduction, principles may come into conflict when one considers that they are as different as "women and children first" and "all men (cf. people) are created equal." Or they can be as different as "to each according to his needs" and "what's good for the goose is good for the gander."

Kennedy valued peace and security. And he supported the principles that he pledged to uphold when he was sworn in as president. But, despite saying that he valued peace, on another occasion he chose to invade Cuba at the Bay of Pigs, an event that disturbed the peace by including violence and risked retaliation. Do different times and situations call for different values and principles? Which values and principles take priority?

Often a person of integrity sees herself as a person of principle. But since many noble principles are at odds, the question then becomes "which principle?" Such an awareness leads to the revelation that one must also consider…

8 **Cultural context:** For the American cowboy, the buffalo were so plentiful, they had no more value than as edible meat and rawhide. Surplus buffalo were often killed for pure sport. Such a lack of respect deeply offended the Sioux and other tribes for whom the buffalo were sacred. Before killing such a magnificent beast could be considered, there must be a need by the tribe for every part of its body and horns.

Religious cultures typically give greatest value to the unseen, while more scientific cultures value visible evidence. Similarly, economic egalitarian principles ("to each according to their need") are valued in socialist states, whereas "first come first served" and "money talks" principles matter more in capitalist nations.

Kennedy's culture had a history of valuing democracy such that he felt a different level of accountability to his citizens than did Khrushchev, whose culture valued more authoritarian and patriarchal values. The American presidency was also held in check by the principle of a balance of powers, which meant that Congress and the courts provided complementary vectors to the presidency. Kennedy had to take them and their leading players into account. John Kennedy had also been strongly governed by his father, by the values of Roman Catholicism, and by the humanism of a liberal arts education. For Khrushchev, his highest accountability was not to any of these. Neither was it to a supreme court or parliamentary system. Khrushchev's highest loyalty was to the Communist Party, especially the hard-liners within its central committee and their rigid socialist values. The differences within their cultures, not just in their personalities, made it extremely difficult for Kennedy and Khrushchev to make agreements and to reason together.

9 Implications: As noted earlier, Immanuel Kant suggested a neat formula for making ethical choices. His first categorical imperative asked that a person should imagine a world in which everyone follows his or her example when making a moral decision. If my actions might have a ripple effect, even to some small degree, then what are the prolonged implications of my choices?

While implications overlap with consequences, they are often more subtle, long-term, and harder to predict. Some implications may not be seen for months or years to come. The implications of a CEO tolerating sexual harassment might be initially submerged or behind closed doors, but later could include lawsuits and firings. Within his company there could also be a cultural climate shift toward distrust, anger, and fear. Ethical decisions that are made and not made can create distant echoes. When the implications or risks of a choice are unknown, there are even more pieces of the puzzle to ponder.

For Kennedy and Khrushchev, the long-term implications of nuclear war were largely unknown, since no preceding war had featured nuclear weapons on both sides. Still, the tea leaves suggested that reciprocal nuclear aggression could be devastating both within and far beyond the boundaries of the U.S. and the U.S.S.R. In this sense, the immediate consequences of decision—escalation of tension, reciprocal public rhetoric, public deception to citizens, military emergency alerts, diplomatic overtures, etc.—could be vastly different that the long-term implications—world war, death to millions of innocent people and animals, and in a worst case scenario, omnicide.

10 **Proportion and balance:** As noted in the introduction, it is hard to know how much weight to give each of the nine factors above. It may also be challenging to determine what is meant by "balanced." For example, if I am on the college admissions board and female applicants score higher than males this year, do I still admit an equal number of men and women to my college? Or do I give more weight to achievement than to male/female balance or equality? What carries more moral clout, personal merit, or gender fairness?

Does gender balance or imbalance best represent fairness? Who is to say? And what about the unfairness of the past, when women were rarely included or entirely excluded from admissions policies for centuries? Should this imbalance be rectified by admitting more women than men? If so, is there not reverse discrimination against current male applicants with high performance scores who are excluded? Does balance mean that we rebalance previous imbalances? Or current ones? Or both, if that is possible?

Facing difficult decisions, each of the profiled historical characters yet to come, like John Kennedy, had to decide the relative significance of factors above, such as fairness vs. consequences or loyalties vs. principles. In assessing such situations, is it wise to give the same proportion and consideration to each factor, or will one factor (such as the possibility of nuclear holocaust for Kennedy and Khrushchev) outweigh all of the others?

Knowing the hidden implications, factors, values, etc., behind a situation is important. But it is no more important than knowing how much weight to give each one upon the scales of justice.

STILL OTHER FACTORS

Each case is unique and ultimately each decision-maker is, to some degree, subjective. Some people seek to make extremely logical, reasonable choices based upon the factors above. But ultimately other factors, including preference and subconscious bias, may color the picture.

Third parties also enter the plot. As with Julius Caesar, whose soothsayer cautioned him to "beware the Ides of March," others have consulted their augurs, prophets, lawyers, mentors, partners, bookies, consultants, fortune-tellers, clergy, lovers, and even their dice or horoscopes. Even when they took the more rational approach of asking for professional advice, their experts (for example, lawyers, foreign policy or military strategists) were not always people for whom they felt affection, respect, or loyalty. Third-party input has ranged from highly substantial to totally ignored, and from unanimous to highly conflicted.

A myriad of other circumstances—weather, illness, alcohol, limited vision, nutrition, interpersonal chemistry, wild animals, heavy medication, kidnapped hostages, enemy bombardments, insects, and even ill-fitting false teeth—have been silent partners in decision-making. Both prescribed and illegal drugs have impacted vexing choices. Such unseen anomalies may not have been initially noted, yet they later surfaced in journals, interviews, and diaries.

Some such details carried little weight, but others were catalysts to rushed or impaired thinking. These hidden factors sometimes become fascinating clues when determining why a perplexing decision was made.

THE HIDDEN JFK

In Kennedy's case, the extenuating circumstances were numerous. His chronic back pain from a war injury and intensive spinal surgery were often augmented by concurrent pains from colitis, Addison's disease, urinary tract infections, allergies, anxiety, and occasional depression. His mood swings, recurring grogginess, and sleep deprivation were treated by (and by-products of) his consumption of codeine, Demerol, methadone, Ritalin, Librium, meprobamate, barbiturates, gamma globulin, thyroid hormone, and steroids. His back pain was often so severe he could not sleep on normal beds, tie his shoes, nor reach across his desk for papers.

Additionally, FBI director J. Edgar Hoover had been a different type of pain in the back. Hoover revealed to attorney general Robert Kennedy, John's younger brother, that the FBI held evidence of the president's incessant philandering with a mob moll and various staffers, movie stars, and interns. Such fraternizing with female third parties with loose lips and untrusted associates placed great pressure on the president to terminate the sexual, if not pharmaceutical, addictions he used to offset pressure.

Frank Sinatra had also visited John's father, Joseph, reminding him of favors allegedly owed by the Kennedys to the mafia. And yet it was John's brother, Bobby, who as attorney general was concurrently and vigorously prosecuting the very mafia to whom the Kennedys allegedly owed payback. For John Kennedy, this contradiction posed yet another ethical headache.

Some time after the Sinatra visit, Joseph Kennedy's stroke left him permanently speechless. Within the tightly-knit Kennedy patriarchy, John deeply felt such family burdens, and he always puzzled over where to draw the line regarding his loyalty to his father.

A myriad of other background lobbies and relations, including a broken-hearted wife with an often-empty bed, impinged upon Kennedy's emotions and thought. And some of the other women in his life found it hard to take "no" for an answer. When the risk of seeing them again was emphasized by his brother Bobby or the FBI, John was confronted by their angry, if not broken, hearts.

New and ongoing dilemmas in the Middle East, Asia, South America, and the segregated southern states required ongoing attention. Only one year earlier, Nikita Khrushchev had angrily banged his shoe upon a table at the United Nations and shouted "we will bury you" while the international press rolled cameras.

It was against this complex backdrop of dramatis personae and personal pinpricks that John Kennedy faced a choice that could alter the fate of the world.

His decision to choose a blockade, rather than more aggressive alternatives, may have prevented the first nuclear world war and preserved many lives, including our own.

SETTING THE STAGE

In the following case studies, other visible and invisible details combine to set a climate for moral decisions that cast long shadows. Like the Kennedy profile, each of the eleven to follow is, like each of us, unique. And yet in the aggregate, the cases reveal much common ground, and also reveal a path for wise decision-making within an age when our world seems severely ethically challenged.

CHAPTER 2

QUEEN ESTHER:
(492-460 BCE)

ANTI-SEMITISM, FEMALE LEADERSHIP, AND HIGH RISK

A LIFE AND DEATH DECISION

Pressure faced her on every side. On the one hand, if she refused to act boldly, everyone within her race could be executed. On the other, if she did act boldly, she herself could be killed and in no position to save others.

She kept looking at the large coin her uncle's envoy had given her to bribe a guard so she could exit the palace.

But whom could she trust? Which guard? Anyone who intercepted her confidential information could funnel it upward to curry favor with the king.

Esther needed a confidant, a sounding board to discuss her plight. Her Uncle Mordecai would be ideal but recently, whenever she left the court to speak with him, she felt watched by the chief eunuch who shadowed the king's wives. Even talking with Mordecai could look suspicious.

The coin felt heavier in her hand. Would she risk using it?

The royal eunuchs who guarded the harem were no threat to the king since they were castrated, but they were a major threat to each wife. Their reports about unusual trips off campus could cast shadows upon—if not bring the gallows to—those without foolproof alibis.

Thus, Esther searched in vain for a quiet place where she could think about options one and two. Option one meant death to thousands. Option two meant likely death to Esther, the only person who could keep the thousands alive. Was there a third option? Could she ask anyone for advice?

THE ISSUES

Since she lived in ancient Persia, Queen Esther would not have used the terms "Anti-Semitism" or "women's rights." Yet her decision would later be seen as possibly the first, by a woman that would prevent genocide against Jewish people. It was also among the first to pit a woman's leadership against a harsh, male dictatorship.

That is precisely what made her decision so stressful. She, a woman, would be speaking up for Jews, and neither women, nor Jews, had a protected voice within the kingdom—both were routinely ignored and punished. Her odds for survival seemed slim even though she had been crowned Queen of Persia.

Esther was Jewish, so she had chosen a Persian name for camouflage, a name which sounded like and paid homage to the Persian deity Ishtar. Only Uncle Mordecai, and a few friends and family, knew she was Jewish. So far, none had betrayed her secret. However, betrayal had exposed other Jews, and she lived in fear.

What if someone accidentally revealed her secret? Or what if someone was persuaded to do so by a rival? Her husband, King Ahasuerus (likely another name for the Persian King Xerxes), had already condemned all Jews to death, and a king's edict was irreversible.

Esther's uncle, mentor, and ward, Mordecai, tried to convince her to use her royal status to intercede for the Jewish people. Every time she felt the large coin in her hand she thought of Mordecai. But it now seemed her uncle was also being watched. He had insulted the king's prime minister, Haman, by refusing to bow to him.

Esther felt that she too was under surveillance when she left the palace, and the time that all Jews would be eliminated was drawing near.

Queen Esther was keenly aware of the fate of the last queen, her predecessor, Vashti. When Vashti displeased the king, she had vanished. Had Vashti been exiled? Executed? Esther did not wish to find out. Allegedly, the last courtier who tried to speak to the king without an invitation was summarily terminated.

Nor was access to the king guaranteed for a queen. In ancient Persia, harems and court intrigues were commonplace. Female visitation to the king might be by sexual rotation, and male visitation might be rank-ordered by political opportunism. Thus, a queen's entry into a king's chamber could easily intrude upon either his plotting with men or his intimacies with women. Either invasion of privacy could ignite the king's wrath. Indeed, Ahasuerus was known for fits of anger followed by rapid capital punishment.

Of course, it cannot be proven that Esther and her story are historically accurate. Yet, for the sake of honoring both the Jewish and Christian traditions (just as we will honor other traditions in other chapters), I have included this narrative as it was conveyed in scripture and related texts. The story has long been tested against those few, surviving historical documents from the third to fifth centuries BCE. Esther's story holds great influence within Judeo-Christian culture, although it cannot be verified using strictly secular texts, neither can it be disproven.

THE ETHICAL DILEMMA

Her anguish over whether to speak, or not to speak to the king came partly from inside Esther, but external pressures had also come from the lobbying of her mentor, Mordecai—who wished to save the Jews—and from the king's vizier, Haman, who wished to destroy them.

Esther likely said to herself, "If I dare to speak without invitation, I probably won't have a chance to explain. But if I do not speak, I will perish when they discover I am a Jew, and my people will certainly vanish with me." In Persia, the king's law was higher than any other. And the king, acting upon Haman's advice, had already decreed that all Jews would die.

Hence Esther's ethical dilemma was substantial. Was her greater loyalty to her husband—the king—and his supreme law? Or to blood family, God, heritage, and the lives of thousands? Her loyalty to herself was not strictly self-serving. After all, if she did not save herself, whom could she save? And who else could possibly save her people?

THE HISTORICAL BACKSTORY

While scholars have debated the historical accuracy of Esther's story, the book of Esther in the Old Testament, the megillah (the Jewish scrolls/scriptures) of Esther, and the tale of Esther (in Greek and other derivatives), all written thousands of years ago, probably echo historical events. Depending upon the translation of those documents, Esther was possibly an orphan from the Hebrew tribe of Benjamin who was then adopted by her uncle Mordecai.

It seems likely that both Mordecai and Esther were part of the Jewish diaspora overtaken by the Babylonians and conquered by King Darius. Mordecai and Esther were probably relocated to Susa, the winter capital of Persia.

Esther's own relocation was one of the most miraculous in history, not unlike the Cinderella fairytale. Most versions of the narrative report her rags-to-riches transformation as the outcome of a bizarre order of events.

The story began in a royal banquet hall. Prior to meeting Esther, King Ahasuerus was quite merry after many days of indulgence at his feast for thousands of guests. Although queens usually did not attend such concubine-laden festivities, the king nevertheless called for Queen Vashti to appear, since he wished to showcase her beauty. One version of the story states that the inebriated king commanded Vashti to appear wearing only her crown.

Whatever the king's demand, Vashti refused to appear whether as a matter of dignity, decorum, wisdom, or stubbornness. After consulting with advisors and others, Ahasuerus elected to punish the queen, in part to ensure the obedience of all wives to husbands, including any other wives he might choose.

All accounts report that Vashti was stripped of her crown, if not her life. Differing interpretations infer that she was demoted to serve as one of the king's concubines, banished, or killed.

AN EXTRAVAGANT BEAUTY CONTEST

Once Vashti was dethroned, the king devised an unusual competition to determine her successor. The most beautiful girls and women were brought to Susa from 127 provinces. In a manner that would make even Hugh Hefner envious, every contestant was given a full year of beautification treatment prior to spending just one night with the king.

Despite the odds, the unlikely commoner, Esther, greatly pleased the king during their night together. She was soon chosen to be queen and was married to the extremely powerful, yet eccentric, Ahasuerus. Today, Ahasuerus might be labeled as a manic depressive due to his extreme mood swings, and his only medicine—unlimited wine—further inflamed such runaway emotions.

Esther's relationship to Mordecai and the Jewish people remained a secret. She moved into the palace to live with the other contestants and later with the wives of the harem.

A HIERARCHY OF LOYALTIES TO THE JUST AND UNJUST

Serious ethical dilemmas often place a person like Esther in a position of choosing between competing loyalties. Such loyalties often include family, friends, spouse, employer, the state, a higher power, and self.

For example, in Sophocles' famous tragedy *Antigone*, the lead character must chose between honoring her fallen brother, or honoring her uncle and the government. In Esther's situation she had to choose between: 1) a partner who was the government and his powerful friends at court, or 2) her family, faith, and people.

She also had to choose between honoring Haman, the king's vizier or prime minister, who paid the king 10,000 silver talents to eliminate the Jews, or her less powerful but empathetic father figure, Mordecai. It was a choice between private, hidden loyalties or public, expected allegiance to the omnipotent state and its rulers.

Moreover, Esther was caught between loyalty to the visible—the monarchy, marriage, and Persia—and the invisible—her hidden legacy and the greater

Jewish "King" to whom she prayed. Ironically, her God was truly invisible or absent in the Jewish and Christian accounts of Esther. Indeed, in the sacred scroll account, God was never mentioned by name.

In both remaining textual accounts, there is only one allusion to deity in the figure of speech. It is often translated as "another place." Esther is told that help may come from "another place," a reference to the hand of providence, but no deity is mentioned by name. Invisible or not, God was the monolithic force within her faith and, to her view, the author of a greater law than the Persian one.

There were high stakes implicit in these conflicting loyalties. For Esther to show allegiance to God and Mordecai would be to embrace both a heathen faith and a criminal who had violated state policy. By refusing to bow to the powerful Haman, Mordecai had placed a high price upon his own head and further jeopardized all Jews, even though his action might be justified as civil disobedience in future centuries. Still, the relative value of Mordecai's life was complicated because he had not only insulted Haman, but had also saved the king's life. Prior to defying Haman, Mordecai had overheard a conspiracy to kill the king, successfully reported it, and earned favor for being a loyal citizen. So, Mordecai was more than a pardoned criminal, but a "hero" criminal.

Thus, Esther faced moral complexities. From her regal perspective, Mordecai was both a patriot and villain. But from her Jewish identity, he was both her former protector and the intercessor for her people. Nevertheless, her current protector, the king, held the greatest power.

HIGHER ALLEGIANCE

Several ethical systems claim that there are loyalties higher than that to political authority. The most prevalent of these highest loyalties are to deity, to humanity, and to conscience. In one sense, Mordecai's plea to Esther symbolized all three.

Nevertheless, our twenty-first century moral lens may misunderstand Esther's own sense of values. These factors loomed large to her: 1) the king had promoted her above all other contestants and wives; 2) he had the power to name her children to be future monarchs; 3) he had dethroned if not executed her predecessor; 4) among their own people, the kings of Persia were seen as divine with unlimited power.

Did such a savior, benefactor, and protector deserve disloyalty? Was she not accountable to the person who lavished opulence upon her and granted her unparalleled freedom among women? Would she not want her children to become royal leaders?

And what about patriotic duty to the head of state and his prime minister (i.e. vizier)? Surely a queen would be expected to epitomize and exemplify the highest loyalty to the throne.

Several philosophies and religions have posited that there are absolutes or universals that transcend personal and cultural loyalties. For example, many have argued that there are no conceivable moral grounds for genocide no matter what a dictator mandates. In that spirit, can anyone in good conscience owe duty to a tyrant who mandates racial discrimination and elimination?

Whatever her seeming interpersonal loyalties, Esther must have also sensed accountability to a higher moral order. Her daily commandments came from her husband, and yet her spiritual ten commandments came from the King of Kings.

THE DECISION LEADS TO A CUNNING PLAN

The decision she faced was daunting. Fear and doubt was already aging the teenage queen. At times her question seemed to be when she would die, not if she would die, and yet she had already died these deaths on the inside and somehow managed to live another day. Miraculously, no one had reported her.

But the dread that she would be found out was immense. Again and again she dreamed of execution; not only her own, but that of her family and friends.

The coin weighed heavily in her hand. Even worse, the profile imprinted upon the coin's face was that of her husband… if she used it as a bribe to leave his palace, surely he would find out. Her indecision had cost her so much sleep as she faced apex anxiety.

Yet somehow, she imagined that there must be a way forward. The coin disappeared into a hiding place for her valuables. Esther knew she could not use it.

At last, she relaxed. An idea washed upon the beach of consciousness like driftwood. She inspected it again and again. It was the third option. However, the plan she was envisioning would not be easy. Could she dare to follow through?

Step by step, she silently hatched the scheme during the quiet of her walk in the palace garden. Rather than avoiding the pressure from either Haman or Mordecai, Esther would make plans with both of them.

First, she would bravely ask Mordecai to lead the Jews into a period of fasting, an action associated both with religious tradition and spiritual purification. Like prayer, collective fasting could be a means of repentance and surrender to God, and in a surreptitious if not political way, collective fasting by her people would also be a sign of solidarity with Esther.

Esther also planned action within the court. When given an opportunity to speak with the king, Esther would choose clever diplomacy by inviting both the king and his advisor, Haman, to a feast in their honor.

But fear reigned. Despite the ingenious nature of Esther's invitation, she knew that the king might be suspicious of her motives. She also knew that he could deny her request.

And yet, to Esther, God seemed to smile upon her. When she moved forward to speak, the king smiled. Rather than calling for her execution, he extended his scepter toward his queen and asked what she would like. In some versions of the story, he even offered her up to half of his kingdom. As a newlywed, Ahasuerus was still possessed by Esther's beauty and charm.

THE PLAN IS ACTIVATED

This good fortune would enable Esther to make her appeal and reveal her hidden identity to the king and Haman. She prepared the best food and wine. During the seductive feast, once the two men were relaxed after drinking heavily, she unexpectedly revealed Haman as the true villain and made a plea for the salvation of her kin.

Both the king and Haman were taken off guard. The sly, yet seemingly innocent queen had prudently planned the right pre-conditions to increase her odds of success—copious gourmet food, abundant wine, and flattery for the two men—by staging a special occasion in their honor. She also held the king's offer to grant her a sizable wish in her back pocket.

Disturbed by Esther's disclosure which threatened his own irreversible edict, Ahasuerus fled the feast. Now it was Esther who was taken aback, since only the despised and distraught Haman remained in the banquet arena.

Seizing this private moment with the queen, Haman threw himself upon Esther's mercy (and possibly her body) to plead for clemency. The king unexpectedly returned to the feast only to discover Haman's offensive encroachment upon his wife.

HAMAN'S DOWNFALL

Events suddenly took a drastic twist. The king's wrath turned immediately upon Haman. Ironically, he would soon be hung from the huge gallows he had recently ordered constructed for Mordecai's execution. Later, Haman's sons would be killed by the very Jews who had been his target, and Mordecai would be named the grand vizier who succeeded Haman.

Even prior to the banquet, Haman's luck had taken a turn for the worse. Infuriated by Mordecai's disrespect (Mordecai had refused to bow to Haman), Haman had approached the King hoping for approval to hang Mordecai.

Ordinarily, such a wish might have been granted. But just one night earlier, the king's insomnia had led him to read from his chronicles and discover that Mordecai had never been duly honored for saving the king's life. So, before he could speak, Haman was asked by the king how the king should honor "a man whom the king wished to acknowledge." Haman thought the king intended to honor Haman himself.

Haman replied that the honoree should wear a royal robe and be led on one of the king's horses throughout the city. As the honoree approached the people, a proclamation would be shouted: "This is what is done for the man the king delights to honor!"

Pleased by this idea, the king startled Haman by commanding that he honor Mordecai in this way by leading him through the city on horseback. In a state of shock, Haman reluctantly agreed to summon Mordecai. Not only was Haman humiliated by being Mordecai's chauffeur, but he was also mortified by honoring the only Jew who had never bent his knees to honor him.

Summarily, Haman became Mordecai's public herald, and then Mordecai became Haman's successor as vizier after Haman was executed on the gallows constructed to hang Mordecai.

Esther remained safely upon the throne and her coin remained securely in her hiding place. No bribes would be needed to speak with Uncle Mordecai in the future. They would both serve closely with the same king and transplant the Jewish people from death row, to the heart of society.

A WOMAN'S LEADERSHIP IN A MAN'S WORLD

Since she was the winner of a beauty contest as a young commoner, Esther has sometimes been envisioned as the naïve, uneducated pawn of the king or Mordecai. In some imaginations, she may have been undervalued as merely a teen fantasy for a lecherous king.

Yet Esther proved to be far more. She was clever if not cunning, courageous if not fearless. Rather than let a serious ethical decision become a perpetual headache leading her to meltdown, she adopted a strategy that changed the path of the king, the Jews, Haman, and history. She proved to be a leader both among her people and in the royal court.

It is possible to regard Esther's predecessor, Queen Vashti, as the first true feminist recorded in Persian history, given her preference for personal dignity and destiny over pleasing her husband, a drunk, irrational tyrant. But if that is the case, it is Esther who was the first successful feminist, since she established herself as the savior of her people and a force to be reckoned with in court. While no precise record of her death survives, Esther seems to have sustained a successful life as a powerful and charismatic player among both royals and Jews.

Such a rags-to-riches story would have been unheard of in a day when mothers of boys received twice the supplemental allowance as the mothers of girls. A queen might have been all but powerless and resided in a harem with dozens, or even hundreds, of other women—primarily concubines—managed by the royal eunuchs.

In the community where Esther was raised, it was commonplace for parents not only to pay taxes, but to give their daughters to the court. Many became cooks, bakers and maids, but those who were more attractive often became royal concubines.

Esther's climb was from the bottom of this social ladder—she was Jewish, lower class, likely orphaned, and female—to probably the second most powerful person in a vast empire. Moreover, she became a woman with a voice in an otherwise all male chorus. Within the silent world of Persian women, she also became an empowered role model, icon, and heroine.

Ultimately Esther's power was not simply titular nor symbolic. When she commanded Mordecai to lead the Jews in fasting, he did so. When she asked the king to punish Haman and reconsider his edict, he did so.

Esther is arguably one of the most important leaders of the pre-literate world: she prevented genocide and changed the course of history. Along with Cleopatra, Helen of Troy, and Jezebel, she can be seen as among the most influential of all remembered ancient women. But unlike the others, Esther may also be respected as a substantial moral leader who risked everything for a just society.

ANTI-SEMITIC GENOCIDE

Although anti-Semitism is often equated with the Nazi Holocaust of the 1940's, the persecution of Jews has been tragically commonplace throughout history. Plays as different and distant as *The Merchant of Venice* and *Fiddler on the Roof*, and novels such as *Anna Karenina* and *Exodus,* are among those that depict the wide geographical sweep and timeframe of anti-Semitic ostracism, expulsion, exodus, and, in some cases, elimination.

So, like the Nazi Holocaust, the story of Haman's genocide plot may be seen as part of a larger context. Indeed, within The Five Scrolls (1984), Herbert Bronstein and Albert Friedlander have declared that "the events described here, if not historically verifiable, are paradigms of historical events which have plagued the Jewish people in every era." Even the plot structure of the story is part of a familiar archetype for Bronstein and Friedlander: "a certain people are scattered … their laws are different … it is not in the king's interest to tolerate them … every generation has seen these events described in the scroll of Esther." Noted ancient history scholar Edwin Yamauchi observes that persecution of the Jews predates Esther's story. And yet Megillat Esther (Scroll of Esther) portrays a rare triumph in preventing systematic atrocities.

Hitler realized the importance of Esther to Jews as a book of hope and victory. Proclaiming that there might be a "second Esther" if Germany did not win the war, Hitler banned the possession and reading of the story. Undeterred by such censorship, Jewish concentration camp prisoners reconstructed the book. Translating the story of Esther into English as *Megillat Esther* (1972), the scholar and professor, Rabbi Robert Gordis wrote that "Jewish inmates in Auschwitz, Dachau, Treblinka, and Bergen-Belsen wrote the Book of Esther from memory and read it on Purim."

The Jewish holiday of Purim is itself evidence of the importance of Esther's stand. Every year on the fourteenth and fifteenth days of *Adar* (the twelfth month of the Jewish calendar), Esther and Mordecai are venerated, and Haman vilified, by Jewish celebrants and their sympathizers worldwide.

THREE PERSPECTIVES: PERSIA, PURIM, AND PRECEDENT

The word "Purim" refers to the lots that were cast by Haman to determine which day the Jews would be eliminated. Ironically, Purim has become the day on which practicing Jews eat pastries known as "the ears of Haman," which might symbolize the ears of common criminals that were typically cut off prior to execution in ancient Persia.

Following a day of minor fasting, Jews who celebrate Purim gather to worship, read the story of Esther, and make loud noises with noise-makers. Many shout "boo" whenever Haman's name is read. Some wear masks (originally portraying the characters in the Esther story), enjoy drinking, and are

44

asked to be especially charitable during Purim. Although it is considered a minor holiday, Purim is only one of two that the rabbinate have recommended should never be abrogated, even after the coming of the Messiah.

Although Christians inherited the story of Esther from their Jewish legacy, they do not practice Purim. While Christian denominations vary in their relative emphasis of Biblical history and the interpretation of scripture, most celebrate Esther's story as a landmark in courage, loyalty, and godliness. Wherever Christians honor women in the Bible with special courses, workshops, and sermons, Esther is typically treated as one of the leading Biblical heroines along with Mary, Deborah, Ruth, Sarah, and others.

Although there are many translations of the Bible, a comparison of popular Christian Bibles with the Jewish scroll of Esther demonstrates that the story is virtually the same. The difference is that Esther and Mordecai's story is seen as a great moment of deliverance and a type of salvation for the Jewish people, one worthy of annual celebration; whereas for Christians, salvation was brought only by Jesus.

From a Persian and Iranian perspective, it is hard to prove or disprove the life of Queen Esther as a historical character. Noted scholars of Iranian and Persian history such as Touraj Daryaee (University of California) and Lloyd Lewellyn-Jones (University of Edinburgh) do point out that Persian literature of the twelfth through fourteenth centuries refers to Esther (e.g. see *In Queen Esther's Garden*).

As early as the third century C.E. (cf. A.D.), Persians visited a neighboring synagogue and assessed a drawing depicting the Purim story inside (see Daryaee, "To Learn and Remember..." in "For Further Reading"). Yet most of these echoes of Esther reference Jewish accounts, and there is little within Persian history per se, outside of literature, to pin down Esther's existence, let alone her biography.

Like some Western Biblical scholars, most Iranian historians think that the Esther story originated sometime between 400–200 B.C.E. (before the common era), and might be a reworking of the Mesopotamian goddess Ishtar's story. Indeed, if Esther existed, it is possible that she adopted or was given the name Esther or Ishtar to blend in with court parlance since her Hebrew name, Hadassah, would have certainly exposed her true identity.

Within Jewish scholarship itself, there is doubt about the veracity of the entire story. For example, the *Jewish Encyclopedia* notes anachronisms, improbabilities, and mismatches within the writings of ancient historians such as Herodotus. Moreover, there are highly exaggerated versions of the story featuring angels who enter the plot in *deus ex machina* style just in time to twist fate and the storyline.

Historians Damdaev and Lukonin (Cambridge) thought of the work as a historical novel which was likely to be true. Bickerman (Columbia) observed that Esther was a variation on an ancient, popular story echoed in *1001 Arabian Nights*. Leading Rabbis and scholars such as Gordis, Bronstein, and Friedlander (Central Conference of American Rabbis) narrated a wide range of interpretations of Esther—from hoax and satire to patriotic literature, legend, and scripture.

Ultimately, the perceived veracity of the tale depends not only upon the faith and tradition of the storyteller, but also upon the beliefs of the readership. Like so many narratives written B.C.E., it is hard to pin down evidence. Whatever the veracity of each detail, the overarching power of Esther's story paved a path through history.

THE TEN FACTORS

In Esther's case, "allegiance and loyalties" (number six) has already been singled out as among the most important factors. But all ten played a part in the decision-making context and help us better understand the case:

1. **Notions of fairness and justice:** Persian justice was based upon regal decision-making, while Jewish justice was divinely ordained. Esther had to choose between the king's arbitrary moral order and the prescribed Judaic sense of justice, which included "thou shalt not kill," and made clear that God's law trumps human law. Genocide by any other name, even if regally commanded, would have seemed a far greater injustice than disloyalty to an inhumane order.

2. **Impact or consequences:** There can be little doubt that Esther knew her decision would have life and death consequences for many thousands. Even if she lived, one consequence would have been losing the trust of those around her. Since she had deceived the court about her Jewish identity, how could she be trusted in other matters? Another consequence would have been the fate of Haman, Mordecai, and their families if Esther's plan proved successful. For the king, his consequences would have entailed either losing his queen or his credibility as a ruler who looked double-minded. For many innocent children, slaves, and entire families, the consequence would have meant death without trial. Everyone Esther knew would be impacted by her decision.

3. **Ends and means:** Esther had already chosen dishonest means to obtain the ends of becoming queen. Then she had to decide whether to remain

dishonest. Honesty about her Jewish heritage might not have achieved her desired outcome. In a matter with such severe consequences, the means did not seem critical. She was quite willing to scheme since so many lives were at stake. Ultimately, she let her humane objectives justify her cunning means and maintain her cover identity, "Esther," rather than revealing that she was actually "Hadassah." Philosophers have often argued that deception is not justified unless lives or welfare are at stake. In Esther's case, she was willing to value human lives above honesty and transparency, and thus used dishonest means to obtain just, humane goals.

4. **Tone and atmosphere:** Esther's faith required a sacred atmosphere, so it was not unusual that she called for prayer and fasting when tension became severe. However, as a new arrival to the court, she had little control over the tone of Persian regal culture. An atmosphere of anger and bullying ruled royal proceedings, and it was her objective to bring about a more peaceful tone. For Esther, a low tone of "might makes right" could be elevated to a high tone of "right makes right."

5. **Motivation and higher law:** Although on the surface it can be argued that Esther's primary motivation was survival, a more benign reading of her character could claim that her true motivation was piety and humane justice. Clearly, Mordecai symbolized a higher law to her, and it was the laws of her faith and thus of her God which she ultimately honored. Of course, she was also directly motivated by survival—her own and that of the Jewish people. But it would be cynical to assume that she was only propelled by self-interest. By all accounts, Esther was also motivated by a law which included "thou shalt not kill," "honor thy father and mother," and "thou shalt have no other gods before me."

6. **Allegiance and loyalty:** As discussed in greater detail above, Esther's case is ultimately one of conflicting loyalties to her husband and her uncle; to the visible and the invisible; to her court and her people; to political and faith-based codes; and to her Persian king and her divine one. Ultimately, she gave more weight to deity, family, justice, and heritage than to government, position, marriage, and materialism.

7. **Values and principles:** Whereas the king most valued power, Mordecai valued faith. The principle of "might makes right" was in sharp contrast to the sacred, life-affirming principles of the Torah. With hindsight it can also be argued that the feminine values of care and compassion contested with the more patriarchal values of ambition and authority. Ultimately, the

values honoring the feminine and faith overcame those promoting empire and executive fiat.

8. **Cultural context:** Living within a Persian absolute monarchy meant that lives were curtailed when not micromanaged by the king and his vizier. Moral decision-making was only rewarded when it served the king's interests and his chain of command.

   The queen had only nominal power since she shared the king's bed and at times she could be closely shepherded by eunuchs or soldiers. Jews were a marginal, impotent subculture trapped within Persian law and military rule. Hence, Esther's life and culture were tightly controlled and her more hidden thoughts and impulses were guided by her Jewish moral training.

9. **Implications:** The long-term effects of Esther's decision would have profound impact upon humanity. Genocide in Persia might have been copied in other empires and the Jews entirely eliminated, as well as all women who questioned royal edicts, and all wives and queens (like Vashti) who did not fully obey their husbands. Ultimately—although Esther did not realize it—ethnic, religious, and gender history would be drastically changed by her stance.

10. **Proportion and balance:** Clearly, Esther did not keep a checklist by which to weigh these ten variables. She was forced to consider consequences, since the fate of an entire people was in her hands. Loyalties were extremely important, since betraying the king meant death, while betraying her people meant spiritual death. Cultural context, implications, and higher law also figured prominently. Finally, her motivation to preserve her own life and those of the Jewish people while serving her god and faith must be seen as a, if not the, primary factor.

Each of these ten variables held significance in Easter's decision, but it is clear that the three most important were consequences, loyalties, and motivation.

THE LEGACY AND THE INFLUENCE

By the time the great French playwright, Jean Racine, wrote *Esther* in 1689, six of his contemporaries and predecessors had already staged their versions of her story. Variations of the tale have been told countless times. The Mordecai vs. Haman conflict is still enacted and recounted worldwide during Purim over twenty-five centuries after the death of Xerxes.

So, one person and story, whether legendary or real, can exert penetrating influence across both geography and history. Probably more people know Esther's story than that of her husband (also known as Xerxes) despite his historical advantage in status, race, and gender.

Reflecting upon some of the factors identified in the previous chapter, we might ask: what would have happened if Esther could have called upon some of the great thinkers in ethics when making her decision? Aristotle and Confucius might have advised her to find a moral mean or moderating midpoint between temerity and timidity. Immanuel Kant might have suggested that she imagine what the world would be like if everyone made the same moral decision that she would make. He would have requested that she treat all persons involved as valid of themselves, not as steppingstones for her own purpose. John Stuart Mill might have advised her to make the utilitarian decision that genuinely benefited the greatest number of people.

More recently, Carol Gilligan, Nell Noddings, and other feminist ethicists would have encouraged Esther to lean toward care and compassion. The great justice expert, John Rawls, would have urged her not to give preferential treatment due to social distinctions, including race, gender, profession, or religion. The important Jewish philosopher, Martin Buber, would have urged her to "view the other such as the one I am," and thus to make the decision as if those involved were all Esther.

Had she lived backwards in time, like Merlin (King Arthur's mentor), Esther might have also consulted Native American leaders such as Luther Standing Bear, who would have advised that she consider the impact any decision would have upon the earth and next generations. Had she asked advice from Lao-Tzu, credited as the founder of Taoism, he might have suggested that she follow the natural way, that is "the Way of Life," such that she did nothing to manipulate or nudge the unfolding outcome already in motion.

Although it is possible that Esther knew part of this menu of moral choice through intuition, it is unlikely that she thought in terms of principles, theorems, ethicists, and case studies. Whether real queen or legendary heroine, Esther ultimately chose an allegiance to the invisible, to a marginalized minority, and to conscience.

In essence, she also chose Mill's "greatest good for the greatest number," Noddings' emphasis upon "care and compassion," Kant's treatment of people as ends of themselves, and his notion of modeling the moral behavior we wish to see globally enacted. Long before Mill, Noddings, and Kant were born, the issues they addressed loomed large. It might well be argued that Esther's actions would also have pleased Buber and Rawls, if not Luther Standing Bear, Lao-Tzu, Aristotle, and Confucius.

Whether her story is historically true or whether it only rings true in a literary and mythic sense, Esther's dilemma raised the question of whether one may serve a higher order than the state and the vows of (royal) marriage. The question of duty—whether it is ultimately owed to country, to God, to self, to family, tribe or race, to partner, to the truth, or to another—profoundly confronted Esther. Honoring an invisible loyalty, in her case, meant threatening a visible one.

THE BOTTOM LINE

Whatever her fears, Queen Esther answered them with out-of-the-box thinking and ethical *chutzpah*. She set a precedent for social justice by challenging the precursors to anti-Semitism and confronting authoritarian rule at great, personal risk. And for perhaps the first time in the recording of substantial ethical choice, what had been called history became herstory.

Herstory Month is now celebrated as a tribute to women on many campuses and within many organizations. The prototype for this volume, *Profiles in Courage* by John F. Kennedy, does not include women within its narrative trail of political heroes. Indeed, one of Kennedy's concluding chapters is entitled "Other Men of Courage."

Caroline Kennedy's sequel, *Profiles in Courage for Our Time*, does include one American female politician and thus opens the door for considering moral leadership beyond stereotype. It is one purpose of this book to suggest that no demographic—no gender, no nationality, no profession, no race—has a monopoly on ethical leadership. Indeed, the four women profiled herein—Queen Esther, Marie Curie, Rachel Carson, and Malala Yousafzai—were born into quite different nationalities, eras, religions, classes, and outlooks.

No one could be more demographically different from me and many readers of this book than an ancient Persian-Jewish beauty queen who lived in a harem and co-ruled an empire as a teenager. It is time to break the image that those facing the worst ethical decisions or making the greatest moral choices were all middle-aged, white, male, American statesmen.

While each of the primarily WASP (white Anglo-Saxon Protestant) politicians chosen by John Kennedy for his profiles were admirable and inspiring men, it is important to note that every race, faith, country, and profession is populated with both courageous heroes and moral cowards. And great women of all ages, professions, and backgrounds have been important role models no less than men.

Queen Esther, as much legendary as historical, set a precedent for public victory. Her story and herstory widen the frame for us to consider moral leadership beyond all categories. Indeed, the next profile in moral courage during the twenty-first century could be someone at the center of your own demographic. It could be you.

CHAPTER 3

SOCRATES:
(470-399 B.C.E.)

DEATH AS A TEACHING MOMENT

For Crito, the stakes could not be higher. The execution of the greatest man he knew was imminent and yet for Socrates, the stakes were even higher. It was a matter of the utmost principle not only for the present year, 399 B.C.E., but for posterity. The purpose to which he had devoted his entire life of seventy years was at risk.

It was hard for Crito to see straight. Not just the shadowy earth and overcast sky, but his inner struggle blurred his vision.

Crito was approaching Socrates' prison cell prior to dawn. If he hurried, he could provide Socrates with a plan of escape before daylight. The harried and hastened disciple had already arranged safe passage for Socrates and bribed the morally challenged guards.

But Crito, one of Socrates' most devout followers, knew that his greatest hurdle would be Socrates himself. Although unjustly sentenced to death, the seventy-year-old philosopher had peacefully accepted his pending execution by way of drinking a cup of hemlock juice.

Crito winced at the thought of Athens' greatest thinker swallowing the extremely painful poison, which paralyzes and then collapses the respiratory system. He had imagined what it would be like—the nausea, the twitching, the rebellion of the organs, the sustained and severe headaches, and the trapped feeling of no escape once the seizures set in.

Accused of corrupting the youth of Athens and of sacrilegious practices, Socrates had defended himself before a jury of five hundred Athenians, only to be found guilty by the thin margin of 280 to 220. If only eleven percent of the jurors who had voted "guilty" had voted "not guilty" instead, his life could have been spared.

But the numbers did not matter to Socrates, and Crito felt that the escape plan might not matter to him either. He had to persuade Socrates to see the pointlessness and ill effects of what, to Crito, seemed like agonizing suicide. He had rehearsed over a dozen reasons why Socrates should flee to safety.

What would Socrates say to each?

CONVINCING SOCRATES TO LIVE

Just who was this Socrates? Our best guess is that he was born in 469 B.C.E., as the son of a stone mason and sculptor in the Greek city-state (*polis*) of Athens. If historians are accurate, he would have been nine years old when Queen Esther died less than two thousand miles away.

Attracted by natural philosophy and the process of reasoning, he established a reputation as a controversial thinker. He seemed to be an original genius to those inspired by him, and an annoying town critic to many of those in power. He was seen by his followers as a teacher of *arête* (excellence), and thus of the art of bettering one's self and one's thinking.

Within his own Athenian circle, Socrates became famous for original critical thinking. Perhaps the two phrases most associated with him, "know thyself" and "the unexamined life is not worth living," still give evidence of his life's greatest priority. The Greek words *philos* (love) and *sophia* (knowledge/wisdom) are the etymological roots of "philosophy" ("the love of wisdom"). His passion for *sophia* was so great that Socrates has been called a (or even the) founding father of Western philosophy.

No wonder Crito, Plato, and other younger thinkers idolized him. According to Plato, Crito provided no fewer than thirteen reasons why Socrates should flee to safety. But Crito knew that convincing Socrates would be like moving Mount Olympus ... Crito kept imagining the paralyzed, twitching body of a hemlock victim.

Somehow, Crito had to bypass Socrates' steel trap of a mind and open his heart. First, he would make strong appeals to emotion by reminding Socrates that his three sons, one of whom was an infant, would become orphans. So too would protégés like Crito become orphaned without their beloved mentor. They would "lose a friend who could never be replaced."

Crito was also concerned that he and other disciples would look bad for not paying to save Socrates' life and thus for seeming to value money more than their greatest friend. Public opinion was important to Crito since the mob mentality governed matters of life and death in Athenian society, as Socrates himself was only recently reminded. Would Socrates want his best friends to appear callous and negligent?

Crito also knew that Socrates might be concerned about the safety of his friends and the difficulties of exile. Another appeal to his heart was in order. He explained that Socrates' future expenses would be paid by foreign friends who were not in harm's way, ensuring that Socrates' local friends would not be at risk. Crito also conveyed that the noted philosopher would be respected wherever he traveled.

The disciple seemed especially concerned that Socrates would be playing into the hands of his enemies. Allowing an unjust trial and penalty to determine Socrates' fate would only encourage them. Here was the opportunity for a moral appeal. Would Socrates want injustice to prevail?

Moreover, Crito argued that the entire trial and outcome could and should have been avoided. There could be no manliness or virtue in tacitly approving of a manipulated charade, or in abandoning one's responsibility to justice, family, and friends. Crito proffered that the easy way out—suicide—lacked courage.

Again, Crito imagined the twitching, powerless body, and he envisioned what would, for Socrates, be the greatest torture—a paralyzed tongue. This time he would share these horrid images with his mentor. Building to a climactic crescendo, the young student argued that drinking the hemlock would be both a disgraceful and miserable outcome for Socrates and all those who cared about him.

The first rays of morning sun cast long shadows across the cell floor and provided the inspiration for Crito's final, more practical appeal. Crito pleaded with Socrates that the window for escape was closing quickly. An immediate decision was required.

OTHER ARGUMENTS FROM THE GREEK CHORUS

Socrates' friends had no doubt offered other reasons why he must escape. For example, they might have argued that his original thinking must continue to be developed and advanced. Moreover, his followers, who would become future leaders and teachers, needed to be further educated. His critical influence upon Athens and the Greece of his day should be sustained. His wife, Xanthippe, and others not mentioned by Crito, needed him. Most importantly, knowledge and good could not succumb to ignorance and evil.

According to the written accounts of Plato and Xenophon, Socrates had these many arguments to consider. This was not an easy decision for Socrates. He would later concede to Crito, "I am exceedingly desirous to be persuaded of you, but not against my own better judgment." Despite his apparent calm in that moment, he had also spoken earlier, in his court defense, about a fear of death.

Thus, the senior philosopher was faced with a tough ethical dilemma. Would he sacrifice everything in the material world—his wife and sons, career, influence, the ongoing development of his ideas and friendships, and life itself?

Or would he sacrifice what he loved in the ideal world—the very principles for which he stood and dedicated his life?

Exactly what were these ideals that could be deemed more important than life itself? And how did he go about teaching them?

THE BACK STORY

Socrates' unique skill seemed to be the dismantling of other people's opinions. He relentlessly cross-examined their ideas in a manner later called the "Socratic method." He became both hero and villain for exposing mindless opinions underneath the cloak of feigned authority. Such a quest for truth led him to re-examine virtually all assumptions.

For example, at that time Athens honored the beauty of exact mathematical proportion. The Athenian aesthetic was arguably based upon the symmetry of design. Yet Socrates, whose face was notoriously disproportionate and unattractive, argued along these lines: "Are not my eyes more beautiful because they protrude further and thus can see the world better?"

He continued: "Is not my nose the most beautiful because my nostrils flare outward and thus can smell better?" He had made this unique argument from an unseen angle of observation strictly to challenge orthodox thinking. Again and again he would upset the conventional wisdom of Athenians.

Whether or not Socrates held to the notion of his own personal beauty, he was interested in re-examining every platitude and accepted truth against the possibility for error and discovery. Above all, he was interested in thinking about thinking.

Perhaps his most threatening assertion was that he could not truly know anything. Socrates claimed that the most human beings can know is what we do not know. Thus, a wise man is not the one with the most knowledge or best logic, but rather the one who realizes what he does not and perhaps cannot know.

Such ultimate humility seemed like penultimate arrogance to his critics. It was as if Socrates, the one who exposed others' ignorance, had created a humiliating scheme to place himself above everyone in the hierarchy of thinking. He was, after all, the one who claimed to know what he did not know, and thus was a wise man among fools.

Whatever the case, Socrates turned the spotlight away from clever rhetoric and toward self-knowing and truth itself. Aspiring middle-class citizens who employed tutors and sophists to appear educated suddenly felt exposed. In many ways, Socrates seemed to be saying "the emperor has no clothes" about the so-called thinking of politicians and the Athenian mob.

Thinking about thinking could be tolerated in the abstract. But when he started thinking about their thinking, the ambitious and pretentious felt personally attacked by his demolition pedagogy. One of his students had likened the philosopher to the stingray, which numbs its prey. No wonder Socrates raised not only questions, but also anger, jealousy, and resentment.

PERSPECTIVISM

In *The Will to Power*, the German philosopher Friedrich Nietzsche coined the term "perspectivism" to explain the perspectives human beings create to make others look inferior and to elevate our own stature. It is not surprising that some Greeks developed the perspective that Socrates was not so much a truth-teller. Rather, he was a troublemaker, traitor to the state, or an aloof eccentric with his head in the clouds.

This latter perspective was perpetuated in Aristophanes' famous theatrical satire, *The Clouds*, which showed Socrates hanging in the clouds in a balloon-basket. Since Socrates and Aristophanes were elsewhere depicted as friends, it is hard to know to what degree the demeaning comedy was meant to be an affectionate spoof, and to what degree it was a biting lampoon. But it is known that most comedies of the day defended traditional Athenian values.

Whatever Aristophanes' intention, the crowds who saw the play were shown a Socrates who was part con man, part buffoon, and part impractical egghead. His ridiculous students were shown bent over in study so they could simultaneously learn about geology with their faces, and astronomy with their rear ends. By the end of the play, Socrates was symbolically annihilated when his school was burned to the ground.

However admiring or vicious Aristophanes may have intended his caricature, the comic image of Socrates played into the vision of his enemies. Indeed, as part of his defense at his trial, he noted that Athenians had been prejudiced against him due to the misleading images within *The Clouds* and other satires. Beyond any others, Aristophanes' perspective had shaped the public imagination.

However, other views of Socrates differed greatly from the poetic license of theater. Xenophon, the distinguished author, soldier, gentleman-farmer, and follower of Socrates, has provided posterity with a nobler, greater image in his works *Memorabilia* and the *Apology of Socrates*.

Like Plato, Xenophon mixed eyewitness with reported testimony about Socrates' genius, methods, and penetrating influence. While Aristophanes created a foolish Socrates who was out of control, it was Socrates' modeling of self-control, even approaching death, which most stole Xenophon's admiration.

BENEATH THE SURFACE: THE THREE CHARGES

Such stock images of Socrates from admirers and comedians conceal some of the deeper factors that were most at play during his trial and imprisonment. In his trial, Socrates faced three charges: 1) not worshipping the gods of his city-state, 2) introducing new and unfamiliar religious practices, and 3) corrupting the youth.

In a sense, the first two charges could be reduced to one—substantial sacrilege. What is unusual in this first charge is that in some senses, Socrates seemed more spiritual (if not more religious) than his accusers. In fact, he constantly heard an inner sacred voice, sometimes in dreams, sometimes while awake, which gave him specific direction.

The great scholar, A.E. Taylor (Oxford), surmised that Socrates was introduced to and friendly toward the Orphic religion of his day. Another expert, Gregory Vlastos (Princeton), thought of Socrates as a supernaturalist ruled by divine signs and inner instructions, not unlike the later historical figure Joan of Arc.

What seems important is that Socrates was divinely oriented in fact, whereas many Athenians seemed to be religious only in custom. He felt that many simply went through the motions. In his own words during his defense, Socrates said: "I do nothing but go about persuading you, young and old, to have your first and greatest concern, not for your body or for your money, but for your soul…"

Rather than being sacrilegious, Socrates aspired to inspire others toward a higher state of being within their religion. His stand devaluing materialism, hedonism, and human achievement in favor of purifying the soul was threatening to lip-service worshippers, sensualists, and indulgence mongers, no matter how devout their pretense.

At heart, Socrates made a plea for deep spiritual values. Four centuries prior to the rise of Christianity, he seemed to be advocating non-retaliation in a culture that championed the sword, if not "an eye for an eye." Indeed, his life and trial seemed to be excellent examples of a non-violent, non-vindictive ethic we will discuss in depth later when considering Gandhi's practices of *satyagraha* and *ahimsa*.

Always seeking to go deeper, Socrates sensed that the human nature projected onto the Greek gods by human beings was not at the core of divine reality. What mattered was not the gods' affairs (in both senses) with men and women, but rather the quality of one's character. It was more important to be wise than wealthy, and wiser to do good than anything else. So, Socrates was more like a prophet than a heretic or an atheist.

Nevertheless, his claim that he was favored by the Delphic Oracle, and that he was linked with other divinity via dreams and an inner voice, put him on troubling legal grounds. Was he claiming to be above Athenian law due to divine intervention? Was he fully sane? Was he a cult leader governed by hallucinated, supernatural sensations? Given that he questioned everything, was he undermining the traditional religion and advocating a new one? In a climate of hearsay and mob influence, one can sense how those questions arose and circulated.

THE THIRD CHARGE

When closely examined, the third charge Socrates faced—corruption of the youth—may have been far more serious. On the surface it seemed that he was indicted for stirring up young men intellectually and for making them question the status quo. Certainly, such action might disturb those in authority who would have lost face. But was this the core concern? After all, Socrates and others had been questioning convention for decades in the presence of young men (cf. disciples) without facing a trial. What was really going on?

The famous independent journalist I.F. Stone found these questions worthy of a full investigation, so he studied Greek to better understand the original texts. Stone's detective work concluded that the trial was essentially political due to Socrates' association with three young conspirators—Alcibiades, Critias, and Charmides.

Socrates made it clear that none of these followers were paying students and that he was not responsible for their political actions. Nevertheless, to the uninformed and unsympathetic, he seemed partially or wholly accountable for their treasons.

All three former students had been at the heart of political upheavals in 411, 404, or/and 401 B.C.E. In each of these years, a miniature civil war had all but terminated Athens' democracy. To differing degrees, each man had displayed tendencies ranging from betrayal of democracy to outright tyranny. Each would have been seen by Athenians as enemies of the state or criminals. So, although Socrates had loyal followers like Plato and Xenophon, and although he had little if any control over the actions of previous associates, he became a victim of guilt by association, a seemingly anti-patriotic mentor for dangerous rebels.

Seen in this light, jurors must have wondered: "Will Socrates train more violent criminals?" Or, using modern language, they might have queried: "Will Socrates galvanize more terrorists'?"

Moreover, some of Socrates' followers were admirers of Sparta, a rival city-state to Athens. On top of this, he had unpleasant history with one of his primary accusers, Anytus, who seemed to believe that Socrates had prevented the proper education of his son. Anytus was also not amused by Socrates' bristling attacks upon the status quo, and thus upon Anytus himself.

So, there were prejudices in play during the trial about specific youth, including 1) three notorious threats to what might today be called "national security," 2) those sympathetic to Sparta, and 3) the son of a primary plaintiff. Since city-states were vulnerable to the potential invasions of enemy empires and rival city-states, in essence, Socrates was on trial *sub rosa* for a far more political crime that at best threatened public safety, and at worst was outright treason.

The unvoiced fear was that Socrates could inspire not just quasi-slanderous attacks on individuals that would undermine their credibility and stature, but that he might also inspire further conspiracy. So, for I.F. Stone among others, the imprisoned Socrates was in essence a political prisoner.

In Socrates's defense, it could be argued that the charges against him were trumped up, that he had not broken any actual Athenian laws, and that he was only guilty by association, and thus was innocent. But, since the spurious charges were inflated, and the real fears and prejudices were unstated, the underlying motives of the accusers could not be openly addressed.

Neither did Socrates, who could have pointed to his own distinguished record of military service, help his own case by being undiplomatic. Jurors may have also taken into account his lifelong distance from public affairs, which gave him the appearance of being an onlooker and critic, not a citizen-participant. In his fifty years of adult life, he had only once become involved in the city's civic controversies.

At best he seemed like a conscientious objector, and at worst like a parasitic curmudgeon. Whatever the appearance of the trial and the three charges, Socrates' apolitical—if not anti-political—stance, his image as barbed iconoclast, and his range of dangerous associates brought obvious prejudice into the heart of the trial.

Summarily, Socrates had offended virtually every sector within the Athenian mainstream. His open-minded, truth-seeking beliefs were a threat to religious fundamentalists, and his challenge to materialist values made him unattractive to the wealthy within the business community. His stated political preferences were a threat to those in power: he preferred leadership by a single, expert leader over elected leadership by the democratic herd.

Finally, his teachings sought to elevate and distance himself from the sophists, whom he considered pseudo-sophisticated teachers and false thinkers. Hence, sophists, who felt that their credibility and power were threatened, also felt that they had a score to settle with Socrates. Whatever the actual charges and pretenses of the trial, and whatever the tradition of free speech within Athens, there were many who subconsciously, if not openly, hoped to muffle, muzzle, mute, or even murder Socrates.

THE SENTENCE

To modern observers, the trial of Socrates would have seemed bizarre. All participants, including the five hundred randomly selected jurors, sat under a large canopy to protect themselves from intense solar heat. Precise time limits for speakers were kept by a water device that functioned like an hourglass. A facilitator called "the king" officiated but did not participate in determining verdicts.

Only Socrates defended himself. He stated that it was his first time in a court and he stressed that, unlike his accusers, he would speak only the bald truth. The defendant likened himself to the gadfly, which stings the lazy horse (in this case Athens) to propel it forward.

As a central theme of his case, Socrates claimed that the Delphic Oracle had named him to be the wisest man in Athens. Indeed, Socrates asserted that it was his sacred mission to truly educate others by exposing their ignorance. Not to do so would be a violation of divine edict.

Almost certainly Socrates' rigid stance worked against him. A.E. Taylor and others surmised that initially many Athenian politicians wanted only to silence and distance him through banishment, not to kill him. But after his guilty verdict, he was asked to recommend his own sentence. He might well have appeased his critics had he recommended self-exile.

Instead, he shocked many by proposing what must have seemed like a self-serving sentence. On the one hand, Socrates proposed that he pay a relatively small fine. On the other, he also recommended that he be given a seat for life at the table of honor, where only Olympic heroes and distinguished generals sat. Since he had so well served Athens by divine instruction, he felt he should be rewarded.

Such an unexpected and seemingly arrogant penalty angered so many jurors that the second vote, which was taken to determine his fate, was far more condemning than the first. Socrates was sentenced to death by a vote of 360 to 140.

THE DECISION: TO BE THEN NOT TO BE

Saddened and shocked by this death sentence, Crito came to Socrates with a plan of escape. He made his arguments about the needs of Socrates' family and friends, about the unjustness of the trial and verdict, about not playing into the hands of Socrates' enemies, and several other rehearsed points. And he had warned Socrates that the matter of escape was urgent.

How would Socrates respond? On the one hand, the philosopher had mentioned his fear of death and his homage to Crito's arguments. But on the other, he was a man of unflinching principles.

Socrates was clear and determined in his reply: he would drink the hemlock.

Although the query, "to be, or not to be," implies tough ethical questions, for Socrates the final answer was straightforward. He could not contradict his professed lifetime maxims. Nor could he commit treason against the spirit of citizenship. If one expressed integrity in life, so too must one express integrity in death.

Socrates put forth many counterarguments to Crito. He iterated that one should not be persuaded by public opinion. In essence, he asked Crito, "should an athlete prefer the advice of his fans to that of his trainer or his coach?" Socrates implied that he, not his friends and family, was his own trainer and the sacred voice that spoke to him was his coach.

Moreover, Socrates argued that it is not length of life that is to be valued, but rather a good life, a just and honorable one. If he broke the law, his life would no longer be honorable.

Furthermore, Socrates was not persuaded that the injustice of others gave him the right to be unjust—two wrongs did not make a right. So, he replied, "we ought not retaliate or render evil for evil." Employing a clever literary device, Socrates then made the laws of Athens into a character in his argument. He asserted to Crito that the personified Laws, if they could talk, would claim that they had greater moral authority than the individual. After all, he had chosen to benefit from the protection of the laws for seventy years. In essence, a type of contract between an individual and the state was in place. So, like others, Socrates had a patriotic duty to serve in the military and to uphold and abide by the state's laws.

Noting that he had always lived in Athens, Socrates argued that had he disagreed with the laws of his city, he could have moved elsewhere. He also never stated that exile to another city-state should be his just penalty. Instead, he had always chosen to live in Athens and by Athenian law. So, he must die in Athens by Athenian law.

The aging sage continued that even if he did relocate, he was not convinced that he would be welcome elsewhere. After all, he would be a fugitive criminal. Furthermore, for Socrates to engage in law-breaking would give credibility to his jurors' and critics' claim that he was immoral. Moreover, to an Athenian, being exiled did not mean mere relocation, it meant being uprooted, almost like being an orphan.

As for his family, Socrates felt that his friends, if they were true friends, would care for his children. Indeed, Socrates believed that his family and friends could not be above the law any more than he could.

The thinker's most overriding arguments were that the laws were sacred. Justice must be pre-eminent above self concern. Socrates' voice compelled him to take the right action, no matter what his self-interest. In short, he had no choice but to follow his lifelong principles, his conscience, divine instruction, and the laws. As I.F. Stone wrote, "Socrates needed the hemlock to fulfill a mission."

Since he felt that the soul was immortal, there is even a sense that Socrates knew he was ascending to a better place. Crito, like Plato and Phaedo, noted Socrates' strange sense of consistent happiness despite his death row confinement.

More than one author has suggested that the accused faced death with a Buddhist temperament of transcendence and acceptance. By all accounts he seemed reconciled to his fate and determined to stand— and then eternally rest—upon principle.

THE TEN FACTORS

In Socrates' case, some of the ten factors carried atypical weight.

1. **Notions of fairness and justice:** The philosopher's sense of justice was more important to him than his own self-interest and the interests of all those closest to him. Principle was paramount when he argued that if he had benefited from the laws as a citizen, he was accountable to the laws even by forfeiting his life. The fairness of the accusations and trial were not given the same weight as the fairness of the laws, and the sense that equal protection by the law means it is also fair to have equal punishment

by the law. On what grounds could Socrates claim to be exempt from the law with fairness to others? What is just for one must be just for all, so Socrates could not claim to be above the law or an exception to it. What was just for him or his family and friends was not ultimately as important as what was just for the state and its citizens, the very same state and citizens he had so frequently and thoroughly criticized for shallow thinking.

2. **Impact or consequences:** The patriarch did not seem nearly as concerned about consequences to himself, family, and students, as to his reputation and a just society. To be a man of honor, it was more important that he lived and died justly than to unjustly extend his life, albeit to educate and care for others. Although his decision would deeply influence his legacy, he seemed unconcerned about that consequence and the possibly dire impact that his death would have upon those who needed him. More important than tangible consequences were the more ideal ones, which might have come by upholding key principles as discussed below.

3. **Ends and means:** For Socrates, fulfilling a noble mission required dying an honorable death, even if he had been dishonored by his peers. In essence, purposeful suicide was the means to complete his life statement as a philosopher. Ironically, choosing death gave life to his teachings. Electing "not to be" was the honorable means of achieving the ends of upholding Athens and its laws, and thus the greater social good. Justification of this choice to self-sacrifice was also done by a highly rational, fully thoughtful means consistent with his philosophy that true thinking is more important than its impact or outcome.

4. **Tone and atmosphere:** Although the atmosphere surrounding public poisoning is hardly appealing, Socrates was nevertheless concerned about maintaining a civil tone. By abstaining from violence and outbursts of grief and anger, he modeled a spirit of acceptance, community responsibility, and non-violence for his followers. Even at his moments of greatest danger, Socrates seemed determined to be a role model who was logical, even-tempered, and accountable. Tone mattered, and thus he refused to succumb to a vindictive or hostile reaction, which would have lowered him to the attitudinal atmosphere of his critics and the mob.

5. **Motivation and higher law:** When he created the Laws as a character in his dialogue with Crito, Socrates anthropomorphized a body of human agreements (laws) to which he must give allegiance. When he argued that

he spoke for Greek deities, he claimed that he served an even higher law than Athenian law. Both the laws of humans and the gods seemed to dictate that he be ferried across the River Styx. Human law is by its very nature higher than individual will, preference, and justification. Even his sense that he was serving a higher Delphic deity could not grant him exception from his duty as citizen to obey the human laws that protected him, even when they also punished him.

6. **Allegiance and loyalty:** It is surprising that Socrates seemed largely without human loyalties. His wife, Xanthippe, his sons, and his many students mattered less to him than ideals. The loyalty he did profess was to the very Athenian government which had found him guilty. His ultimate loyalties were not so much to people as to abstractions. In this regard he stands unique in this book. While many others in this volume stood tall for principle, most seemed to struggle deeply with the possibility of abandoning or injuring others. For Socrates, the welfare and comfort of others closest to him was not a primary concern. His highest loyalty by far was to ideals and ideas.

7. **Values and principles:** Socrates pulled the rug out from under those who greatly valued money, status, and power. So, he was ennobled when he proved that he valued something more than his own money and survival. He preferred thinking, truth, and justice over material and social advantage. Ultimately, the ideals and ideas for which he died (as immediately above) were reflections of strong democratic, legal, and egalitarian values, as expressed in principles such as "all are equal before the law," "none stand above the law," and "my country right or wrong, but nevertheless my country."

8. **Cultural context:** It seems curious that a family man of seventy years old would appear unconcerned about the fate of his wife. However, pre–Hellenic Greece did not value women, embraced slavery, and supported a city-state government in which each patriarch and polis could govern its own affairs. Even if Socrates' wife and other women, children, and slaves had mattered deeply to him, it is not likely they would have been very important to Plato and the other men who later wrote about Socrates. Within Greek intellectual culture, women, slaves, and children were all but invisible.

Moreover, Athenians strongly valued the strength of their state against rival city-states and conquering powers. Even hints of treason and those who inspired the treasonous were not to be tolerated.

Finally, Greek education did not value critical thinking in the way that modern Western thinkers do. Sophists, high-priced tutors, and others who taught social climbers to appear fashionably educated carried more clout and support than those who taught the quest for real truth and the confession of human ignorance.

9. **Implications:** The long shadow cast by Socrates has helped to mold philosophy, liberal arts (where Socratic questioning is a cornerstone), the academy, and Western civilization. Since his death punctuated and martyred his life, it has become almost a part of his philosophy and definitely a part of his impact. Socrates' hemlock and Newton's apple may be the best-known plants within the history of ideas.

   But it is hard to imagine that Socrates could have known about these long-term implications of his stance. Indeed, he seemed to be abandoning and traumatizing the very disciples who would extend his legacy. His larger concern seems to have been the implications of law-breaking and abandoning one's principles. In that regard, he was more concerned with the implications of his actions for Athens and its laws, and for his own reputation, which would be preserved in dying by the same principles by which he had lived.

10. **Proportion and balance:** Unlike Plato's student, Aristotle, who advocated a "golden mean," Socrates did not seek to find balance and compromise. Loyalties, tone, and consequences did not weigh as much as civic justice and ideals. Indeed, what is memorable about Socrates' death is not only the strange democratic sentence and toxic outcome, but also his choice to value ideals above family and survival. Faced with a similar ethical decision, most people would have welcomed Crito's egress. In his reply to Crito, Socrates certainly did not give significant weight to all ten factors. Ultimately, abstract justice and loyalty to principle mattered more than life itself.

THE LEGACY

After describing Socrates' final moments and words, Plato wrote: "So ended our friend, the man we held best, wisest, the most upright of his age." In the public imagination Plato has remained Socrates' best advocate, friend, biographer, and publicist.

Depending upon the context, Socrates may be seen as a (or the) founder of Western philosophy, a new type of Greek hero, or a committed moral prophet.

Within the current conventional thinking, he is still viewed as a radical thinker of strong ethical vision, who has inspired and provoked millions for over twenty-four centuries.

Like Moses, Joan of Arc, the prophet Muhammad, Jesus, and the Buddha, among others, he faced great resistance for what he self-described as his divinely ordained role and views. Like Plato, Aristotle, Kant, and others, he also attracted great response to his original and independent pursuit of truth. Whether or not he corrupted the youth, he certainly excited them about what Rousseau would later call *"le gai savoir,"* or the joy of learning.

Prior to Socrates, the prototypical Greek hero behaved like a military conqueror and looked like a bronze Adonis. For later generations, Socrates transformed this image of a hero into someone who followed the dictates of conscience above all, no matter the cost.

Thanks to Plato's writings, Socrates also elevated the roles of logic and critical thinking above blind faith and conventional wisdom. Although there were many pre-Socratic thinkers, many ancients and moderns alike regard(ed) Socrates as the root of much subsequent, substantial thought.

By elaborating the notion of "the soul," Socrates had already prepared a place for Christianity to develop the concept four centuries later. He also served as a role model and inspiration for Plato's academy, one that lasted nine centuries until it was closed by Emperor Justinian.

In one sense, Socrates might be seen as the founder of the modern Western university, in which reason and (self-)critical thinking perch at the apex. As Taylor wrote, he "has been, directly or indirectly, the teacher of all thinking men since his own day." Of course, women and men from many other cultures have also been acknowledged as parents of important thought.

Regarding his life of great influence, there is no more dramatic and arresting story than Socrates' deliberate choice to die for an ideal. Whatever the merits of Crito's and other critics' arguments, it is unlikely that Socrates' influence and example would loom as large had he yielded to their preferences.

Socrates has bequeathed to posterity not only the notion that "the unexamined life is not worth living," but also the conviction that the unexamined death is not worth embracing. Although for others the question "to be, or not to be" might be a difficult ethical dilemma, his own ethical standards of accountability, consistency, and integrity were too high to justify "to be" if the laws argued otherwise.

In the final analysis, it was neither personal survival, nor political, military, and financial success that mattered most. Rather, it was an unwavering commitment to his vision of truth, sacred mission, conscience, and character. For Socrates, there could be no higher stakes.

PURPOSEFUL SUICIDE IN THE TWENTY-FIRST CENTURY

Had Socrates been born into a Christian home, he might well have been taught that suicide is a sin. And had he been born into the family of an Islamic suicide bomber, or a Japanese Kamikaze pilot, he would have been told that suicide for a higher purpose is noble. Time and culture alter the interpretation and value of actions.

It is not clear that Socrates would characterize his decision as suicide, despite what others might say. During war it is common that we say a soldier "sacrificed" himself that others might live. Did Socrates sacrifice himself such that his ideas and principles might live? Or was his death suicide? Was it Athenian justice? Or unjust political punishment?

Whether suicide or sacrifice, or something else, the final ethical decision to die is most profound because it is the last decision one can make. There is no posthumous chance to change one's mind.

SOCRATES IN THE CLASSROOM

It is easy for me to hold Socrates up as an exemplar regarding his thinking and questioning. In the classroom, one may admire his reasoning, iconoclasm, and resilience. But I am reluctant to hold Socrates up as a role model for students when considering his purposeful death.

Why invite others to risk dying for a cause when there is no guarantee the cause itself will not die? And who can say what one might accomplish in death that would not be exponentially amplified in life?

After all, the terminal choice is irreversible.

So, when students ask me, "is there any cause worth dying for?" I reply, "if so, then it must be worth living for!"

CHAPTER 4

JOHN ADAMS
(1735-1826)

PEACE AT ALL COSTS?

WHAT IF ...?

Have you ever wondered what might have happened if history had taken a different turn? What if Napoleon had won at Waterloo, or Hitler had repelled the Allied forces on D-Day? What if the atom bomb had been a dud, or Salk had developed an ineffective vaccine for polio? Suppose Nelson Mandela had never been freed from jail? Or Queen Elizabeth I had ruled another twenty years? What if Martin Luther King's, Mahatma Gandhi's, and Abraham Lincoln's assassins had missed?

Such changes need not be political. Suppose Bette Davis was selected to play Scarlett O'Hara in *Gone with The Wind*, or Jackie Robinson was permitted to play major league baseball two years earlier? What if Mother Theresa or Malala had died as a child, or Martin Luther had changed his mind about the pope and Catholicism?

Although it is impossible to know the outcome of each of these hypothetical events, it is safe to say that unforeseen changes might have occurred. If we were alive, we might be speaking a different language, fighting in a foreign army, or working within a different profession if our parents were guided by different events.

Indeed, we might have different allergies, be married to a stranger, or descended of a different family or race if the past was significantly altered. All human decisions have shaped history in unpredictable and sometimes profound ways, and each change can lead to a chain reaction. For example, if Frederick Douglas, Pocahontas, Emperor Hirohito, Jack the Ripper, or Susan P. Anthony had married one of your great-grand parents, whom might you be today?

WHAT IF JOHN ADAMS ...?

So where would world events be without John Adams, the second president of the United States? If he had never lived, would it have mattered? After all, he does not appear on Mount Rushmore with the presidents considered to be most significant. He was not re-elected to the presidency, was often unpopular, and was strongly criticized by both his own Federalist Party and the opposition Republican Party.

And yet, had Adams never lived, our lives would be substantially altered. Without John Adams, George Washington probably would not have been selected head of the Continental Army and elected president of the United States. Without Adams, important treaties and loans may never have been secured for the fledgling colonies.

Arguably, without John Adams, the young colonists would not have built a navy, and might well have lost the Revolutionary War. Without the second president there would have been no John Quincy Adams, his son who was later the sixth President of the United States. Without Adams' encouragement, Thomas Jefferson may never have drafted the Declaration of Independence, nor have seen it adopted by Congress.

So, it is important to ask: "What might have happened if John Adams had solved his most difficult ethical decision differently?" What if his momentous decision about war with France had changed? History tells us that he struggled with that vexing foreign policy matter at length and in depth.

What if he had chosen a different ethical approach? Thousands of lives, the survival of a vulnerable infant nation, and a lasting peace were at stake. Had he chosen a different path, Americans might all be speaking French—if America (as we know it) had even survived.

THE DILEMMA

It was over two thousand years after the deaths of Queen Esther and Socrates, in a fledgling new country thousands of miles from Persia and Greece, on one of those intolerable summer days—the horrendous heat and humidity, coupled with his wig and jacket, seemed insufferable. If he opened the windows, the wasps and mosquitoes would be everywhere—but should the windows remained closed, he felt he would pass out from exhaustion. How could he possibly think about the dilemma that would not go away?

It was undoubtedly the most difficult decision of his presidency, if not of his life. All throughout the year, President John Adams had struggled with what to do about the French. The very nation that had been America's strongest ally during the Revolutionary War—France—was now seizing U.S. ships, cargo, and sailors—all but declaring war upon the United States.

Large beads of sweat poured down his forehead. Was this from the smoldering heat, or the decision? Probably both. What about the window for fresh air? He could see the wasps and sense the mosquitoes rallying for an attack. The window remained closed.

What was he trying to think about? Oh yes, the French. Unlike during the Revolutionary War, when the colonies could count on the Marquis de Lafayette and the Comte de Rochambeau for loyal support, France more recently had been ruled by a disagreeable chain of authority. Such potentates first included a five-person committee called the Directory, which had descended from France's reign of terror. Later, the cunning, manipulative foreign minister, Talleyrand, took over and now the ambitious, treacherous Napoleon Bonaparte was seizing unprecedented power.

John Adams would have preferred not to work with any of these, and was especially appalled by Talleyrand, who had demanded a $10,000,000 loan for France from the relatively impoverished new country. On top of this, Talleyrand insisted that he personally be paid $250,000 as a sweetener to open negotiations. Adams felt that a bribe by any other name would be repulsive.

Concurrently, Napoleon continued to seize power, having conquered Italy, invaded Egypt, and made clear his intentions against Britain and the United States. If left unchecked, Bonaparte would name himself emperor and aspire to world dominion.

Adams had realized all too late that the salty sweat would leak into his stinging eyes. So, he pressed his handkerchief pressed against each, which only intensified the stinging, he found it hard to think about the French with other dilemmas so close at hand—the handkerchief… the window… the humidity… the gnats… the heat… and the mosquitoes…

Still, he knew he had to think this through.

Of great concern were the domestic effects of preparing for war. Adams knew that fighting France would mean creating a strong U.S. Continental Army. Retired former President George Washington had made it clear that he could no longer serve as an active commander-in-chief. Instead, Washington, too old for combat, would only remain as a figurehead if he could appoint his own commanders. And Washington's choice for field marshal, second in command only to Washington, was Alexander Hamilton.

Despite his high regard for Washington, Adams could only tolerate such a scheme if Hamilton remained head of a small, impotent army. Whatever his brilliance as a financier and political party builder, Hamilton seemed just as ambitious as Bonaparte. Both Adams and his wife, Abigail, had witnessed Hamilton's back-stabbing chicanery firsthand.

Indeed, Hamilton, while feigning friendship, had worked repeatedly against the president behind his back, and had sought to govern indirectly by controlling members of Adams' cabinet. Hamilton seemed to be a megalomaniac, a known womanizer, and a master manipulator. President Adams dare not risk having such a man at the head of the army if it grew powerful enough to mount a *coup d'état*.

The sweat. The drenched handkerchief. Was there a dry one somewhere? Where was his drinking water? What about the window?

While supporting Hamilton posed a threat to Adams and the nation, not supporting him posed an equal threat. Alexander was the strongest voice within Adams' Federalist party. To oppose Hamilton could mean political death, a divided party, and Hamilton's heated revenge. Known for dueling, mobilizing opposition, and spreading scandal, Hamilton had already been instrumental in undermining Adams' bids for election. There was little doubt Alexander also had the power to block the president's re-election.

Although hardly a party sycophant, Adams had long been aligned with most goals of the Federalists and could not win election without their support. The rival Republican party would undoubtedly back their leader, Vice President Thomas Jefferson. So, Adams sorely required Federalist backing to secure a second term in office. But now the Federalists wanted a war with France—one led nominally by General George Washington, but actually by General Alexander Hamilton.

It was not only the Federalist Party that backed Hamilton. Increasingly, it was the mood of the nation to favor anti-French militancy. Bands of militia were forming again, and patriotic songs were sung by audiences in theaters. Adams himself had taken to wearing a uniform and sounding like a leader poised to defend American ships and mobilize his military.

He was deeply moved when hundreds of letters poured in pledging patriotic loyalty to him, and when crowds stood in the theater to salute Adams and the new republic. He had never been more popular.

So, on the one hand, his own nation and party, coupled with France's bellicose behavior, seemed to be prodding Adams toward war. And yet, he could in no sense empower Hamilton, draw swords with Napoleon, or endanger thousands of lives. After all, he had lived through the gory horrors of one treacherous war—the American Revolution—and he did not wish to be the author of another… especially one he could lose.

He stood and went to the window. He just had to open it. The heat was sweltering. But there were swarming enemies within sight… and what of the bugs he could not see? Were they lurking, just like the thousands of soldiers not yet visible in the line of fire?

JEFFERSON IN AND OUT OF THE SHADOWS

Bringing further pressure against war, and against Adams, was his own vice president, Thomas Jefferson, who led a strong opposition Republican party. As much as anyone, Jefferson felt linked to the French due to their invaluable support for the American Revolution, and now due to the democratic passions of their own revolution. Loving France's parallel quest to be rid of monarchy, Jefferson felt it was America's responsibility to uphold French patriots no matter what their foibles.

Jefferson was not only backed by Republicans throughout most states, but also by another popular citizens' uprising sparked by "Citizen Genet." A visiting French zealot who traveled the states seeking to enlist troops and fund his own country, Genet had appealed to the president and anyone who would grant him an audience. But Adams, among others, found Genet overbearing and inflexible. Adams similarly felt that Jefferson had gone too far in endorsing Genet and the more extreme elements of the French Revolution and chauvinism.

Jefferson had become a sharp double-edged sword for Adams. Together they had led the Spirit of '76, weathered the Revolutionary War, championed the Declaration of Independence, and formed a winning alliance. But recently, Jefferson appeared to be ruled by his own ambitions, and seemed an untrustworthy conspirator against the president.

As Adams thought about Jefferson, the word "vice" was being enlarged in Thomas's title—not the word "president." All of Jefferson's vices were now coming to the fore. And the word "president" could be reserved only for Adams himself, although he sensed Jefferson plotting to capture it. So, Jefferson had to stay *vice* president. Yet Adams felt all the maneuvering by Jefferson's cohorts—most of it clandestine and below the belt.

Where was the other handkerchief? The sweat was now dripping onto the desk. What to do about Jefferson? About the French and Napoleon?

AN AGONIZING DECISION

President Adams felt sandwiched between the pincers of party politics. There was not only the vice president's scheming—he also felt caught in another vice of popular opinion and personal conscience. He had taken an oath of office to protect the nation and the Constitution. But which was more important: short term protection from the marauding and muscle-flexing French—or long-term protection from the bankruptcy, bloodletting, and heartbreak, if not defeat and captivity, that a prolonged war could impose upon an infant nation?

Ethically, there was also the question of numbers—how many possible casualties? How many millions of dollars? How many ships, arms, and battalions were required to face a juggernaut like Napoleon? How many of these would be wasted?

But in the back of his mind were the more heart-wrenching questions about numbers that only a president can face—how many teenage deserters would he have to hang or pardon? How many anguished parents would try to meet with him each day to plead for deserter sons facing execution? How many prisoners, spies, gangrene amputations, frostbite deaths, malaria cases, and smallpox losses of soldiers, medics, chaplains, and sailors who never fired a bullet? How many families destroyed by soldier suicide, homicide, desertion, and infectious diseases? How many libelous stories in a scathing tabloid press, which would blame him for each defeat and for the loss of life during victories?

He had been through all this territory when Washington's troops perished by the thousands, fighting soldiers with superior arms on the one hand, while fighting winters and disease (without shoes) on the other. The president knew few families who had not lost a son, a father, their land, a home, their life savings, or their all to the revolution. And the country needed sustained peace to create enterprise, foster prosperity, relieve debt, educate new leaders, build hospitals and roads, and address dozens of pressing domestic stress points from slavery to inflation.

RISK AT EVERY TURN

Beyond all this, Adams heard loud rumblings in the background.

In the eighteenth century, everyone faced daily pressures that are hard for a twenty-first century reader to fathom. Almost any disease could be fatal or lead to an epidemic. Entire cities had to be evacuated or quarantined, and Congress was not magically exempt. Again and again, Congress would lose members of their families to smallpox, dysentery, dropsy, scarlet fever, and other tragedies. Indeed, upon occasion Congress had to be closed or evacuated from Philadelphia to reduce the risk of ongoing fatalities, or to flee the invading British.

The treatments for many diseases at that time, such as bleeding the patient and inoculation by puss injection, could be worse than the disease itself. Patients and their caregivers were not protected against the onslaught of endless spiders, snakes, gnats, mosquitoes and other venomous and disease-transmitting creatures which populated the New World. Nor were many illnesses properly diagnosed.

There was little relief from extreme cold and heat. And what protection there was, such as multiple open fireplaces in most homes, meant an atmosphere of smoke-filled rooms, which in turn could lead to bouts of coughing, undiagnosed illnesses, and lung pollution.

Women were particularly disadvantaged in a world of dangerous childbirth, high infant mortality, large families, long days of physical labor, and access to few manufactured products and medicines. Women frequently cared for the ill, including dying children and relatives. They knew few of the privileges of men. Abigail Adams brought this inequality to John's attention by asking him how he could fight for the freedom of men, but not of their partners.

Slavery, although especially populous in the South, was also commonplace in other colonies, and servants' lives frequently resembled those of slaves. American citizens who were or who seemed to be mentally ill (or "lunatics," as they would have been called), if they survived, were often locked away in underground dungeons, trapped in another form of slavery. Life was plagued with issues of survival and freedom for most of those living in this new world.

Consequently, it seemed that Adams and other leaders were always swimming against the tide. They were boxing with one hand tied behind the back. For example, if a president failed to raise taxes, the country was paralyzed and would continue to underpay its congress and army. However, when he did raise taxes, there were rebellions and the accusations of oppressive government, not unlike the charges against King George III.

Rebellions and assassination threats reminded him of his own vulnerability, as did the loss of a son to alcoholism, a daughter to cancer, and many relatives and friends to epidemics. He would eventually live long enough to see his beloved wife Abigail die of typhoid. Already she had been confined to bed for eleven weeks. She had remained consistently in what she called her "dying bed" with severe fevers, melancholy, insomnia, and chronic fatigue.

Even when she was well, Abigail was often ministering to one or more diseased or bereaved relatives. She would frequently take in broken-hearted family members when their partners had proven unfaithful, incompetent, or had disappeared. At one point, Abigail was caring for seriously stricken relatives in the rooms on both sides of her own. Such was the world of John Adams' "dearest friend," whom he considered his top advisor.

Even when he moved to the new President's House, later to be known as the White House, the building was under construction, barely furnished, and filled only with slaves performing construction work. From this new setting, communication with Philadelphia and Boston could take days or weeks, and communication with Europe sometimes took months. Indeed, a treaty was signed in Europe which might have changed the outcome of Adam's re-election bid. But news of that signing did not reach him and Congress until weeks later after the electors had voted.

In the aggregate, Adams faced some of the worst conditions of any president. These included betrayal and opposition by his own cabinet and vice president; the loss of his mother, two children and the near death of his wife; ongoing sensational, severe defamatory ridicule in the press; inflammatory public attacks by the heads of his party; a strongly divided Congress; a European immigrant society with mixed loyalties to France, Britain, and the United States; constant and epidemic threats to health, sanitation, and welfare; economic inflation, corruption, and resistance to taxation; mobilized political rivals within both the opposition and his own party; and his ongoing physical denouement.

Prior to the presidency, Adams had faced numerous obstacles. Life-threatening illness in Amsterdam; a hazardous voyage across, and almost to the bottom of, the Atlantic; and an almost-lethal winter trip through the Pyrenees, were just some of his challenges abroad.

Such reality looked little like the surviving romantic portraits of the Founding Fathers. Like Washington, Adams would find the presidency more than threatening to his health.

Indeed, ongoing crisis was the backdrop for what biographer John Ferling described as "a crossroads in his presidency." Ferling emphasized Adams' own words when he wrote: "A terribly difficult decision had to be made… 'I am old—very old and never shall be very well—certainly while in this office,' Adams lamented."

OF REPUBLICANS AND...

In the twenty-first century, it is not difficult to imagine the gridlock of a stubborn two-party political system. The current decade has included a fiscal cliff, multiple government shutdowns, a health insurance standoff, partisan filibusters, impeachment procedures, and other issues that remind citizens of the hazards of rigid, adversarial party loyalty. Republicans and Federalists of the eighteenth century were just as likely to draw strict party lines and to incessantly debate rigid positions as modern Republicans and Democrats are today.

Thus, most legislative confrontations might have seemed like politics as usual, both today and during Adams' presidency. What would seem highly unusual in the current political arena was that Adams' primary rival was his own vice president. Unlike the current political arrangement, whoever garnered the second-highest number of votes in a presidential election became vice president, irrespective of party affiliation.

So, while Jefferson had been a close colleague and friend during the American Revolution, later Vice President Jefferson felt that Adams imposed too much centralized government upon the populace, and thus the president no longer honored the true spirit of independence. The Jefferson-Adams relationship had moved from one pole to the other. During the first Congress, Adams had served as an unofficial mentor to the younger Jefferson while the two worked together in a subcommittee to draft the Declaration of Independence with Benjamin Franklin.

Throughout the Revolutionary War, and while both served as diplomats in Europe, Jefferson and Adams enjoyed each other's companionship. They even arranged a private vacation together, taking a tour of gardens throughout the English countryside. Both loved education, farming, books, science, the classics, and the new republic. Like the other founding patriots, they were also united by a hatred of oppressive English royalty and a fear of hanging for treason.

But once they were no longer rebels and became the new government, each man took a different path. Jefferson continued to support the revolution both in France and in the domestic fight to keep individuals free of restraint. As president, Adams felt compelled to press for a strong government and sensed that the French Revolution had gone too far. Adams even seemed to oppose the original American Bill of Rights when he reluctantly signed the Alien and Sedition Act, a law that allowed for the deportation of immigrants, and which penalized anti-government free speech.

What Adams could not foresee was that Jefferson was so opposed to the Federalist approach that he would betray him. Jefferson went to great lengths to covertly block Adams' policies. Unlike Adams, who as former vice president had supported the policies of President George Washington, Jefferson openly spoke and voted against many of his current president's ideas. Indeed, Jefferson secretly bankrolled a muckraking journalist, James Callendar, who wrote for the *Aurora* tabloid and lead a smear campaign against Adams.

Possibly the unkindest blow of all was Jefferson's behind-the-scenes advice, if not instruction, to the French government. While Adams wanted his diplomatic team to be fully received and quickly heard by French authorities, Jefferson secretly advised the French ambassador that France should draw out negotiations as long as possible. Portraying Adams as an old curmudgeon, Jefferson gave every impression of being the younger, loyal friend to whom France should secretly listen. Jefferson's influence in delaying negotiations played an important role in defeating Adams and undermining his popularity.

So, John Adams was crossed and manipulated by his own Republican Vice President Jefferson on the one hand, and berated and betrayed by his Federalist Party leader Hamilton on the other. The only thing worse than the intractable opposition both Hamilton and Jefferson faced from each other was the surreptitious, malicious opposition Adams faced from both.

Although Jefferson and Adams would eventually rekindle their friendship through correspondence after retirement, the scars of the Republican-Federalist rivalry ran deep. In 1793, two congressmen, Lyon and Griswold, actually fought each other with cane and fire tongs on the congressional floor. In 1804, Jefferson's Republican vice president, Aaron Burr, killed Federalist leader Alexander Hamilton in a duel. Many other rivalries led to bitter acrimony. Despite his Federalist tendencies, Adams was too independent to consistently toe the party line. He would eventually be called "a man without a party."

VALUES ABOVE ALL

Often behind a tough ethical decision are conflicting values.

Early in Adams' legal career, he had demonstrated highly valuing fairness by defending British soldiers accused of murder in the Boston Massacre. He was committed to a just trial and reasoned deliberation about evidence, no matter how disloyal he seemed. It did not matter to him how unpopular the outcome might have been. But he also valued the rights of colonists and the safety of his family. So, he had to weigh such values prior to accepting the job.

John Adams' values had been formed early in life, in the cradle of a Puritan Massachusetts and Harvard education that mixed the classics with Protestant theology. Mentored by a father who had modeled integrity and even-handedness, Adams tempered his Christian dogma with open-mindedness and his scripture with Plato, Shakespeare, and Cervantes.

Although he read the Bible frequently and attended church until his final years, Adams, who might be called a quasi-Unitarian, was never a fundamentalist evangelical. He advocated tolerance, and at the end of his career he tried unsuccessfully to reform Massachusetts law so that it would provide equal protection to Judaism. Never a slave-owner, his political values were epitomized by human rights and civic justice.

Pulitzer Prize-winning biographer David McCullough aptly likened Adams' disposition to the eagle shown in the great seal of the United States. Within the eagle's left talon are thirteen arrows that symbolize war. The right talon holds an olive branch, a traditional symbol of peace. In heraldry, the right talon was always given greater preference so, while the eagle is prepared for both war and peace, overall, the symbol favors peace.

Such would be President Adams' response when confronted with the possibility of war. He would recommend arming U.S. frigates and preparing for conflict with his left talon, while setting a course for peace through diplomacy with his right. In that pacific spirit, while working constantly with his ambassador to the Hague, he simultaneously sought to send a delegation or emissary to France for negotiations.

Tolstoy might later have entitled Adams' career *War, then Peace*. The two great chapters in his public life were war with Britain, followed by the pursuit of peace with France. With his left talon he pursued funds to build a stronger navy; but with his right he negotiated for peace via third parties. Only a goal that he valued more than peace could motivate Adams to choose war if diplomacy failed—a goal such as liberty in the face of rapacious conquest by abject tyranny.

THE ETHICS OF NUMBERS

While Adams was determining a national itinerary, in England the legal and moral thinker Jeremy Bentham was developing and promoting his theory of utility. In his latter years, Bentham would be joined by a much younger John Stuart Mill, who would be seen as his co-author of utilitarian theory. Their ethic of social reform aimed for practices that brought the greatest possible happiness to society. To the extent that such pleasure or happiness could be quantified, it would be called "the greatest good for the greatest number," and be known as utilitarianism.

In modern terms, "cost benefit analysis" derives from this intention to weigh potential gains vs. losses or, in utilitarian terms, likely happiness vs. likely pain or social malaise. Whether he ever tried to mathematically weigh the full costs and benefits of war with France, Adams certainly considered some of the numbers of what was at stake. On the one hand, he risked a divided country, rebellion against taxes, lost credibility, a military coup by Hamilton, and huge human and financial losses if the country went to war. But if he steered toward peace, Adams would give France a large military advantage—including license to loot U.S. ships and the incentive to invade and conquer the colonies—and he would lose party support, national popularity, and likely re-election to the presidency.

In this context, just what was the greatest good for the greatest number? Whether or not he had heard of Bentham, Mill, or utilitarianism, as an elected official, was Adams accountable to the majority and their preference? If so, the greatest number wanted war. Correspondence arrived daily from hundreds who wished to enlist and support the president by defeating the French. But following this majority would mean interpreting "the greatest number" in the short term. Such a majority *du jour* might be determined in a plebiscite, but would it matter in light of what Adams sensed about the long term?

The "greatest good for the greatest number" might well pertain to posterity. After all, the number of people injured, orphaned, killed, bankrupted, captured, evicted, raped, pillaged, and invaded during a lengthy war might matter far more than the number currently enraged by French bullying.

In such a case, a utilitarian ethic is not as simple as comparing the number of people likely to be happy vs. the number of people likely to be hurt. For example, if six people each donate a pint of blood to save the life of an accident victim, it is not only the numbers that must be considered. After all, the six people will quickly recover, but without the blood transfusion, the accident victim will die. So, most would agree that the welfare or happiness of the one matters more than the loss of the six in that case.

Thus, utilitarianism considers more than the surface numbers attached to happiness and pain. Mill thought that intensity, duration, fruitfulness, and likelihood must also be taken into account. For example, a visit to the dentist might generate pain for the duration of one week, but it could lead to years of pain-free gums and teeth, and thus to a fruitful overall experience. The intensity of pain at a dental visit could be high, but such pain could be far greater in years to come if a gum condition were left unattended. Similarly, the likelihood that the dentist can eradicate the condition, rather than just provide momentary relief, must be taken into account.

So, for Adams, the number of possible casualties and dollars could not tell the whole story. He also had to consider how long the war might last, how intense and involved it could become, how likely he was to win, and what fruit could come or wither from victory or loss. Even if he could have predicted all of this (and he could not), there would still have been other factors to consider.

One of the most troubling matters in prediction is the role of uncertainty. Without knowing all the variables, it is hard to estimate likeliness or fruitfulness. Neither Adams nor Napoleon could foresee what storms might arise at sea, or determine the possibility of epidemics, bank collapse, supply depletion, insect invasion, blizzards, miscommunication, desertion, crop failure, extreme heat or cold, and human error. Napoleon had already realized that no matter how superior his armies, they could not contend with the sub-freezing cold of the North or malaria of the South. Both had overcome his troops. So, decision-making involved uncertainty and great risk.

There was also the possibility of misunderstanding. Indeed, by the winter of 1798, Adams began to realize that he had misunderstood the French government. Both the French and American militants, like the sensational tabloids, sought to convince him that war was inevitable.

Yet, repeatedly Adams received private communications suggesting that the French government did not want war with America. One after another discrete message reached the president, and Adams' emissary, Eldridge Gerry, although distrusted by many, returned from Paris bringing the perspective that France sought peace. Dr. George Logan, a Republican citizen-diplomat, also returned from France with a positive message from Talleyrand to Adams. Even George Washington wrote Adams supporting the view that France sought peace. Two more confirming messages arrived from Talleyrand himself.

Finally, a man whom Congress would not quickly forget, William Vans Murray, Adams' minister resident (i.e. ambassador) to the Hague, had written persuasively to the President. Adams' eyes and ears in Europe, and a supportive Federalist, Murray had met with French and other officials and was convinced that war with America could not help the French.

To Murray it seemed that France, already at war with Britain, feared a possible alliance between the English and Americans. France had also requested a large loan from Adams to support their escalating war budget. Moreover, Napoleon realized he could not fight successfully in those parts of the New World where his troops had been emaciated by malaria.

When all of this was considered, it seemed common sense that France was only feigning aggression and actually sought peace. War was not inevitable. The greatest good for the greatest number became clearer cut in Adams' thinking.

FEBRUARY 18, 1799

The heat, humidity, gnats, flies, and sweat-soaked handkerchief seemed far behind him. Eventually, the swarming wasps and mosquitoes outside the window had disappeared. Many months had passed, and now the problem was not the heat but rather the lack of it.

It was February. A lot had changed, including the frozen ground and fresh air all around. Although shivering, Adams finally felt confident about his thinking.

Armed with the information from Murray, at last John Adams could make the decision, one in concert with his original peace-making pledge to Congress and the nation. The pressure from all sides had been intense. Yet he was now certain that he could be and should be a peacemaker.

On February 18, 1799, Adams made what biographers consider to be the bravest act of his life. Without consulting Abigail or his cabinet, he sent a courier to Vice President Thomas Jefferson, who would read Adams' unexpected message to the Senate, which included these words:

> I nominate William Vans Murray... to be minister plenipotentiary of the United States to the French Republic... to discuss and conclude all controversies between the two Republics by a new treaty.

Although Congress would force a compromise such that Adams would have to add two more envoys who would accompany Murray, the die had been cast for peacemaking.

Ironically, while peace seemed assured abroad, war-like reactions struck Adams at home. Threats of assassination, vituperative tabloid articles, and Federalist protests assailed him like a school of piranhas. With his aspirations for active military leadership dashed, Alexander Hamilton wrote a biting and costly public attack upon Adams' leadership.

It seemed clear to the president, if not to others, that he had sacrificed himself to save the country. Already distanced from the Republicans, the president suddenly found himself equally isolated from the shocked, hostile high Federalists within his own party. Politically, he no longer had a leg, let alone two, to stand upon. But he had made his decision. John Adams would seek peace.

THE TEN FACTORS

Once again, several of the factors were important to the leader in the hot seat, John Adams, when choosing between war and peace.

1. **Notions of fairness and justice:** Is it just for thousands of young men and their families to be sent into an unnecessary war? Is it fair to a young, vulnerable nation to impose a great economic and human debt and the risk of lost sovereignty? Ultimately, Adams was not concerned with being fair to Federalists and Republican zealots, nor to the French, nor ambitious rivals like Jefferson and Hamilton. Adams' greatest sense of justice was to the innocent—the many thousands who would suffer due to the ravages of war, their families, and the citizens who had elected him. He had to be accountable to those who trusted him to serve and protect the nation, whatever his personal sacrifice and whatever the notions of fairness held by others.

2. **Impact or consequences:** As a successful and dedicated lawyer, Adams was always concerned about a just outcome to any decision. Possible tragic consequences may have been his most important consideration—losing a war with France would have led to a dire outcome but winning might also exact an extremely high toll in dollars, a currency newly adopted in 1785. Adams was also keenly aware that he might lose re-election, career, and public approval. So, the possible outcomes could be costly and extreme, but the costliest by far would be war.

3. **Ends and means:** In this situation the means of action, violent war or non-violent diplomacy, was crucial to a desirable end. Adams was also concerned that the ends he determined be influenced by the right means of communication. It was not always clear whether the information he received about France was accurate when the messenger had a different end in mind. So, he ultimately chose a pacific means, trustworthy diplomacy, which was parallel to the desired end of international peace.

4. **Tone and atmosphere:** Obviously a harmonious tone seemed far more important to Adams, despite the belligerent atmosphere catalyzed by Hamilton and his followers. Although for Hamilton's group, war would have meant the romantic overtones of glory, vindication, and triumph, Adams recalled all too well the atmosphere of deep fear, agony, chaos, grief, and death from the Revolutionary War. Despite the backstabbing of his rivals, Adams sought the elevated tone of transparency, honesty, and civility.

5. **Motivation and higher law:** The Founding Fathers had spoken through Jefferson's language about "inalienable rights," and were motivated by the principles inherent within Christianity, freemasonry, and democratic theory. Although killing had become a way of life, and Adams had to make his own decisions about whom to pardon and execute, ultimately the divine law "thou shalt not kill" took priority over the human law honoring "an eye for an eye" and other reciprocal violence. Like Socrates, Adams sought to honor the laws and ideals no matter how unpopular they might prove to be. His greatest motivation was to save lives, including the life of his young, vulnerable country.

6. **Allegiance and loyalty:** While Jefferson, among others, had argued that America owed great allegiance to France in light of France's backing of the colonies during their hour of need, Adams was unconvinced. Highly independent, he did not seem strictly loyal to political party, patriotic anti-French zealots, nor his unfaithful presidential cabinet. His greatest

allegiances seemed to be to his wife, the most stable of his children, very trusted friends, and his personal notions of wise governance. As a patriot, he had given great allegiance to George Washington, his fellow Founding Fathers, and the new nation. Whatever allegiances he might have to his political party and other politicians who had supported him, his highest loyalty was to his country, especially those within it who lacked voice.

7. **Values and principles:** A lover of Shakespeare, one of Adams' key principles might have been "to thine own self be true." He valued the health of the country, the integrity of his own policies, and his ability to sleep with a clear conscience above popularity and personal wealth. In making his decision, he greatly valued the survival and prosperity of others. Adams also seemed to value a higher power, the sovereignty of individual men, and the well-chosen words of the Declaration of Independence— "life, liberty, and the pursuit of happiness."

8. **Cultural context:** Although there was a patriotic culture in 1799, to some extent America remained many cultures. Most colonists were immigrants, or the (grand-)children of immigrants, such that Dutch, German, French, Spanish, and Portuguese were influential, if not spoken languages throughout many colonies, and American Indian (cf. Native American) culture had penetrated into imported customs in diet, lifestyle, and governance. Although most of the Loyalists to the British crown had fled to Canada and England, British culture was still deeply rooted. In 1799, perhaps the greatest cultural divide Adams faced was the tension between the Francophiles and the Francophobes, a tension also reflected in the two political parties.

   The notion of being an American involved the forging of a new culture with distinctive values empowering individual men as in no other country. Women, indentured servants, slaves, and relocated Indians were still entrapped like their colleagues worldwide. But large numbers of immigrant white men were enjoying a new lifestyle with far more personal comforts and choices than elsewhere. Preserving and building upon this new libertarian culture was a high priority.

9. **Implications:** Perhaps the greatest long-term implication was the success of an experimental nation. Although America had only narrowly defeated the British, there were no guaranties that such a political novelty as young and economically unstable as the United States could sustain sovereignty, especially when facing Napoleon. Ultimately, the stability, if not survival, and success of the entire country and laboratory for democracy were at

risk. Many other implications cast their shadows—the future of international relations, possible war in Europe, the legacies of the Federalist and Republican parties, the role of John Quincy Adams in future government, and American freedom from French imperialism. But as always, implications are tealeaves that often cannot be clearly read. So, Adams could only speculate about their nature and importance.

10. **Proportion and balance:** It is these implications mixed with more immediate consequences which both proved most important. In the short term, Adams' own sons, like those of his neighbors and colleagues, might well have been casualties if war should have broken out. But the greatest casualty could have been the "Sons of Liberty." Patriotism and pacifism could be conflicting values for some. But for Adams, these were congruent and important values most influential in his decision-making. Being a patriot meant being a pacifist in this situation, and he gave great weight to both.

CENTURIES OF CONSEQUENCES

It seems obvious that our world would be quite different had Adams succumbed to war. The U.S. would not have doubled its land size via the Louisiana Purchase of 1803 had it been at war. Americans might well have lost the War of 1812 to Britain if they had been previously or concurrently fighting another world power.

It is difficult to know how else the world map and populations would have changed if a Franco-American war had erupted. Having fought incessantly with England, Native Americans, and disease, Americans might have discovered that another serious war would have emaciated or broken the fledgling nation. Even victory would have been costly, since war often depletes resources, (wo)manpower, morale, leadership, families, and the economy.

And what impact would this have had internationally? Since France had formed an alliance with America during the Revolutionary War, would others have formed different alliances during the war with either America or France? Which countries might gain or lose power? And which would lose thousands of young men?

Could Jefferson have become president if it meant fighting his beloved France? Would James Madison, Andrew Jackson, Abraham Lincoln, and other future stars have become household names if they or their fathers had been killed in combat? Napoleon, Talleyrand, and future French royalty might also have had entirely different biographies.

Such changes would impact yet other changes that define our twenty-first century lives. Would we be alive? Would Americans be speaking French? Living in another country? Who can say?

The initial question, however, has a definite answer. Had John Adams never lived, America and the world would know a different narrative. It was said that Washington was "first in war, first in peace, and first in the hearts of his countrymen." Conversely, Adams now knew that if he and his country were to be "first in peace," he could not be "first in the hearts of his countrymen."

But who can say how many thousands of lives, including the life of his country, Adams saved? He felt the deep pain of a seemingly lost career and reputation for well over two decades. Yet arguably he gained "the greatest good for the greatest number" for well over two centuries.

FACING UNKNOWNS

In our own work it is often difficult to predict how our decisions will impact the future, especially that of those yet unborn. Many of us face tough judgment calls impacting the lives of others, seen and unseen.

Those who use the utilitarian ethics model for making difficult decisions in this century often use the language of "cost/benefit analysis" to weigh the relative numbers of lives, dollars, and resources which might be saved or lost by any given decision. Such a process includes the attempt to compare what could be gained and lost as a result of a difficult ethical choice.

While such numbers analyses have their place, and might give preliminary indications of tangible net gains or losses, using such tools usually triggers the question: "What cannot be measured?" It seems likely that Adams knew he could not measure the deep pain of parents who would lose their children, nor calculate his own worth if he lost self-respect. It is likely that he was familiar with the question: "What profits a man if he gains the whole world but loses his soul?"

Adams also could not measure the odds of national survival. The information he received from France was not always reliable, and often self-contradictory. Nor could he tell if Napoleon would truly win the war, given Napoleon's dominance in major battles on the one hand, but his losses to weather, distance, and disease on the other.

It is often easier to measure dollars, lives, and hours than intangibles such as personal fulfillment and national success or morale. When asked by students how much weight to give to numerical analysis and measurement, I let them know that cost/benefit comparison can be a practical tool, so we learn how to employ it in the classroom. However, I add that this approach is an incomplete indicator of some of the most important factors involved in many ethical decisions. At that point some students ask: "What do you mean?"

My reply: "What is the weight of your own conscience? What is the measure of your own integrity? What is the cost of losing both?"

CHAPTER 5

WILLIAM WILBERFORCE:
(1759-1833)

CHEATING WITH INTEGRITY?

"In my law books I might have stumbled across something and I
want to propose it as a strategy. *Nosus Decipio*. It's Latin.
Loosely translated, it means… 'we cheat'."
—James Stephen

Nosus Decipio. The words haunted William as much as the strategy they
suggested. "We cheat."

It was not surprising that this was the recommendation of William's brother-
in-law and noted legal expert, James Stephen, who was known for his creative
approach to the law. But should it be something that he, William, would ever
consider?

William was so pre-occupied that he never saw the mud and fox excrement
on the lawn as he paced. Wiping the reminder of his pet fox from his boot,
William struggled with this concept of "cheating," since his life had been
committed to two great purposes. One was the reformation of morals
throughout England, a doctrine that certainly would not favor cheating. The
other was to end the horrific slave trade. For decades he had failed to pass
effective legislation in Parliament, and he had tried everything he could think
of… except cheating.

There it was again, mud beneath the weeds. His foot had sunk at least two
inches, enough to mean both boots would need polishing once again.

After so many years of William's frustrated efforts, James was not only
recommending cheating, but proposing that William, a member of Parliament,
do so in the broad daylight of England's House of Commons and House of
Lords. Such deceptive maneuvering would be witnessed, if not publicized, by
English royalty, clergy, press, and eventually the public. Nevertheless, James
was an authority on international trade law, and could be trusted for savvy
advice.

So, what did James have in mind? William closed both eyes and tried to
imagine. He pictured his cohorts and enemies in Parliament. With the backing
of their Abolitionist allies, William and James would have to attempt new

parliamentary tactics to end slave-trading. Their previous attempts had only catalyzed an increasingly polarized parliament.

The damned damp boot again! He looked down fearing the worst.

The reality was that those who favored slavery would organize and vote down anti-slavery bills, if not in the House of Commons, then later in the House of Lords. But what if an effective bill could be passed which seldom mentioned slavery? A bill that, on the surface, seemed to be about an entirely different issue? What if Wilberforce and his Abolitionist colleagues remained silent about this new bill, as if it were unrelated to their purpose?

What if the new bill was proposed by someone seemingly neutral on the slavery issue? What if it was presented as a strictly patriotic bill that could help England win the ongoing war against France?

Such a plan would be highly tempting from a political standpoint. It would draw support from the prime minister, from the Crown, from the war leaders, and from all those who, in general, voted for anti-French legislation. It might just work.

Yet, earlier in his life, William had made what he considered to be his most important decision—to become a devout Christian. It was a decision that affected every other choice he made, every day, from his founding of the Church Mission Society to his leadership within the Society for the Prevention of Cruelty to Animals in London. At times his devotion made it difficult for him to be a politician. Indeed, due to periods of severe illness and the stressful, cloak-and-dagger politics of cheating by many others, William had often contemplated resigning from the intense, manipulative atmosphere of the House of Commons. And it was precisely the manipulation, betrayals, immoral attitudes supporting slavery, backroom deals, and cheating that made him long for a more pastoral and sacred life.

Yet, in the past, he had always been able to find a way to—at least on a personal level—match the moral with the political. But now he must consider: *Nosus Decipio*—we cheat.

Would he?

The decision loomed even larger than his zoo, with dozens of pets, like the fox, who left presents on the lawn. Pacing the pasture repetitively, and all but blindly, did not make the matter easier.

He was also not fully aware that an American president, John Adams (Chapter 4), who was over twenty years his senior, was facing his own ethical challenges within his own parliament, called "Congress," over three thousand miles away. But Wilberforce was aware that he had both allies and enemies in the newly established United States.

WHAT WAS AT STAKE?

It is well documented that William Wilberforce's conscience constantly propelled him to end the slave trade at all costs. More than once he had smelled the stench of disease and death itself on ships that packed hundreds of Africans so tightly on the lower decks that they could barely move. Sleeping on hard, splinter-ridden wood floors, these slaves lied in vomit, urine, insects, blood, and excrement, as they felt chains and leg irons wear their skin to the bone. Slave berths were reported to be as small as four feet by eighteen inches per person, and there was no protection from extreme heat, cold, starvation, seasickness, or contagion. Even fifty feet away from the ships, Wilberforce could pick up the mingled aromas of blood, urine, vomit, disease, and filth.

William had heard many firsthand reports from runaway and freed slaves, and former ship captains about living aboard the slavers. Breathing the constantly contaminated air of diseased companions, slaves watched as the dead, the dying, and sometimes the disabled and resistant, were pitched overboard to be devoured by the ocean. In 1781, like many of his compatriots, Wilberforce was shocked to discover that the captain of the slave ship *Zong* had thrown 153 slaves, some very ill, over the side of the ship to become shark food.

What happened prior to and following these voyages was hardly better. Free African men, women, and children were captured, including by some of their fellow Africans, separated from their families, beaten or whipped, held in slave trading forts and prisons for weeks with little food and no understanding of their future. Once the lucky survivors of the voyages reached the Caribbean or America, they were auctioned to slave holders, and worked in sugar cane factories where giant fires routinely burned the workers, or on cotton or tobacco plantations, or they became sex workers to their owners... all without pay.

Some disobedient slaves had been boiled alive in sugar cane syrup. Few witnesses protested, since doing so would risk meeting a similar fate.

The penalties for slow or interrupted work, and especially for insurrection or rebellion, were chilling. Stephen Tomkins' book, *William Wilberforce: A Biography*, includes white and black eyewitness accounts of slaves brutally killed in front of their families, hung by the ribs with large hook incisions until dehydrated, and publicly savaged. Stephen himself had attended a trial in which four slaves— who seemed innocent—had been found guilty of murder, and were burned to death as a deterrent to others. Since slaves were legally considered to be property, owners could threaten, torture, and dispose of them as they wished.

Although not all owners were cruel, even the average or better slave owner could randomly buy and sell, beat and overwork, micromanage and underfeed his slaves at any time. To prevent the theft and escape of slaves, many were routinely branded, manacled, and collared in heavy irons. Women were frequently raped by their owners and foremen, and were then expected to rear their illegitimate, mulatto children.

Although much of this cruelty has become common knowledge today, in Wilberforce's time such treatment was not commonly known— and, when it was, such mistreatment was not seen as unnecessarily cruel. William Wilberforce stood as one of relatively few who could not imagine how a country claiming to be Christian and civil could tolerate such conditions, let alone rationalize a large, highly profitable industry that transported thousands of shackled, often dying humans every year.

At the very core of his religious experience were such teachings as "love your neighbor," and "do unto others as you would have them do unto you." During his conversion, Wilberforce was particularly moved by the story of the Good Samaritan, a narrative about one man bending over backwards to assist another of a stigmatized race. All seemed starkly clear to him that slavery was precisely the opposite.

But, if there was anything as vexing as slavery, it was the obstacle course preventing its removal. Those who wished to abolish slavery were labeled "Abolitionists," and portrayed as unrealistic extremists. Many slave traders and their allies were affluent merchants who could bribe or lobby members of Parliament to demean Wilberforce and uphold the status quo.

Rather than hearing humane, reasonable voices supporting his concerns in Parliament, initially Wilberforce was confronted with fabricated stories about how well the slaves were treated. He also listened with disbelief to fellow members of Parliament, who spoke of how poorly these Africans would fare without owners and a livelihood. In Parliament, it was also argued that if Britain did not own and trade the slaves, then their French enemies would obtain them and thus gain the edge in manpower and war. These concocted, far-fetched arguments seemed endless, and yet hopelessly entrenched in the minds of Wilberforce's colleagues.

Other promoters of slavery appealed to fear. "They outnumber their owners and will murder them if they are unchained!" was a common refrain. Rumors were planted that freed slaves might even travel to Britain to seek revenge upon slave profiteers, including those who had collared them. Another widely circulated myth was that killing the slave trade would also kill the economy. "Wilberforce will ruin England and our business" became another common refrain.

In short, the "fanatic" and his supporters were up against not only a powerful, successful slave-trade fleet, but also an army of clever politicians, lobbyists, merchants, and lawyers. These apologists for slavery worked not only by day to defeat Abolitionist legislation, but also by night to send death threats, publish inflammatory propaganda, bribe and mobilize supporters, and, in Stephen's words, "to cheat."

The most intimidating death threats targeted his wife and family. So, while Wilberforce's mission seemed imperative, his opposition seemed impossible.

FOR JUSTICE AND HUMANITY

Given the tactics of his opponents and the grave injustice of slavery, why shouldn't Wilberforce fight fire with fire? Why not deceive one's opponents in pursuit of a greater good? Why not cheat?

Because everything about his character leaned the other way. By the time of his death, Wilberforce would be portrayed as England's leading secular saint and called "the Washington of humanity" by an Italian count. But George Washington, a slave owner himself, had repeatedly deceived the British generals in order to gain a tactical advantage in war by cleverly circulating erroneous rumors to his enemies about the movements of his troops.

The famous general and president had told outright lies to create inaccurate intelligence reports that fell into British hands. To save lives and possibly win the war, Washington had cheated repeatedly.

Still, Wilberforce was not literally at war with his opponents in Parliament, and he had a reputation for great integrity and generosity of spirit. Such generosity extended in many directions—frequently, he invited the poor to dine in his home. In1801 alone, he donated the modern equivalent of $120,000 to feed the starving.

His generosity also extended to many types of animals, whom he kept as friends in and near his home by the dozen. Although his fox was sometimes feared by strangers at the door, it was among his favorites. It was for their sake that he also labored to co-found the SPCA.

He was known as a major benefactor to many celebrated causes for animals and humans alike. To his followers, William was a great humanitarian who fought for justice with his pen, mouth, hands, and purse.

Wilberforce was also known for his selflessness in striving for the larger good. Consistently he sacrificed health, political success, privilege, and comfort to fight for the marginalized and the exploited. He selflessly offered his leadership role within the Abolitionists to less accomplished colleagues such as

Abington (who declined), and he would rather promote God and others than himself. Frequently, friends and family would discover that he was recuperating at home due to exhaustion and illness after intense sacrifice. Even what little time he had for personal pleasure was devoted to supporting his church, family, and friends.

Would such a man wish to lose credibility by becoming a cheater? After all, although he participated in gambling and heavy partying in his Cambridge University days and later at the men's clubs of London, all of that had disappeared after his life-altering conversion. The most influential people in Wilberforce's life now were evangelists such as John Newton, the author of "Amazing Grace" and other hymns. Newton, as a former slave ship captain, had written that he was "a wretch" who "once was blind but now I see." The poet William Cowper, staunch ally Thomas Clarkson, religious benefactor John Thornton, and Wilberforce's devoutly religious uncle and aunt were also among the many moral vectors who shaped young William into a man of great faith and a beacon of integrity.

Thus, those who sought to dig up dirt to spread rumors usually came up empty. He was a loving and loyal parent and a dedicated husband to his young wife, Barbara Spooner. And the other leading ladies in his life, such as Hannah More, were far from flirtatious. They were typically fellow reformers, religious leaders, and Abolitionists.

Some of the most famous moral leaders of his day had supported him. Shortly before his own death, religious giant John Wesley had written him: "If God be for you, who can be against you?" The Americans Benjamin Franklin, Thomas Jefferson, and John Jay had demonstrated great admiration for William's stand against slavery.

Next to the Bible, one of Wilberforce's favorite books was *Pensées* by the French-Christian philosopher Blaise Pascal. Not surprisingly, William's role model in all moral decision-making was Jesus.

Would such a man want to trade his reputation as a spiritual leader for that of a political con man? Would such a man wish to be forever branded a dishonest and untrustworthy cheater? He knew with great certainty that his political rivals would enormously inflate even the slightest character flaw in a defamatory way, should he reveal it.

THE ETHICS OF ENDS AND MEANS

Idealists and absolutists such as the German philosopher Immanuel Kant have argued that people should never intentionally lie. After all, if a society permits lying, how can people know who, if anyone, is telling the truth—and thus there can be no trust or glue holding the society together. Moreover, if deception is acceptable, there is little means for ensuring accuracy, accountability, or protecting the truth. And if individual deception is acceptable, what is to prevent government, religious, educational, and other institutional deception?

However, there are those who are more subjective. Friedrich Nietzsche noted that humans develop perspectives that protect and promote their—or should I say our—own base of power. Certainly, deception has been and is sometimes part of the repertoire of human behavior when one wishes to build or protect power.

Indeed, self-deception can be one of the first steps leading to deceiving others. And deliberate deception may also be one of the ways that we obtain and maintain power, which Nietzsche asserts is a primary human motive.

So, while Wilberforce ideally needed an unblemished reputation and humanitarian approach, realistically he also needed power. And he was not an absolute purist about deception. Even among those for whom deception is not desirable, there have been special exceptions in which the "end justifies the means," and thus deception is sometimes not only justifiable, but arguably necessary. For example, why spoil a surprise birthday party for a friend by revealing the secret to him... just to avoid deception? Why tell a three-year-old that there is no tooth fairy, Easter bunny, or Santa Claus? To push to the extreme, why truthfully answer a serial killer, rapist, or pedophile who demands the location of his next victim?

In the Cuban Missile crisis described in chapter one, President Kennedy and his doctor chose to lie to the American people about his health so he could avoid public panic and meet with key advisors. Other presidents and world leaders have lied about their health or concealed plans, including military invasions, when they felt it was a matter of national security.

Indeed, in 1986, National Security Advisor aide Oliver North famously lied to Congress and the American people about the Iran-Contra dilemma. North defended himself by saying: "Lying does not come easily... but I had to choose between lives... and lies."

Many philosophers and leaders have claimed that lying is permitted when lives are at stake. And Wilberforce was keenly aware of the many African lives at their breaking point.

Thus, the Abolitionist "fanatic" would hardly be alone as a public official who rationalized deception in the pursuit of saving the lives of many, and the health and freedom of many more. It was not just a matter of preventing the slave trade of his day—he knew that he could also prevent the premature death and cruel treatment of thousands, if not millions, of would-be slaves in future generations.

Moreover, when one considers ends and means, the slaves themselves were already being treated as a means to an end, and not respected as an end of themselves. While Kant forbade lying, he also stated that human beings ought never be treated solely as a means to an end. This second categorical imperative of Kant's, which insists that all people be individually respected and not used as steppingstones, is certainly violated by the very notion of servitude. Slavery uses people as a means for reducing personal workload and for increasing fortune without care, respect, or the permission of those involved. Violating many notions of human rights such as privacy, "life, liberty, and the pursuit of happiness," health, vocational and relational choice, and family protection, slavery implicitly involves both highly problematic ends and means.

So, Wilberforce might have asked, "do two wrongs make a right?" Does the termination of horrid inhumane treatment justify the use of deceptive means? His ends—the abolition of slavery for thousands alive and millions yet unborn—seemed of the utmost importance. And he had already tried every legal and ethical means he could think of, using legitimate parliamentary procedure for two decades.

He realized that to model deceptive means would perpetuate, if not magnify, the trickery already present in Parliament. And he knew that misleading cleverness, no matter what the gain, would seem base and un-Christian to those who looked to him as a moral leader or role model. It deeply bothered him that he might never be trusted again once he was known as a cheater.

Yet, on the other hand, how could it be immoral to commit a minor sin by the few in order to terminate a major sin by the many? In this case, given that no other alternative had proven effective, did not a highly noble end for humanity justify a questionable means by a handful of activists?

OVERCOMING CENTURIES OF FAILURE

In the Wilberforce era, slavery was a deeply inculcated human practice. After all, the Greeks, Romans, Egyptians, and most ancient cultures had thought of slave trading as routine. Throughout Europe, Asia, and the New World of Wilberforce's youth, forced slavery was a deeply embedded, time-honored practice. Even many of the indigenous tribes discovered by explorers had their own slaves. Indeed, some of the English and European slave practices seemed mild when compared to primitive tribes who used slaves for human sacrifice.

The result was that Wilberforce was very much working against the national and international status quo. However, abolitionism also had deep historical roots. The fights for freedom, whether by Spartacus or Moses (who said to Pharaoh, "Let my people go"), were well known. In Wilberforce's case, he had sought to pass appropriate legislation since 1787, nearly two decades before Stephen advocated *nosus decipio*. He was soundly defeated in the early years, losing over ninety-five percent of the votes within the House of Commons. Each year thereafter, it was as if he had to push the boulder of Sisyphus up the mountain, only to be defeated once again.

In his 1791 legislation proposal to the House of Commons, despite great eloquence and debate that lasted until three in the morning, he was nevertheless defeated by a vote of 163 to 88. Although occasional compromises seemed to augur progress—from five percent in favor of abolition to thirty-three percent in only three years—Wilberforce still interpreted them as defeat. After all, a compromised piece of legislation that recommended the very gradual abolition of slavery seemed impotent—any delay meant the captivity, punishment, and death of thousands more slaves. And what was to prevent such postponement from being a precedent for yet other delays?

During the 1790s there was the illusion of progress. By 1793, the Foreign Slave Bill was defeated by only two votes. The very next year the bill passed in the House of Commons only to be defeated later in the House of Lords. Even when William felt confident of victory in 1796, his opponents played a cruel trick by giving coveted opera tickets to many voters, such that they played hooky from the evening session. Wilberforce narrowly and unexpectedly lost the vote, seventy-four to seventy due to chicanery. Already, he had faced a decade of defeat despite the semblance of progress each year—Sisyphus indeed.

The mathematics of all these votes made little difference to the slaves. They were sold, whipped, and exiled from their families in a similar manner as if the votes had been a unanimous "no." Wilberforce and his friends—Fox, Clarkson, Stephen and others—were exhausted. Something different had to be done.

STEPHEN'S BREAKTHROUGH

It was this backdrop of sustained frustration that made Stephen's novel, clever idea seem tempting. His proposed bill would allow Britain to search and seize other ships, and thus relieve them of their cargo. This would give the British the upper hand against the French in war, because such cargo could provide enemies with supplies, resources, and, as Stephen had noticed, slave power. If the British raided neutral ships to seize or liberate their cargos, this would seem like a time-honored war strategy, and not an Abolitionist tactic.

What sea captain would want to fill a ship with hundreds of slaves, whom he must feed, if he could no longer unload and sell them? Not only would the foreign slave trade become crippled, but a blow would be struck against the British slave trade as well. Since slaves were often transported to midpoint destinations before being transferred to British ships, the supply of such slaves would also be depleted, and thus handicap the British traders, not just their rivals. In short, such a tactic, although disguised as an anti-French patriotic measure, would mean that slaves would be unloaded and never reach their destinations.

In an era of staunch British chauvinism, any tactic that increased military advantage over the French seemed laudable. The Crown, prime minister, military leaders, and most of parliament were likely to endorse such patriotic measures without looking for a seamy underbelly.

The more Wilberforce contemplated it, the more alluring Stephen's strategy, which derived from his book, *The War in Disguise*, must have seemed. But to succeed, the staging of the bill would require clever theatrical role-playing and cooperation among all of the primary characters. Wilberforce would have to deceive in other ways, too. He would have to feign indifference to the bill, remain silent on abolition, and turn his attention to other issues in the House. All of the other usual suspects promoting Abolition would also need to feign disinterest and help to distract parliament.

The cabinet and other higher-ups would have to present and support the bill as a warhorse without mention of slavery. New friends of Abolition in the House of Lords would need to be quietly courted. And those who drafted the bill would have to both create and hide an anti-slavery policy within a policy, embedded within the bill's carefully crafted language.

In short, all those involved would need to tacitly follow a common script to create and transport a Trojan Horse to the opposition. *Nosus Decipio.* "We cheat."

THE VALLEY OF THE SHADOW OF DEATH

Another factor playing into the background of Wilberforce's decision to move forward with this strategy was his history of poor health. Again and again, William had faced death and barely survived. As a result, he never knew which of his efforts would be his last. Within his own family he was also frequently close to death—his mother had nearly died, and his father and sisters had all passed prematurely.

Severe fevers, intestinal poisons, digestive collapse, and colitis had frequently kept William bedridden. He credited his doctors, loving family, God, and a life of morning prayer and worship for his narrow escapes. But by the same token, he knew that life in Parliament provided enough stress to make each pending vote his last. More than once he had smelled the stench of death on the slave ships, and he had felt death's call within his own body. If he was going to make one last effort, it had to be then or never. Stephen and other allies were waiting for his reply.

THE DECISION

In an ideal world, Wilberforce would have never been a cheater. In a perfect society, William would have aspired to continue modelling upright stature for his peers and the next generation. In a world where all people consistently lived their spiritual faith, he would have been more transparent, direct, and open.

But he did not live in such a world. The "fanatic" recalled that Reverend Newton and other mentors had encouraged him to work for change in the secular world, rather than retreat to the cloistered life of the monastery. And in the secular world, he had learned that "all's fair in love and war" … and politics.

Even his role model, Jesus, had used verbal evasiveness and cleverness when replying to the slippery Pharisees. The statesman knew that "God helps those who help themselves," and many an otherwise-respectable statesman had used questionable tactics and strategies during elections and parliamentary proceedings. Moreover, the people William would be hurting economically— slave traders, plantation owners, bribed politicians—would not and could not be harmed to the same extent as the slaves who were being shackled, stolen from their families, whipped, and thrown to the sharks each month.

He reasoned that the problem of deception or cheating in Parliament was really a misnomer. It was more a matter of gamesmanship than cheating within the fiercely competitive arena of politics. And if you did not use every tool possible to win that game, others more deceptive and aggressive would beat you.

If there was one lesson he had learned during two decades within Parliament, it was that neither prayer nor moral uprightness alone could win the vote. You also had to take action, build alliances, learn the players, speak the language, know the opposition's weaknesses, and, if and when the moment called for it, even employ minor sleight of hand for a higher purpose. Was this one meaning of "God helps those who help themselves?"

Finally, his clenched teeth and hardened frown began to relax. The decision had been made. Ultimately, in this politicized context, Wilberforce could make and rationalize a clear-cut choice. Although such action did not come easily, he would explore—if not implement—Stephen's plan.

He would bounce the idea off of his life-long friend and fellow strategist, Prime Minister William Pitt, and he would also ask God's forgiveness in pursuit of His greater purpose of "loving your neighbor."

And yes, he, William Wilberforce, would cheat.

THE TEN FACTORS

Although there is no evidence that he systematized a checklist such as the one below, there can be no doubt that Wilberforce discussed and debated most of these ten ethical factors not only in Parliament, but with allies, friends, and family.

1. **Notions of fairness and justice:** His primary rationale for considering cheating was the profound unfairness he associated with the slave trade. Not only with slavery itself, but with the separating and deporting of African families without their consent, while giving different rights and privileges to English and European families, was discriminatory and, to his view, inherently unjust. Notions of "Biblical fairness" (i.e. slaves existed in all cultures mentioned in the Bible) and of "fairness within one's caste," etc., were at odds with Wilberforce's sense of democratic and humane fairness. Justice was another matter, since slavery was indeed legal and thus just within an English parliamentary context. But that was exactly why he struggled to change the law. English justice did not compute with universal or divine justice.

    Although the notion of "cheating" seems inherently unjust because it is de facto unfair to those who are cheated, Wilberforce came to the conclusion that it is not unjust to cheat cheaters. To his view, slave owners and traders were cheating human beings of many of their basic rights and perpetuating an extremely unjust system. His parliamentary cheating would pale in comparison to the larger theft of millions of people from their homelands, families, and civil rights.

2. **Impact or consequences:** The true ethical tension for Wilberforce was between his desire for different consequences (a victorious vote) and his allegiance to the tone of honesty (see below). From his perspective, he had exhausted all honest means without the desired impact. Thus, in order to

achieve a victorious consequence or outcome, he would have to consider deceptive practices.

Consequences carried immense weight in this case, because the fates of millions of people in future centuries were held in the balance. However, the immediate consequences of winning by cheating could have cost Wilberforce his reputation as a person of integrity, and the trust of many of his peers and those for whom he was a role model. He decided to accept these short-term consequences for the sake of the long-term impact: the abolition of slavery in England.

3. **Ends and means:** As stated above, the ends or consequences became so important to Wilberforce that he was willing to consider sacrificing his typically noble means. Exceptional injustice meant considering a rare exception to his usual means, and also an exception to his typical...

4. **Tone and atmosphere:** Wilberforce wished to maintain a trustworthy tone. His faith was steeped in the high standard honoring the sacredness of life. And yet even the commandment "thou shalt not kill" had exceptions, such as self-defense and the rules of war. Similarly, couldn't one make an exception to "thou shalt not lie" when facing deceptive political enemies? Must tone be universal, or could one lower one's standards in selective arenas, such as when an artist employs poetic license? Couldn't one be more aggressive—and even manipulative—when countering a bully? For example, a bully who engaged in slave-trading, which separated children from their permanently exiled parents as a side effect?

However, he also sensed that if he clouded his own atmosphere, he was modeling a tone at odds with the wholesome world he was advocating. William also knew that his followers, friends, and family looked to him as a Christ-like role model and as their advocate. What kind of model and advocate would he become once seen as untrustworthy and hypocritical?

5. **Motivation and higher law:** As a man of faith, William held himself accountable to a higher law. In order to be able to sleep with himself, his motivation had to be to please the god he believed in, and to honor a law higher than that of English torts. He was motivated not so much by a sense of human justice, but by one that he might have argued was inalienable, divine, and inherent. Given the notion of *agapé*, also known as unconditional love, permeating his faith, Wilberforce was motivated by intense compassion and could not tolerate the suffering of humans and

animals. It was his obedience to higher law that propelled his lifelong passion to change human laws.

He sought to change the laws of the earth to conform to the laws of heaven, and not the other way around.

6. **Allegiance and loyalty:** On the one hand, this statesman had sworn allegiances to the Crown and his country. And yet he felt an unsworn allegiance to humanity at large, especially to victims and the voiceless. His loyalty to his family and their safety had to be taken into account no less than to his followers, including the runaway slaves who looked to him with hope for reform. Despite his enmity toward slave-owners and the businessmen who supported them, he also knew that as a member of Parliament, he held at least some measure of accountability to English business.

   Moreover, as a Christian he was also expected to follow the commandment: "love your enemies." In that sense, he held an allegiance to all human beings. But most of these people, including the church and civic leaders he admired, already had a voice in their own affairs. Slaves did not. Ultimately, despite many other allegiances, William's priority allegiances were to 1) God and 2) voiceless victims. This primary loyalty to God bound him to obey His command: "Do unto others as you would have done unto you." He could not imagine anyone wanting to be "done unto as" slave traders and owners did.

7. **Values and principles:** Clearly, Wilberforce highly valued human freedom and dignity. The question became whether or not he also valued honesty so highly that he would place it above other values. Christian principles such as "love your neighbor" and "love your enemies" were, as explained above, strongly both in play and in conflict. More secular principles, such as "to thine own self be true" and "all men are created equal," were weighed in Parliament and in his head. Adam Smith's principles of economics honoring an "invisible hand" that drives the markets was used to justify the slave trade, but Wilberforce understood the counterbalancing "no man should be only a means to an end" principle as well. Ultimately, the principles and values that seemed to matter most were those that honored individual human choice, dignity, and sovereignty.

8. **Cultural context:** As noted above, not only Wilberforce's host culture, but most known cultures of his day, welcomed slavery and modifications, such as indentured servants. Bribery and corruption were commonly

accepted parts of political culture, including the buying of elections. Royal and aristocratic power held a vector of authority. Women, other than royalty, were almost entirely without voice and totally without vote. Spokespersons for minority rights were typically trivialized or demonized. The landscape of a tradition-bound, white, patriarchal culture created a difficult obstacle course for human rights activists.

9. **Implications:** Wilberforce knew from correspondence and intercessors that actions taken in one country could have long-term implications in others. Terminating one part of the slave trade meant sending a message to foreign governments and crippling the overall slave economy as well. Freeing living slaves also meant preventing the enslaved lives of their children and grandchildren. William was enough of an idealist to hope he was helping to ending all—not just regional—slavery, and so the implications of his actions could be drawn upon a broad canvas.

But there were other implications, such as bankruptcy and the collapse of many slave-related businesses and careers. And there were the far larger costs to be incurred by those who would be forced to pay laborers, rather than to merely feed and house slaves. Yet for Wilberforce, the greatest possible implication would be a moral one: victory would assure that far fewer people could legally own other people. And any moral victory would set a precedent for other ones. In his scriptural terms, the implications were that "good would triumph over evil," and ideally would be more likely to have momentum to do so elsewhere.

10. **Proportion and balance:** We have no record of how much relative weight Wilberforce gave to all of these factors, yet it is clear that he gave most of them much consideration. Few people ignore death threats and the possible loss of reputation, and he was never one to disrespect the truth. Nevertheless, he gave so much weight to liberty, fairness, compassion, and especially to the sacred dignity of life, that in retrospect it seems hard to believe that these would be overshadowed by allegiance to rigid belief, tone, and reputation, especially within a political context. He gave greatest weight to the sanctity of life, and the divine principle that "we are all made in the image and likeness of God." Ultimately, he gave fresh meaning to his mentor's commandment: "He that is least among you all, the same shall be great," and gave greater value to spiritual principles than to the political values of his colleagues. That said, ultimately, results did matter to Wilberforce, and so he also gave value to humanitarian outcomes, which, in this case, involved using deception to obtain.

THE WILBERFORCE LEGACY

After much deliberation, Wilberforce and Stephen finally approached Prime Minister Pitt with their plan. Presumably, they asked to speak with him discretely, so as to move away from others nearby. It is surmised that the prime minister, also an abolitionist, smiled wryly to himself after giving a private congratulations to his two friends, as if to collude with mischief-makers.

Whatever the conversation, whatever the atmosphere, whatever was heard or not heard, history tells us this much: Pitt surreptitiously agreed to the clever end-run, which supported his goal of defeating the French. Wilberforce and Stephen then huddled privately with other allies to hatch a full-blown, clandestine plan for tricking the opposition. Part of their strategy was to flip their process by running the camouflaged bill through the House of Lords first, to give it legitimacy and momentum. In 1806, it passed there easily by a vote of forty-three to seventeen.

Later, the bill would not only pass in the House of Commons, but also pave the way for the monumental victory the Abolitionists had long pursued. In 1807, without the need for further deception, Wilberforce proposed an anti-slavery bill that passed 283 to sixteen. After almost two decades, the anti-slavers had reversed the vote and garnered support from almost every corridor.

Sisyphus was finally a free man, and so too would be thousands of Africans who would no longer be captured and deported.

As for Wilberforce, he became a national hero, if not a saint. His fame rapidly spread, reaching international levels.

In 1814, Thomas Jefferson, who had succeeded John Adams as president, encouraged American Abolitionists by citing Wilberforce's example and reasoning. By 1858, the "great emancipator," Abraham Lincoln, said, "every American schoolboy should know the story of William Wilberforce." Frederick Douglas called the triumph a "victory for the whole human race."

None of them mentioned cheating.

After William's death, his new prime minister proclaimed, "millions unborn will bless his memory." Noted historian F.K. Brown wrote that there was not any major reform group or charity that was not helped by Wilberforce's generosity, whether in spirit or in coin. John Jay observed that he was "good among the great and great among the good."

The legacy of William Wilberforce lives on concretely in the numerous institutions bearing his name worldwide. However, it lives most vibrantly in the important scientists, artists, pacifists, statemen, athletes, parents, advocates, engineers, teachers, doctors, lawyers, civic leaders, and others who have made a far different contribution to humanity than they would have had they, like their ancestors, been sold into slavery.

In his own way, Wilberforce had lived out the words of the negro spiritual known as "Let My People Go":

You need not always weep and mourn
Let My people go!
And wear these slav'ry chains forlorn,
Let My people go!

Go down, Moses,
Way down in Egypt's land;
Tell old Pharaoh
To let My people go!

Wilberforce had told the rich and the powerful to let God's people go. And finally, the Red Sea had parted.

Along the way, Wilberforce had to wrestle with a vexing ethical decision, but in the end, he was more than convinced that it had all been worth it. For if it took an ounce of cheating to save a ton of humanity, he would not let the letter of rigid beliefs trump the spirit of human dignity.

If there is one more takeaway from Wilberforce's life that stands out, it is the power of persistence. His early attempts were crushed by overwhelming majorities and his cause seemed laughable even to moderates. But, for decades, he remained convinced that his ethical stance, no matter how unpopular, was morally persuasive and humanely essential.

How does that apply today? What are the difficult decisions in our lives where we may be tempted to succumb to pressure?

Cannot conscience still be trusted as a moral GPS for the twenty-first century? As I tell my students, "in this era in which we are told that everyone is sleeping with everyone else, there is only one person with whom you must be able to sleep—comfortably—yourself."

CHAPTER 6

MARIE CURIE:
(1867-1934)

RADIANT AND AT RISK

Her heart, kidneys, and head had never felt so much pressure.

The heart was broken. The kidneys required surgery. The head contemplated suicide.

And yet, there was even greater pressure to make a quick decision. Was it necessary that she immediately leave Paris to return to Warsaw? Her brother, Josef, had pleaded with her to do so. Her eldest sister, Bronislawa, doggedly insisted. The dean at the Sorbonne and others at the highest levels demanded her exodus.

Sadly, the French public agreed. Indeed, an irate crowd had stoned her house, forcing her to move in with friends.

Large beads of sweat poured down an ashen face. Or were they tears? Or both? People closest to her had described that face alternatively as pale, fallen, lifeless, and pure white. Nothing could amaze or amuse it under the present conditions. It had aged twelve months in just one.

For Marie to remain another month might add another year. In one sense, it felt like she was trapped in a time tomb, and it would always be 1911—but as she stared in the mirror, she thought it must be 1931. At forty-four, Marie looked like a sixty-four-year-old version of her mother, returned from the dead.

It would not have surprised her to know she would soon be hospitalized, and then moved to a sanitarium. She was losing too much weight along with her mind.

This apparition called Marie had been told she could stop all this by quickly departing Paris. And yet, by moving to Warsaw, she would abandon her dream, her purpose, her centrality within the scientific world, and the man she deeply loved. She would also abruptly uproot her family. It seemed unthinkable to leave—and unthinkable to stay.

Marie had to think of others. Her two daughters had been raised in Paris and would be deserting their friends, their educational paths, and possibly their bright futures. But she also needed to consider her other family back in Warsaw, Poland, the land of her parents who had sacrificed so much for her. Poland remained home for her brother, Josef, the prominent cardiologist, and for so many others keen to welcome their prized celebrity and long-lost Polish cousin back home.

But what of her French friends, protégés, closest colleagues, confidants, and students who needed her? What about the leading-edge scientific circle of which she was a centerpiece?

And though she could hardly talk about it, her heart also continued to return to the question: "What about Paul?"

PAUL IN THE REAR-VIEW MIRROR

In Marie's Paris, Paul Langevin had precipitated the best of times and the worst of times. Long before he was her paramour, Paul had been a precocious assistant of her husband, Pierre, and a promising young physicist. Before long, Langevin had become a dear friend of the family and a prominent rising star at the Sorbonne. It was the best of times.

After Marie's husband perished in a tragic accident in 1906, Paul became her comforter. But, according to the French tabloids, he had come too close for mere comfort. The scandal papers had discovered that after he had comforted her, she had also comforted him, and one comfort led to another. For both of them, this had created such wonderful feelings, and her heart raced just to remember them.

Such intimacy had led her to a dream about their future life of science and pleasure together. It had also led to the deepest, most affectionate correspondence. In a whole new way, it was the best of times.

Yet there were three problems. Paul was married. Marie was a celebrity. A tabloid possessed their love letters.

While the more liberal press sought to defend Marie's honor, the boisterous, gossip-driven scandal rags quickly embellished the story and mounted a multi-pronged smear campaign. Beyond the alleged tryst itself was the melodrama of the martyred French wife, Jean Langevin, with four children supposedly abandoned by their father. Then there was the anti-Semitic allegation that Marie was Jewish. According to town gossip, her father had been a converted Jew, and in other inaccurate articles, she was allegedly German, "an anti-patriotic foreigner," and a concubine. None of these allegations were true.

One scandal sheet, *Le Petit Journal*, had published a fabricated letter from Marie to Paul, advising him how he could rid himself of his shrewish wife step by step. The defamatory buzz spread like brushfire. It was the worst of times.

Even more spectacular were the daily descriptions of ongoing duels fought to defend the honor of Langevin. Various journalists, born during the Dreyfus era of "*J'Accuse*," were fueled by French chauvinism and anti-Semitism even though Curie was actually not Jewish.

Any attempt by authorities at the Sorbonne to show decorum and decency by protecting the privacy of Curie and Langevin was twisted into yet more yellow journalism. Now the story would read that the powerful, elitist university was bullying and censoring the people's press and a vulnerable, abused mother.

That Marie was also a mother was seldom mentioned. Neither was the lack of any evidence that Marie and Paul were physically intimate, nor could it be proven that they had written any, let alone all, of the quoted and paraphrased love letters.

No wonder Marie looked ghoulish. Her daughter had recently fainted after reading a headline, and Marie looked as if she had fainted inside. She had evacuated her daughters from their country home, which had been stoned, to live with friends in the city. Yet, such forced relocation and keeping a low profile felt more like imprisonment.

And what of Paul? Anything they might say to each other henceforth could be broadcast, out of context, by the so-called journalists. Nor could she see or be seen with him. And how could she explain all this to her daughters, colleagues, and students? No wonder she was "whiter-than-white" and alternatively stunned, incensed, and despondent.

Then there were the people who were obscene and making scenes behind the scenes. Even the muckrakers could not print some of the names she had been called. Nor would they print the murder threats "Madame Langevin" had made against Marie. After all, Jean Langevin had to be sympathetically portrayed as the victim, and Marie was being cast as the foreign home wrecker.

There were tales of hush money and other bribes given to the mother of four, and to the yellow press, through third parties, to sanitize and withhold parts of the story. Both the circus and the sideshows featured fiction, corruption, and caricature.

Beneath all this was the unspoken threat that Marie posed to the French double standard. Within "*La Belle Epoch*," it was widely known that men of stature often maintained and were even expected to keep subservient mistresses. Yet women of stature must remain above reproach.

Marie had also been a major threat to the male-dominated European scientific community. The rigid Parisian patriarchy narrowly prevailed, but was severely frightened, when she came within two votes of being admitted to the all-male French Academy of Sciences.

Whatever was said on the surface, women were jealous that she was admired by men of influence. Yet, men of influence were jealous that she alone had won two Nobel Prizes, and in two different fields—physics and chemistry. Although her husband had shared the first Nobel Prize with her prior to his death, she had received the second on her own. At that time, no other man or woman was accorded such scientific prestige.

After all, she was *the* Marie Curie, who had first won fame near the turn of the century with her husband Pierre Curie for their experiments with radioactivity. But now that story was playing differently in the press. Suddenly, it was being parroted that she had "ridden Pierre's coattails," and was not really an authentic scientist.

Indeed, many believed that she had dishonored Professor Curie's memory. Some dirt peddlers went so far as to claim that he had known about the affair, and thus his accident was really a suicide. He must have deliberately thrown himself beneath the carriage that crushed him.

These were the tall tales of revisionist history she had to endure in the tongue-wagging tabloids. So, the ghastly pale Marie seemed headed for a nervous breakdown amidst a sea of vitriolic arrows. She could not even return to her own country home without risking her life and injury to her daughters. Why, indeed, should she remain in Paris?

STANDING HER GROUND

And yet it was impossible to leave her life trajectory, and her sense of commission.

Marie was mystified that she was staring into her friends' mirror and looking at an exhausted, humiliated old lady. This was not the woman on a mission, whom she knew so well. How could she abandon her purpose?

And yet the face was that of a zombie. She did not possess the energy to chase away a vagrant spider approaching her, let alone take on a rumor-driven city.

Just as Newton had asserted that for every action there is an equal and opposite reaction, she was aware that for every argument supporting her likely exit, there was an equal and counter-balancing rebuttal compelling her to stay.

For example, on the one hand, a delegation from Poland, led by a fellow Nobel laureate, had invited her to teach at the University of Warsaw. There, she would be a national celebrity and well supported.

But on the other hand, the argument for her to stay was that her shared dream with Pierre was always to establish a substantial lab in Paris. Right then, with two Nobel Prizes and a desk full of other honors, she was much closer to creating that substantial radiology lab at the Sorbonne. And the Sorbonne was far more geographically and intellectually central to the scientific community than the University of Warsaw. Moreover, Marie's team of top colleagues, including Paul, worked primarily in France.

Madam Curie felt a strong compulsion to push discoveries within atomic, if not sub-atomic, physics to their limits. Her work promised humane and educational gifts to mankind. X-rays and other radiation treatments were being developed in medicine, and she felt an ethical responsibility to use her expertise to serve humanity. She sensed a mission to make every imaginable breakthrough possible.

Could she accomplish that in Warsaw? Russian imperial rule in Poland had been cruel and castrating to the intelligentsia, and she was wary of losing her academic freedom. Indeed, Marie had disturbing memories of the Russian Czar hanging the brother of one of her Polish friends. Authoritarian Russian dominion of Poland forced students to lead double lives by studying their own Polish culture surreptitiously in the underground "floating university."

Yes, in Poland she would be a national hero relatively free of scandal, but at what cost to her research? To science? To humanity? The Russian government could even close the university, ban women, punish independent thinking, and censure her experiments. The risks were sky high.

And yet, Warsaw was also compelling. She had remained very close to her Polish family, to whom she had written long, affectionate letters since leaving Warsaw in 1891 at the age of twenty-four.

But her husband's French family had taken her in as their own, and Pierre's father had become the primary caregiver for both of their daughters. In fact, during the scandal Pierre's brother was among her strongest supporters. Although abandoned by some colleagues, most of Marie's Paris family, like her own daughters, became even closer during the maelstrom.

There was a moral counterpoint to consider as well. Although Marie might bring her small family to greater safety and peace of mind in Warsaw, if she left Paris, she would appear to confirm the rumors. By fleeing and taking the lower ground, she would in effect be saying that she was guilty as charged.

Shouldn't she stay to refute all the embellishments and libel? To leave would be to accept exile and fan the flames of defamation.

There was also an ongoing battle with patriarchal authorities. Dr. Curie wanted to hold her own as a world class thinker and an equal in research. To leave would have meant that she had been successfully ostracized, and that women need not apply for leadership roles in science, the academy, and indeed in society.

Although she would not have used the word "feminist," Marie felt a strong responsibility to work toward equality, nurture younger female scientists, and be a leader above gender as well. If she absconded to Warsaw, all this would come undone. And she was painfully aware that had she been a man (especially a French man), a subterranean romance like hers would have been accepted as part of the status quo.

It seemed that every reason to stay also came with a reason to leave. On Nov. 11, 1911, the telegram had come from the Nobel Committee awarding her the second Nobel Prize, this time in chemistry. Surely, this distinction would establish her long-term scientific value to France and the Sorbonne, and would outlive the passing storm.

But then the other shoe dropped. The Nobel Committee was having second thoughts. This time they had written that she should not come to Stockholm to receive the prize until after the anticipated Langevin divorce proceedings. Her heart broke again as she realized the power of the tabloids to undermine her global, not just local, reputation and professional status.

Another reason to stay, the second Nobel Prize, had turned into another reason to leave. She feared the public would hear that she was no longer travelling to Stockholm to receive the prize and put the pieces together. She could imagine how this story would run in the press.

A HOST OF FACTORS

There seemed to be too many pros and cons, not to mention undisclosed feelings, to consider them all rationally. And there were also unknowns. Could she and Paul ever have a positive relationship again after the divorce and aftershocks had passed? Would she be named in the divorce proceedings as the other woman?

The stress of the scandal was destroying her health. But wouldn't moving her family be equally stressful? Was she stable enough to pack and move? She had been suffering from a chronic infection of the ureter and frequent high fever.

Before his death, Pierre had weakened and slowed down considerably, which made her wonder if the radioactivity also had negative effects upon both of them. Indeed, her exposure to radiation was so frequent that it might explain some of the mysterious pains and retardations in her body.

Then there was her fear of being spied upon. Jean Langevin seemed to have gone to great lengths to steal the love letters. It often felt like Marie or Paul had been followed by someone who would uncover more dirt for Jean or the newspapers. Would she ever know privacy again in Paris? Would her children?

Curie had always felt a fierce loyalty to Poland, in part because it had been eternally persecuted—by Bismarck, by the Czar, by imposed educational inspectors—and she felt great empathy for the Polish people, her people. Her father had sacrificed much for her, and she had been pulled frequently by a longing in her heart to return to him. Sadly, she was still on the train to Warsaw when he passed away, and arrived too late. Marie felt ongoing guilt.

Curie's mother had died when she was only nine. After that, the tightly knit family had all been so loyal to Marie, and to each other. Had she been loyal to them and to Poland?

Would it not alleviate the suffering of her daughters, and her own anguish, to be a true daughter of Poland and return to native soil? And yet...

And yet, what a loss. Adding it up, she would lose her freedom, resources, her primary mission, the Sorbonne, the Curies, close friends like the Burrels and the Perrins, time, her daughters' educations, scientific status, health, the chance to clear her name, and all those she served—junior colleagues, students, mentees, Polish immigrants, and medical associates.

On top of all that, there were principles and values she believed in that she wanted to fight for, which included the truth of her own situation, full freedom of thought and scientific inquiry, equality of women and foreigners, respect for human beings and their privacy, the future health of humanity via radiation therapy, accountability to her followers and colleagues, and the integrity of taking a strong stand rather than escaping responsibility.

And yet, staying in France would mean asking her daughters to face death threats. Would that be fair? Would that be necessary? Would that be wise? Could that be tragic?

CHRONIC ADVERSITY

Marie was no stranger to adversity. Both her mother and eldest sister had died when she was a child. Her father had been demoted due to the control of Polish educators by the Czar's minions, and thus she found herself becoming agnostic. It was difficult to believe in a god who would take away her mother, her sister, her father's stability, and any sense of public safety. She had once stayed up all night comforting a friend whose brother was scheduled to be executed by the Czar's lackeys the next day.

As a young governess, Marie and the son of her employer fell in love... only to be told by his parents that she, a lowly employee, was beneath his station. She felt jilted and crushed by a cruel class condescension. And yet there was no escape. By contract she was required to continue employment as their governess for two more years.

Later, in order to make ends meet as a young student in Paris, Curie had sustained a life of poverty. She would starve herself until she fainted and sleep wearing all of her clothes to barely avoid freezing.

After she married Pierre Curie, the young couple adapted an old shed for their research, since the university could not afford a modern laboratory. When they closed the windows to avoid the freezing winter, Pierre and Marie constantly inhaled toxic fumes. In the summer, the heat became overwhelming. Raising two children during the long hours of research proved taxing, and their third child was sadly voided by a miscarriage.

Even with fame came the excessive problems of notoriety.

As a private person who wished to continue her work, Marie was appalled and smothered by a steady stream of well-wishers, parasites, interviewers, and curiosity-seekers who visited at all hours. Privacy seemed impossible.

Far worse, Pierre's decline in health, and then depression, signaled some hidden problem, which was later alleged to be radiation poisoning. In April 1906, his skull was crushed by the wheel of a heavily laden carriage after he had slipped and fallen on a Paris street while opening his umbrella.

Four years later, Pierre's father, who had been the backbone of family domestic care, also died. Maria had lost the two rocks of stability in her home and had to make major adjustments to care for her daughters—and for her heart. Two of her very best friends had departed.

Yet another shock came when one of the most distinguished leaders in science, a powerful friend named Lord Kelvin, claimed that radium was not an element. Much of Pierre's and Marie's research was based upon the discovery of two new elements—one of which was radium, a primary source of "radioactivity," a term Marie had coined. Kelvin's claim was devastating and, if shown to be true, could have destroyed the bedrock of the Curies' research and reputation.

Thus, despite many awards and accomplishments, her life was regularly punctuated with fear, shock, and tragedy. The early stages of fear had emerged during the clandestine, illegal underground courses she took in the "floating university." Even in childhood, there had been the chronic fear of being discovered and persecuted by the lethal Russian regime.

So, Maria was no stranger to fright and suffering. Indeed, both she and Pierre had inexplicable, intense pains. They had lost the tips of their fingers to radium.

Still, nothing could have prepared her for such vitriolic intensity. During the autumn and winter of 1911, the conservative press dubbed Marie the "Vestal Virgin of Radium." She received both spoken and written threats that she must resign from her job and she must leave France. After all, she and Paul had "divided the Sorbonne," and there could be no peace with her on campus.

The event became so traumatic that there were no entries in Marie's lab notebooks between October 1911, and December 1912—fourteen months! And her daughter, Eve, who deeply felt the impact as a child, only minimally and defensively noted the Langevin events in her lengthy biography about her mother. Indeed, Paul Langevin was only mentioned in passing as a colleague. The event became a family burden too heavy to name, let alone bear.

So why should Marie remain within the heart of pain, persecution, and Paris?

FOR SCIENCE AND PIERRE

The young immigrant Marie had received not just one master's degree, but two, and then a doctorate. By 1894, she had met the prominent, young French scientist, Pierre Curie. At first, Marie had pursued the handsome professor to obtain laboratory space. But soon it was Pierre who was pursuing Marie for romance. By 1895 they were married and bicycling around France for their honeymoon.

It was the same year that German physicist W.C. Roentgen had discovered what he called the "X-ray," since in mathematics "X" signified an unknown quantity. In 1897, Marie gave birth to two children—one named Irene, and the other called "radioactivity," a term she coined in an important scientific article. She would nurture and protect both for the rest of her life.

Shortly thereafter, she would discover what she claimed to be two new elements, "polonium" (named for her native Poland) and "radium," which became her fascination and primary exploration for decades to come. While Pierre's father watched after young Irene, Pierre and Marie tended their more radioactive progeny in their converted-shed laboratory.

Of great significance was the discovery that the atom was hardly static or uniform. Prior to the Curie's work, scientists had maintained the notion that atoms did not change size, weight, or composition. But the explorations of Pierre and especially Marie confirmed that atoms could decrease their size by giving off rays or energy.

Like Roentgen and their French colleague Henri Becquerel (with whom they shared their first Nobel Prize), the Curies were suddenly the Magellan and Columbus of physics, exploring a new, invisible universe of charged rays and dynamic "weight-loss" atoms, without knowing the implications of their expeditions.

Within her doctoral thesis, later viewed as among the most significant in science, Madame Curie studied Becquerel's newly identified "uranium rays." Soon, she would be demonstrating that the radioactivity of these rays could be an actual property of atoms. Doing so proved to be a precocious and significant contribution to science.

Supporting her throughout these voyages was a strong and equal partner, Pierre, with whom she would soon have a second child, Eve. It proved ideal for Marie to have Paul as a sounding board for her experiments, and vice versa. Although only Pierre spoke in Stockholm when they received the first Nobel Prize, and although only Marie spoke when receiving her second (Pierre had died eight years earlier), each accurately and proudly acknowledged the other.

The prolific Pierre had published twenty-five influential physics papers between 1898 and 1903. But suddenly, the Curies were so in-demand after winning their shared Nobel Prize that his publishing completely stopped. They were invited to so many events, whether together or alone, that their individual and tandem research seemed terminated.

The Curies had endured and accomplished so much together that all of Marie's future dreams had been for them—as a unit. Her deepest loves—for science and for Pierre—called for her to create a new laboratory or institute in Paris. After Pierre's death, she had secretly shared those dreams with Paul, who also deeply loved science, Pierre, and Marie.

If she could not publicly say her dream was not only for Pierre, but also for Paul, she could continue to say that it was for science and for Pierre as she moved toward her goals. And since the Curie family had adopted her so thoroughly, she felt as much French as she was Polish.

How could her first loves and her adopted country be left behind? She had done everything *with* Pierre in France. How could she not do everything *for* Pierre in France? After all, she was not just Polish. When weighing her decision, she had said to others: "But I am now almost French. And I am now a Curie…"

FOR WOMEN

One reason Marie had been involved in the Polish underground "floating school" was that women were not allowed in Polish universities. Even when she entered the Sorbonne, Marie was only one of twenty-three women among two thousand men enrolled in the sciences. Throughout Europe, women were often referred to as the "weaker sex." It was not uncommon for a wife of great strength or candor to be sent away to an insane asylum.

116

The double standard was deeply ingrained in the university culture. Whenever Pierre and Marie travelled to England or Sweden to make a speech or present a paper, only Pierre could publicly represent them.

Marie Curie had experienced both French and male chauvinism when being told what she could not do or have. She had seen firsthand some of the many female students who were failed on exams while their male counterparts of equal intelligence were passed.

It was within this patriarchal monopoly that her accomplishments seemed all the brighter. She was the first female professor at the University of Paris, and the first woman to receive a doctorate in France.

Although no woman was admitted into the French Academy of Science until 1979, Marie came closest almost seventy years earlier. No man would win two Nobel Prizes to equal her feat until Linus Pauling did so fifty years later. She raised two talented young daughters, one of whom would also earn a Nobel Prize.

Marie loved the companionship of other women and remained close to her sisters. Her greatest publicist and patron was the female editor of *The Delineator,* an American woman's magazine. Curie was also among the foremost promoters, employers, mentors, and supporters of young female scientists.

Clearly, gender politics was an inflammatory agent in the scandal at the Sorbonne. Paul Langevin was not being asked to leave France, yet Marie was already all but exiled. As a woman, an agnostic, a Pole, a widow, a perceived Jew, and a female leader outside the French Academy of Sciences, Marie was a strong threat to the status quo. Even after Pierre's death, when she was offered a stipend as his widow, she declined it by saying "I'm perfectly capable of supporting myself."

The French were disturbed by such a woman who, according to them, did not know her place. Yet, women of all ages were inspired by her independence, motivation, and achievements. To this day Madame Curie is a potent role model, not only for women, but for all scientists, pioneers, and leaders. Although she did not use her pulpit to advance feminist political rhetoric, she lived her life as if to say, "see me as who I am, not as a category."

Dr. Curie had felt the injustice of rampant discrimination for many years, so she saw the scandal through that lens. She was being vilified not only for threatening the French social order, but for doing so as a woman. Whatever she did was not just for science, foreigners, Jews (actual or otherwise), family, or Pierre—it was also be done for women, especially those who looked up to her.

A COURAGEOUS DECISION:

Nothing had changed about her situation. Her heart, kidneys and head had never felt so much pressure.

The heart was broken. The kidneys required surgery. The head contemplated suicide.

No wonder the mirror still pictured an exasperated, ashen old lady of only forty-four years. She could neither erase one wrinkle nor darken one hair.

"*Je suis francais,*" she said half aloud.

It meant, "I am French," and she had said it years ago to test her accent. Although the lips moved slightly, the face remained frozen, as if embalmed.

"*Je suis francais,*" she said a little louder as the lips moved further.

She was no longer listening to see if she sounded more French than Polish. Marie sounded almost French. Nor was she testing her tired larynx to see if she could still speak. She could see that she was still alive... marginally.

The center of the mirror moved more dramatically as she spoke firmly. "*Je suis francais.*"

Marie knew what she would say when next she was pushed toward a move to Poland. "*JE SUIS FRANCAIS!*" would be her emphatic answer.

And she would add to it. "I am French! My daughters are French. My husband was French. I will not leave my country!"

There was far more to this declaration than met the ear. She had thought the matter through and realized that her heart, daughters, work, adopted family, accomplishments, husband's legacy, and ongoing dreams were all in France.

"*Je suis francais,*" she said dramatically as the mirror's mouth enlarged yet again—and she thought she no longer recognized an old woman, but rather an awakening tiger.

Marie would stay and fight. Professor Curie would stay and teach. Madame Curie would remain and honor her husband. Dr. Curie would study radioactivity and chart a new, invisible galaxy. Nobel laureate Curie would travel to Stockholm and receive her well-deserved prize. Marie Curie would take the higher road.

For Marie, "*je suis francais*" was not simply an acknowledgment that her French accent now overshadowed her Polish one, nor that she had been part of the Sorbonne for two decades. It was not even an awareness that her children were far more French than Polish, nor that she had an unsorted mountain of honors and credentials in her office, the majority of which were French.

It did not mean that almost all of her possessions and writings were now local, not imported. Nor was it simply a statement about her legal citizenship.

"Je suis francais" had a deeper meaning—that she was not a quitter. What she started in Paris would be finished in Paris. Neither was Marie a doormat. Wherever she was being pushed back by chauvinistic hyperbole, she would stand to exert the force of truth. If she had made one mistake, she would not make another.

The mirrored face all but stood at attention. She could almost detect a smile trying to erase the scowl. Whatever the cost, whatever the pain, whatever the tarnishing of her fading image, she could win the war of science despite losing the battle of reputation.

"Je suis francais!"

THE TEN FACTORS

The ten factors of ethical decision-making shed much light upon the Curie decision:

1. **Notions of fairness and justice:** Marie painfully observed victims of persecution in her childhood and was quickly sensitized. Discrimination by nationality, gender, and ethnicity were unacceptable, and the "Sorbonne Scandal" was fueled by all three. The word "chauvinism" was coined employing the name (Chauvin) of a French soldier so patriotic that his actions were seen as excessive and exclusionary. Seeing both French chauvinism and the broader application of the word "chauvinism" of all kinds as extreme and discriminatory behavior, Marie felt that fairness necessitated a more balanced approach. Both insiders and outsiders, and both genders, should be honored. All should participate on a level playing field no matter what the customs of the day. Reputation should also be on an equal basis. If men were permitted to have concurrent romantic and sexual relationships without loss of honor, so too should women. Justice could not exist outside the boundaries of equal treatment.

2. **Impact or consequences:** Curie sensed that her discoveries could have far greater impact in France than in the politically censored and unstable climate of Poland. Already, radium and the property of radioactivity seemed to have significant potential for medicine. She projected that ongoing experiments could have humane consequences for mankind. Of course, there were other consequences to be considered, including those bearing upon her daughters' safety and potential achievements. And more far-reaching impact would be upon the Curie and Langevin families, close friends and Polish relatives, the Sorbonne, Paris, the Nobel Prize

Committee, and even upon France and Poland. Many people stood to be further damaged, and in some cases quite unfairly.

3. **Ends and means:** Marie did not have to struggle with ends vs. means questions as much as others chronicled in this book. But each journalist who gained access to the unauthenticated love letters had to decide whether to treat Marie and Paul as a means to sell newspapers, or as human beings and thus, in Immanuel Kant's terms, an end of themselves. Was Marie still a human being, or a news object? Similarly, her employers had to ask: was she primarily a status ornament (and later a black eye) for the university, and thus viewed as a means toward their public relations? Or was she an end of herself, and thus a colleague to be supported through thick and thin?

4. **Tone and atmosphere:** In matters of sex and romance, Marie honored the discrete tone of Victorian euphemism and privacy. For her, these were matters not to be discussed in living rooms, let alone by the press. By moving to Poland, she would have allowed the tawdry, tabloid tone to prevail in a country where there was virtually no press libel law. Although at one level, the scandal was about Marie and Paul, at another level it was about whether slander and sensationalism could trump truth and scientific evidence. Should not the tone of reasoned discourse and factuality prevail over the conventional wisdom of amplified gossip? And should not a moral code protecting privacy prevail over the low-tone, anything goes, gossip-driven Parisian worst practices du jour? Whatever others might have done, she stood for a tone of civility.

5. **Motivation and higher law:** Unlike Gandhi's and Wilberforce's appeals to higher, divine (whether Hindu or Christian) law, Dr. Curie was motivated to discover and verify the higher law of nature itself. She was also motivated by such strong attraction to Paul Langevin that she was willing to sacrifice most other priorities and key values to maintain the amorous relationship. Since the second, romantic motivation could not be consummated, she would ultimately be driven by the first—the quest for scientific law and discovery. Her hope was for a universe in which all would be motivated to discover this higher natural law, rather than by the quest for power and dominion over supposedly secondary classes, genders, and races.

6. **Allegiance and loyalty:** As in Queen Esther's case, the nature of her allegiances was one of Professor Curie's most vexing dialectics. Her loyalty to her blood family was offset by a loyalty to her in-law Curie

family. The loyalty she felt to France was as strong as the one to Poland. Her allegiance to her daughters and their safety might have meant fleeing France, but allegiance to her many colleagues, protégés, and students meant staying. The leading men in her life—her father, brother, Pierre, and Paul—were no longer visible, but they were also equally divided loyalties. And a loyalty to Paul might have meant, against all odds, staying, in hopes that they could ride out the storm and someday reunite. Still, a loyalty to her father's memory, a father she had deeply loved and ultimately betrayed (at least from her own guilt-ridden perspective), would have meant returning to Poland. The sum total of all allegiances left Marie torn down the middle.

7. **Values and principles:** One of the most important values to Marie was truth. Both Curies had quested for the truth of an atom's precise makeup, properties, and weight for decades. She also sought truth based upon valid evidence from journalists, who unfortunately valued profit above objectivity. Privacy was an equally compelling value that she coveted no less when she was famous than when she was infamous.

   The principle "what's good for the goose is good for the gander" and "all people (not just "all men") are created equal," underlined her longing for gender equity. Meanwhile, the principle "to thine own self be true" was behind her quest for professional, academic, and personal freedom. But she had to face the truth inherent in a natural law stated by fellow scientist Sir Isaac Newton: "For every action, there is an equal and opposite reaction." Although she knew at some level that her dalliance with a married man, and one with so many children, would do harm to others, the "opposite reaction" principle did equal harm to her and her own children.

8. **Cultural context:** Despite the brocaded pseudo-civility of Parisian culture, Marie's France was no less controlled by power plays and masculine monopoly than was Esther's Persia, Carson's America, and Malala's Pakistan. It was a world in which it was unthinkable for most women to receive a college education, or to have "mattresses" (i.e. male mistresses). The rules of the game were set by European male tradition and expectation, rather than primarily by ethics. The crowds that had so easily turned against Marie Antoinette, Dreyfus, and Robespierre could also betray a Nobel laureate. The Belle Epoque mores and a lengthy legacy of French mob rule played a part in Marie's cultural *Stimmung*. Within this culture was the subculture of the Parisian elite, who had rigid rules about who might enter their membership.

121

9. **Implications:** As noted under "consequences," Marie Curie knew that there could be dire long-term implications for her daughters no matter what she did. The two girls could be forever harassed and ostracized—if not harmed—as Paris outsiders if they remained. But uprooting them from their friends, adoring relatives, and educational mentors could also have been an irreversible shock, especially if it meant they were branded by scandal for life. But the larger implications for humanity could not be seen as clearly as these immediate consequences to her daughters. Although she might have been able to sniff out a potential for her discoveries, she could not have known at the time that they would later save thousands of lives. Still, these long-term implications and their promise propelled her forward.

10. **Proportion and balance:** While some of the ten factors held little importance to Marie, factors such as conflicting loyalties, consequences, justice, and truth-telling greatly mattered. Privacy, academic freedom, gender equity, and reputation also impacted her decision-making. And while she could no longer speak of it, she greatly valued romantic love. The pressure of many people offering advice, directives, and even threats was not insignificant. But what mattered more was her own inner radar and sense of destiny, and the hidden hope against hope that someday this might all blow over, and she could once again see Paul. As an ethical decision, there were many vectors of influence, but ultimately the greatest proved to be the uncompromised purpose of a mission yet to be accomplished.

THE LEGACY

Dr. Curie's honored place in scientific history would long outlive her critics and rivals. Her two Nobel Prizes were only the most prominent of over a hundred awards and citations she received over a thirty-five-year period. By 1902, the French Academy of Sciences had already given the Curies many distinctions. Pierre and Marie were also honored guests of the Royal Institution in England and awarded the Davy Medal. Despite her narrow miss at being elected to the French Academy of Science, she was selected for the French Academy of Medicine.

Later, her daughter Eve would write that Marie had earned a pile of honorary degrees that were never sorted, counted, or listed. Following World War I, Dr. Curie also received an important military medal for service to France. Her trips to the United States were not only to receive honorary degrees from Yale,

Columbia, and other leading universities, but also to receive a most treasured prize—a second gram of radium valued at $100,000, presented by the president at the White House.

Of great importance to Dr. Curie were: 1) the establishment of the Radium Institute, and 2) her financial ability to draw top scientists together. The next generation of Curie-inspired inventions were offspring that included sonar, quartz watches, ultrasound, electronic appliances, TV tubes, and mobile telephones.

Curie's contemporary and fellow Nobel laureate, esteemed physicist Ernest Rutherford of Cambridge, said that Marie was the "foremost woman investigator of our age." Biographer Barbara Goldsmith added that the "obsessive genius" was "as rare as a unicorn in the field of science."

Since the "Sorbonne Scandal" savaged Curie's character, Albert Einstein's counter-balancing comment is most striking. The famous German physicist, with whom she had hiked and often conversed, wrote: "Marie Curie is, of all celebrated human beings, the only one whom fame has not corrupted."

Of course, the human use of radioactivity turned out to be a mixed blessing, as Kennedy (Chapter 1) and Truman (Chapter 8) would discover when agonizing over the possible use of nuclear weapons. Rachel Carson (Chapter 9) would have other doubts about the healing use of radiation during her chemotherapy.

It is hard to know whether the use of radioactive substances protected or endangered more lives in the long run. For example, those living and dying in Hiroshima, Chernobyl, Three Mile Island, and similar locations could not know the long-term impact of radiation poisoning upon their children, grand-children, and neighboring communities. Questions about how and when to utilize uranium's and radium's progeny greatly expanded the discussion of social, if not anti-social, ethics.

Nevertheless, during World War I Curie became involved in a highly pro-social use of her "nuclear family." Her greatest applied use of radium is one far less known than her work in the laboratory, and it became her largest humanitarian accomplishment.

During the first Great War, it became obvious that technologies showing X-ray silhouettes could save thousands of lives. Previously, military battlefield surgeons and medics often had to guess the location of fractured bones, broken bayonet tips, bullets, and shrapnel lodged inside wounded soldiers. When used properly, the new X-ray machines could show the precise positions of such foreign objects, and thus prevent hundreds, if not thousands, of deaths and amputations.

In 1914, Marie personally perceived the need to bring such X-ray machines close to the front lines. She persuaded wealthy friends and associates to donate cars that could be equipped with X-ray technology.

Such transformed vehicles, which looked next-of-kin to ambulances, could be driven into battle zones when casualties were at their peak. Eventually, a fleet of twenty "petite Curies" (as they were soon called) was assembled. Their drivers and technicians examined literally millions of wounded soldiers and were credited with saving thousands of lives.

While it is unknown what would have happened had Marie returned to Poland, it seems unlikely that she would have created her fleet of mobile lifesavers. Often accompanied by daughter, Irene, Marie drove a petite Curie herself, and greatly assisted both military and medical efforts throughout World War I. Ironically, she helped to save the lives of those who had thrown stones and written scathing vitriol about her indiscretion. And in other cases, she saved the lives of their relatives, friends, and neighbors.

Eventually, Dr. Curie was pictured more as a national heroine than as a black widow. Not only had she chosen to stay in Paris, but the French chose her to be the first woman who, due to her own accomplishments, would be buried in the Pantheon, Frances's exclusive national cemetery for celebrated citizens. If you listened closely, you might hear her proudly say, *"Je suis francais,"* from her coffin as she was permanently laid to rest.

THE FIRST STONE

Christian versions of the Bible report a story about Jesus of Nazareth being asked to give advice at a public execution. In his day, it was commonplace for women known to be adulterers to be stoned to death by a crowd. When such a woman who was taken in adultery was brought before him, Jesus was alleged to have said to the crowd: "Let he who is among you without sin throw the first stone." When no one hurled a rock, the woman escaped.

Nineteen centuries later, French Christians had apparently forgotten this moral teaching by Jesus. They stoned Marie's house after her adultery was reported and continued to hurl barbed words long after the stoning. A Parisian public shaming followed a public stoning.

But Marie's crime was not really fornication—a charge that has never been proven. Her crime was rather a dramatic break with public expectation.

The Irish wit, Oscar Wilde, reportedly said: "If there is anything worse than being seen with your mistress, it is being seen with your wife." The statement would be neither funny nor vintage Wilde if it did not contain at least an ounce of truth. Indeed, Wilde was commenting not upon what was moral in his society, but rather what was fashionable within upper class Britain.

Similarly, for Marie, her sin was not so much against morality, but against French *à la mode*. Living in Paris, the epicenter of the fashion world, her exposed behavior was not civic *haute couture*. She had broken a segment of the Napoleonic code written with invisible ink.

Had Marie fled Paris, she would have been forever stigmatized as a social pariah and sinner against these unwritten laws of La Belle Epoque. By remaining in Paris, she lived to see the fashion mores change, and she walked to the front of the runway by modeling lifesaving selflessness throughout the Great War.

Ultimately, Curie is remembered neither for the Sorbonne Scandal, nor for the petite Curies and her humanitarian coup. Instead, in the twenty-first century the headline of her life features her "Nobelity" more than her nobility. The lead story about Curie is now her understanding of radioactivity, not her social fall-out.

Dr. Curie has become a great icon of scientific discovery rather than of cultural non-conformity. Ironically, her character was proven at precisely the moment she was accused of having none.

Today, the Langevin scandal seems figuratively buried with hundreds of other historical sideshows. And Dr. Marie Curie is literally buried in Paris within a Pantheon of national legends, including two exceptional French physicists with whom she is finally reunited—Pierre Curie and Paul Langevin.

CHAPTER 7

MOHANDAS GANDHI:
(1869-1948)

FIGHTING FIRE WITHOUT FIRE

"You'll have to divide my body before you divide India."
—Mohandas Gandhi

INTO THE FIRE

Every part of his body cried out for nourishment. It was becoming harder to move such frail, emaciated limbs. The hunger was intense, and the numbness was increasing.

And yet, this was a skeletal torso and wan complexion to which he had become accustomed. He had denied himself so many pleasures, and even necessities, it seemed his body had come to expect the pain and steps toward starvation.

Water was his only luxury. It felt like a momentary feast whenever he received an ounce. Mohandas had been fasting for four days. At the age of seventy-seven, recovering from illness, the tiny giant was already at risk. He could not think clearly as his energy emptied. An already difficult decision became more taxing.

The skeleton in a sari was trying everything he could think of to prevent the division of India into two nations, and he was willing to sacrifice his own life to stop the runaway violence. Mohandas Gandhi had recently arrived in the city of Calcutta, which felt like a civil war zone between Hindus and Muslims. Journalist William Shirer reported: "At the risk of his life, Gandhi had gone into the blood-soaked streets of Calcutta littered with corpses and the debris of burning buildings…"

And now, it was as if every food aroma in the house was guided toward him. Each mention and memory of meals and every smell seemed ten times stronger than usual. Sometimes his guests were unaware of their own scent. But the odor was there, especially the smells of fruit, spices, and vegetables.

He could detect it, as if by olfactory radar, in the next room. The reclined Mahatma could anticipate enticing smells travelling from room to room without passport.

In light of the half million people who had already been slaughtered by rival Muslim and Hindu factions throughout India, and the growing intensities likely to erupt on India's Independence Day, the worst seemed yet to come. Biographer Olivia Coolidge wrote: "Calcutta was like a city doused in gasoline waiting for the first firecracker of independence to set it off." Many Muslims were passionately in favor of creating their own nation they hoped to call Pakistan; but they were violently opposed by the much larger Indian majority of Hindus.

So, he had decided to fast, and to let it be known that he would not break that fast until peace prevailed in Calcutta. He had long ago tired of the violence against his people, and now he was tired of the violence among his people. Mohandas was mentally and emotionally exhausted from it all and, due to the fast, he was physically drained as well.

Having faced so many stressful incidents, fasts, and periods of illness, his exposed ribcage seemed hollow. It was as if he could hear his stomach screaming, "I NEED FOOD!"

And yet, his commitment was to win the inner battle with appetite and desire. So, the clock on the table no longer mattered. Wherever the hands pointed, even at mealtimes, he would abstain.

WHY STARVE?

As he had done for five decades, Mohandas Gandhi had walked toward the epicenter of a human earthquake hoping to prevent violence and promote unity. As a Hindu, he had asked a known Muslim leader, Shaheed Suhrawardy, to live with him and make appearances together throughout Calcutta wherever they might dampen the flames. Despite the immense risk to both lives, they agreed to live with a few others in a modest dwelling with only one latrine. Because they were positioned in a boundary zone between Hindu and Muslim sectors, it was if both men had one foot in each world.

In spite of Gandhi's great reputation as the father of Indian independence, as a man worshiped by millions, he received death threats and was aggressively assailed by *goondas*, the rioting gangs engaged in arson and murder. On more than one occasion, militants had smashed the windows of the temporary Suhrawardy–Gandhi dwelling. The frail, elderly Gandhi was almost hit by a hurled brick and a flailing hand club just before he began his fast.

Although there were interludes of peace throughout Calcutta during their days together, Gandhi and Suhrawardy had wondered if their efforts were in vain. Once again, violence had erupted in late August, though only days earlier,

Hindus and Muslims had marched together through the streets chanting, "long live Hindu-Muslim unity," and "long live Gandhi." But soon the recurring disruptions were so great that police had to use teargas to disband *goondas* storming the unguarded Suhrawardy–Gandhi abode.

Amidst such pending disaster, Gandhi knew that he must employ a more drastic and potentially suicidal weapon to obtain any chance of long-term peace. So, on September 1, 1947, he had announced to the world that he would fast until peace was sustained citywide, and until ongoing harmony was guaranteed by the leaders of all factions—Hindu, Muslim, and to a lesser degree, also the Sikhs.

He fully realized that this decision might mean a fast until death. And after four days, he was already wondering if he was reaching the point of no return.

"Food," his body demanded. "Food!"

But he was an old hand at ignoring and harnessing the interior urges. Alternatively, he could pray, chant, sleep, or ask for water.

As word travelled that the revered *Mahatma* (sage, master, or great soul) might be sacrificing himself in reaction to their violence, both sides began to change their self-righteous attitudes. Suddenly, the Muslims, who constituted only twenty-three percent of Calcutta's population, realized they might be blamed and vindictively slaughtered *en masse* for causing a Hindu demigod's death. Concurrently, the Hindu zealots realized that they might be shamed by more moderate Hindus, if not by all of India, for forcing the beloved *Mahatma* to martyr himself.

On all sides, the mood seemed to be shifting. Now on the fourth day of fasting, even the hostile *goondas* had penitently dropped their weapons at Gandhi's bedside. Many others who visited, including the governor, doctors, and leaders from both factions, pleaded with Gandhi to end his fast and not his life.

Still, he had to remain vigilant and abstinent. The *Mahatma* knew that terminating the fast might allow the trigger-happy hotheads on both sides, armed with grenades and machine guns, to return to reciprocal slaughter. He faced a difficult ethical decision that could impact the lives and deaths of thousands, if not millions—in this context, he was asked to answer the time-honored question, "to be or not to be?"

And he faced a far less philosophical question ringing not only within his ears but throughout the body: *"Food?!"*

THE MOMENT OF DECISION

Gandhi knew that if he broke his fast, he would only have oral promises from local leaders that violence would end. Similar verbal oaths had previously been broken. It was also possible that, despite their best intentions, none of these leaders could control the hotheads leading the civil unrest.

The *Mahatma* realized that, given his distrust of spoken pledges, he should persist. Against all medical advice and common sense, he could demonstrate that one life was far less important than the peace and unity of his people.

He did not wish to resume an off-and-on fast, continuing to eat each time violence disappeared. Doing so would mean that each of his actions would be less publicized and potent. He wanted the violence to end once and for all. Each life was precious— and each murder was pointless.

Yet, on the other hand, millions of people counted on him to remain their living savior. One friend advised him: "You can do far more for humanity if you live than if you die." He could no longer advise, inspire, or lead once deceased.

More than anyone in India, and possibly in the world, he had proven effective when modeling and implementing massive non-violent efforts to obtain Indian independence. He had actually opened stubborn, authoritarian minds and hearts. Who could possibly take his place? Shouldn't he live to fast another day? What of his children, grandchildren, lifelong friends, protégés in training, worldwide correspondents, and advisees? Could he risk abandoning them due to his fanatical passion for principle? In a house divided, would peace be any more likely without the master peacemaker?

Gandhi had been riddled with recent illnesses and had needed periods of retreat for recuperation. He knew that an exhausted, frequently ill, aging body could not last without nourishment. Four days for Gandhi was comparable to perhaps eight weeks in the life of the twenty-five-year-old Irish hunger striker, Bobby Sands, who died after 66 days. Although he had fasted for weeks when he was younger, healthier, and stronger, Gandhi was now approaching his seventy-eighth birthday, just one month away. Each day of fasting could be his last.

Hence, there were counterbalancing vectors pulling at Gandhi to either prolong or break his commitment. And millions of radio listeners awaited his decision. To be... or not to be?

THE SACRED SECRET WEAPON

Mohandas Gandhi was famous for his arsenal of weapons that did not employ violence. Honoring the Hindu ideal *ahimsa* (non-violence), he developed a series of non-action actions over five decades, which came to be known by many names—passive resistance, non-cooperation, and especially the powerful Indian concept of *satyagraha* (truth force or soul force), a name Gandhi himself had given to non-violent resistance.

Mohandas envisioned *satyagraha* as a compelling moral vector, with the potency of a courageous, loving, persistent spirit standing against that which is ethically wrong. The *satyagraha* arsenal included many tools—strikes, the public burning of registration documents, sit-ins, symbolic imprisonment, and work stoppage, to name a few.

Some *satyagraha* tools were so subtle, they were almost invisible. For example, as the *Mahatma* sat at his spinning wheel for hours making his clothing from indigenous thread, he seemed miles away from political centers and military activity. Yet, the spinning was a constant reminder to the public that he had led a boycott on British clothing in India, and was in solidarity with those who wore only home-manufactured cloth. Indeed, the spinning wheel, which became a symbol of both home rule for India and of *satyagraha*, was his constant companion in photographs publicized all over the world.

Perhaps the most sacred and easily controlled weapon of *satyagraha* was the personal fast. As biographer Robert Payne observed, Gandhi refined and customized it, beginning with minor fasting in his early years in South Africa. Later, he learned to employ much more dramatic life-and-death public fasts in India.

The fasts evolved from strictly spiritual solo events, to far more political, orchestrated dramas that involved publicists, doctors, allies, and radio broadcasters for international impact. It was these more customized, mass publicized political fasts, designed to achieve a specific political outcome, which could be construed as a non-violent weapon, whether against extremists, the British, or polarized factions.

For Gandhi, the original and ongoing purpose of fasting from all food (and on many occasions also from speaking, sex, and other comforts) was spiritual. Within his own understanding of Hinduism, with which he mixed elements of Jainism, Christianity, Islam, and other religions, effective fasting permitted him full detachment, with 1) no temptation of the flesh, 2) little if any consciousness of self, and 3) adoration of God. In Robert Parker's words, "… he entered the Divine Essence. Then, when he returned to the world, he brought with him the commands of the Divinity."

As the years passed, Gandhi discerned that fasting also seemed to have a specific impact upon his environment, and thus upon the issues and causes to which he devoted himself. In essence, Mohandas perceived that by purifying the body he would augment the powers of the soul, and thus accrue the strength to impact, if not dominate, surrounding events. In Parker's words, "the soul grew as the flesh was subdued… and there flowed out ever-widening circles of power that were ultimately invincible."

In effect, the ascetic devotee sensed that depth of "in-reach" was in direct proportion to the length and breadth of "outreach." Gandhi's oft-quoted maxim, "we must be the change we wish to see in the world," referred in part to this inner change that brings outer change in society. A corollary to his maxim might state that the deeper the inner, personal peace, the greater the prospects for outer societal peace. Or, in related words, the greater the inner cleaning (including fasting), the greater the odds that outer disruptions will be cleaned up. In short, "in-reach" equals outreach.

Gandhi had learned that this inner drama could also become public theatre. Like a well-constructed play, the later fasts would begin with a public announcement foreshadowing the forthcoming narrative. Then the audience would become engaged in the suspense regarding possible outcomes (Unity for India? Punishment for the bellicose? Changes of leadership? Expulsion for the British *raj*? Death for Gandhi?). Daily radio reports would bring updates in the plot (Gandhi is ill; Nehru tries to persuade Gandhi to quit fasting; riots cease in Calcutta, etc.).

Thus, as a strategist, he knew how to escalate the suspense to boost the audience share of those listening. Indeed, he would use the tool of escalation in many of his activities. For example, during an act of non-violent resistance, at first one man would be jailed, then several men, then women and children would be incarcerated, each commanding greater attention from the media and public. In the case of fasting, the play would end with a grand, dramatic climax—a hero rising from his deathbed as disaster is averted.

So the 1947 fasting decision was not just about one man's diet or life. It was a well-rehearsed, developed performance aimed at global impact. When well executed, the spiritual, political, and theatrical implications of such performances were deafening.

While the dramatic radio plot would focus upon the one celebrated life that was at risk, Gandhi aspired to focus attention upon the millions of other lives at stake. And although his brain was fading, his fasting strategy was well engraved in long-term memory. The scream for food competed with the cry for peace.

WHY BOTHER?

After so many years of beatings, massacres, jail and near starvation, why didn't Gandhi retire instead of confronting an urban nightmare? After all, as a fading elder, he had more than paid his dues. Indeed, his life had been devoted to overcoming discrimination and achieving liberation. He had publicly opposed British landlords extracting the last drops of money from Indian farmer peasants. He had personally experienced and fought the authoritarian condescension of both South African and British conquerors.

Among his own people, he had fought against the rigid caste system. Gandhi especially championed the rights and humanity of those enslaved by the word "untouchable." In a country where women also seemed indentured through the traditions of child marriage, abusive patriarchy, imposed widowhood, irrational cultural death sentences, and frozen domestic roles, Gandhi found both categories of slavery—caste and gender—unacceptable.

Mohandas had deliberately lived in small towns in the Indian countryside. Year in and year out, he had confronted the pressing problems of widespread dysentery, failing education, and horrible sanitation.

Nor would he ever acquiesce to the status quo, no matter how much Indians were taught to be submissive. However, the penalties for resistance and reform, especially against the British and rival factions, were severe. For example, within less than one hour, fifteen hundred Indian men, women, and children were slaughtered by the British army in a courtyard. In another instance, one hundred and seven women and children had fatally hurled themselves down a well to avoid being violated by the men of a rival faction.

Similarly and tragically, Hindu men had killed fifty of their own women to "save their honor" from immediate desecration by rapacious Muslim extremists. Amidst such turmoil, the *Mahatma* had deliberately created and lived in *ashrams* where untouchables, Muslims, Christians, and Hindus ate together, shared the same chores, and worked for social transformation.

The short, thin, traditionally clad elder had become known as the prince of *satyagraha*. Although some of his attempts at unified passive resistance had failed, many other actions were successful. Some perceived him as a second Christ figure. After all, he had taught entire peoples how to turn the other cheek. Facing violent bigots and substantial armies, he had successfully fought fire without fire.

In short, his life was too fully invested in reform and human dignity to look the other way. Since he had faced the razor's edge of apartheid; been beaten, derided, and imprisoned for years; fasted repeatedly for other causes; faced great pain and discord within his own family; and taken on the strongest empire

133

in the world at the time—another day without food would hardly be threatening.

Gandhi's mythic stature had become all but super-human. Over the years, thousands made pilgrimages to talk, learn, work, and pray with him as if he could bring the advice, magic, deep forgiveness, or healing of a saint. The British viceroy of India, Lord Mountbatten, called Gandhi a "one-man boundary force" who was personally disarming a fractured India. Later, Albert Einstein would write that generations yet to come "will scarce believe that such a one as this ever in flesh and blood walked across the earth."

FAR BEYOND THE ORDINARY

By observing Gandhi's modest origins, one could not have predicted his future. Neither a member of the elite Brahmin caste nor a gifted student, he might easily have lived a quiet, ordinary life in his hometown. Had he been born fifty years earlier, history might never have recorded his name.

By the time he was thirteen, Gandhi and his two brothers were part of a triple marriage ceremony arranged to spare his father the expense of three separate weddings. Ordinarily, such an early marriage would have shackled a young Indian teen from a middle caste with many family responsibilities and a mundane job for the rest of his life. But the emerging gentrification of India, coupled with the expanded training of a new wave of Indian professionals, meant that more families were selecting one young son to become a banker, newspaper editor, urban merchant or, in Mohandas' case, a lawyer.

Sent by his family to London to be educated about the British justice system, Gandhi became even more aware of injustice. After law school, his first major job was as a barrister representing fellow Indians in South Africa.

In that land of apartheid, the green lawyer observed what seemed to be an eternal parade of racial injustice. Indeed, within a month of arriving in South Africa, where blacks, coloreds, and whites were segregated, he was bodily ejected from a train for traveling in the wrong cabin. Although he had purchased a first-class ticket for the train in London, after he boarded in South Africa, he was instructed that first class was reserved only for whites. After debating his rights with the conductor, he was man-handled and thrown from the train to the ground at the next stop.

Fortunately, the *Mahatma's* strong exposure to the Jain religion as a child had taught him tolerance of all faiths, peoples, and outlooks. So, Gandhi quickly learned to work cooperatively with the multiple belief systems and races throughout South Africa. However, there was one outlook to which he was intolerant—intolerance itself—and he quickly found himself, as legal counsel, pitted against those who protected entrenched intolerance.

Nothing had prepared Gandhi for the pin-cushion life he would live once he represented victims of discrimination. As a "colored boy" facing rigid imperial regimes in each city and country, he was like one David facing an army of Goliaths. But the experience of waging a perennial uphill battle against inequality thickened his skin and taught Gandhi skills which would serve him until his final fast.

These skills developed into avocations that allowed him to multi-task as a one-man activist organization. So, he become his own:

1) publicist: including initiating and writing for his own publications and befriending many journalists and influential writers.

2) networker: including developing alliances in Europe, Asia, Africa, and North America.

3) petitioner: writing literally hundreds of petitions, proposals, legal amendments, and other documents.

4) fundraiser: the young lawyer learned never to spend without financial reserves, so fund-raising became a way of life.

5) *satyagraha* master: through boundless trial and error, he discovered which modes of non-violent resistance were effective and would gain the most popular support.

6) educator: whether as lawyer, social activist, or friend, Gandhi was constantly teaching others about *ahimsa*, *satyagraha*, civil rights, coalition-building, and the Hindu spiritual text, *The Bhagavad Gita*.

Beyond all this, he mastered another profession for which he had interned as a devout Hindu child. In addition to the six roles above, and to being a husband, community organizer, and father, Gandhi also lived the life of a priest.

PERPETUAL SANCTIFICATION

In childhood, Gandhi had been taught the traditions of fasting, ceremonial prayers, and Hindu rituals. His life became one of perpetual sanctification through prayer and abstinence.

After waking, sometimes as early as four in the morning, he would begin each day with prayers, and then bless his world again in the evening just prior to sleep. Fortunately, during childhood, his family priest read from both the Islamic *Koran* and from Hindu sacred texts, so Gandhi became accustomed to holding both religions in esteem.

When he encountered Christianity, the young legal student was taken by the "Sermon on the Mount" and by the story of the good Samaritan. The latter account of one man caring for an injured man from an ostracized race when others ignored this victim, seemed the very antithesis of apartheid and of the British *raj*.

So, Gandhi questioned the Christianity of the imperial regime, and embraced the more genuine Christianity of the New Testament. He soon became fond of quoting the Bible verse "without vision, the people perish."

Thus, Gandhi's spirituality, while based in Hindu roots, grew to include whatever teachings seemed accurate to him. His religion transcended, yet also included, all religions and other eternal wisdom to the extent that their principles rang true. Perhaps the most important text in his life was the Hindu *Bhagavad Gita* (*The Song Celestial*), which he not only read during times of soul-searching, but which became the basis for the spiritual talks and workshops he gave.

Gandhi frequently chose to build and live within spiritual communities, known as *ashrams*, to maintain a holy atmosphere and to worship with those close to him. Even in jail, his cell became his *ashram* as he followed the highly disciplined cycles of prayer, meditation, and occasional fasting throughout the week. During much of his life, one day of the week was reserved for strictly enforced silence, a practice he sought to maintain even when constantly in demand by guests and aspiring disciples from several continents.

All abstinence—from speech, from food, from distraction—was epitomized when in 1906, at the age of thirty-seven, he decided to practice the ultimate Hindu withdrawal from the sensual world—*brahmacharya* (celibacy)—despite his wife's concerns. From Gandhi's perspective, such self-control over inner drives harnessed and harvested his power in more profound ways.

So, the *Mahatma's* fasting must be seen in this larger spiritual context, in which less is more, abstinence is potency, and retreat from human nature leads to sensing divine nature. While he was not ordained as a priest, his life was that of a holy man and to many he even became an informal guru.

Hence, Gandhi's fast in Calcutta was just the visible tip of an iceberg backed by decades of priestly self-discipline. The *Bhagavad Gita*, or *Song Celestial*, of the cosmos sang through his body and consciousness as they were cleansed. With the shrinking of the body came the enlargement of the soul and the divine forces of transformation.

Similarly, every food that Gandhi ate had a disciplining impact upon his health and inner state. His vegetarian diet was carefully chosen and monitored. He often requested that foods be transported to him whenever possible in prison and when traveling, to maintain a highly specific balance of nutrients.

Of course, circumstances such as the riots in Calcutta prevented access to fresh fruits and vegetables. In similar situations, his fast from the foods he found essential was imposed rather than deliberate.

While Gandhi's rationale for fasting might seem irrational to those who are scientifically inclined, upon further reflection, his thinking must be seen as universal. Even Newton's third law ("for every action, there is an equal and opposite reaction") is next-of-kin to the Christian notion of sowing and reaping ("you reap what you sow") and the Hindu concept of karma (current action produces next-life reaction or reward). In the English vernacular, this law is often worded as "what goes around comes around."

For Gandhi, every action within had a corresponding reaction in the outer world—so obtaining inner peace was essential if he was seeking to unify a pacific India. Even Newton might follow this logic. Strange as it might seem to many, Gandhi's inner spiritual world was his infrastructure for changing the political structures of nations. Indeed, one of his favorite books was Tolstoy's *The Kingdom of God is Within You*, which similarly posits that the inner predicts the outer. Tolstoy also frequently extolled another of Gandhi's favorite themes: non-violence trumps the immense wastes of war.

ONE OF THE PEOPLE

Despite this constant spiritual approach, there was nothing condescending about Gandhi. On the contrary, he personally cleaned the *ashram* latrines, fed the animals, and was in effect a fully self-reliant servant. Initially, such labor was a source of irritation to his family members, who sharply reacted to performing the mundane and presumed impure work of untouchables.

At the core of spirituality for Gandhi was the doctrine of service to others, no matter how humbling the task. Biographer Judith Brown wrote of his belief that "only by service to humankind could one draw close to truth, to ultimate reality, and thus to one's own deepest self." So, although he frequently encountered friction with friends and family, the *Mahatma* was seldom too tired to serve them. Indeed, he added even greater service by mentoring many young people and inviting Madeleine Slade (later named Mirabehn), the visiting daughter of a British admiral, to live with his family as an adopted child.

The people Gandhi served were from all walks of life. On the one hand, the Indian statesman Nehru, whom Gandhi mentored, was of high Brahmin pedigree. On the other hand, Gandhi deliberately chose to live and work with peasants to experience, if not eradicate, their poverty and poor health.

Most cultural, regional, and global leaders within India became the *Mahatma's* friends and admirers. British, African, European, and American journalists, diplomats, clergy, and activists were never far from his door or correspondence. He was influenced not only by Tolstoy and spiritual texts, but also by authors as different as Thoreau, Raychandbhai, and Ruskin. By the time of his Calcutta fast, Gandhi had eaten, spoken, and prayed with thousands upon thousands, including representatives from almost every faith, nation, class, and caste.

None were excluded from his service. Gandhi deliberately performed the manual labor of untouchables so they could rest or work with him. Similarly, none were too mighty to escape his reproach. He wrote to everyone from Hitler to Churchill about what he thought would bring the world to a state of justice.

As a man of the people, the *Mahatma* sought to hear their voice. As a self-made leader, he struggled to be their voice.

THE MOMENT OF TRUTH

The moment of truth had come on September 4, 1947. Gandhi had said he would fast until peace was restored and the leaders of the various factions had committed to harmony. Although lip service was at that point being given to making peace, and although he was assured that no violence had occurred in Calcutta that day, the *Mahatma* remained unconvinced.

To some degree the longing for food had been reigned in, although when he listened to his body, it was unhappy. He felt as weak as the malnourished children he was hoping to save.

If he broke the fast, he knew many more might die. After all, even some of the peacemakers who had recently traveled into the city border zones had been slaughtered. But if he continued the fast, he would greatly increase the odds that he would pass the point of no return and wither into a coma.

Would he listen to the promises of the people? Or to his own inner voice? Back and forth he had weighed the options until he was certain of his next move. Neither of the two extremes he had considered would work.

So, he would take the third option.

From his bed, Gandhi summoned the strength to think about an alternative. Slowly, he could compose his thoughts.

Mohandas then stated that unless all representative leaders converted their oral commitments into signed covenants, he would continue the fast irreversibly. He demanded that their sworn commitment to peace be in writing to share with the world. And he declared that, if this peace was ever broken, he would continue his denouement into the next life. The next fast, he affirmed, would be irrevocable and irreversible. To slightly paraphrase the famous words of Patrick Henry, Gandhi was stating: "Give me accountability—or give me death."

THE THIRD WAY

The esteemed Greek philosopher Aristotle had claimed that there was always a third path between extreme actions, the golden mean. Aristotle thought of this third path as the mean between deficiency and excess.

For example, a deficiency of courage might well be perceived as cowardice, while excessive courage might be deemed foolhardiness. But an admirable character trait would be the third and middle option, courage itself.

Using another example, regarding excess, if all people are eternally promiscuous, there would be negative consequences in the forms of overpopulation and sexually transmitted diseases, not to mention challenges to morality and relationships. But, when considering deficiency, if the entire world were to become celibate, the death of humanity would ensue.

Similarly, if all people were to consistently and excessively eat, gluttony would precipitate the end of the human species. However, if all people ceased eating, such inaction would also lead to omnicide.

Ultimately, the golden mean has proven to be a valuable tool in vexing ethical dilemmas as well. Of course, the ethical dilemma must be reasonable to begin with. Otherwise one might say that Hitler should have killed only three million Jews as the midpoint between killing six million (excess) or none at all (deficiency). The mean is not necessarily mathematical and is not meant to be applied to absurd hypotheses such as the commission of genocide. The golden mean is a way of finding reasonable compromise between insufficiency and overkill.

While Gandhi had not publicly mentioned Kant, Mill, and other great ethicists, he had ruled out their approaches to this dilemma. And while he did not reference Aristotle, nor Confucius, who also advocated following a central way, ultimately it was the path between deficiency and excess that Gandhi had selected. And, of course, he had also been influenced by several of...

THE TEN FACTORS

1. **Notions of fairness and justice:** As much as anyone is this book, Gandhi was driven by a personal desire for human fairness and a professional quest for legal non-discrimination. He perpetually encountered pre-ordained notions of "role justice" or "empire justice," which opposed the principles of divine and human equity that he believed paramount. Although he reluctantly tolerated some aspects of the caste system, ultimately Gandhi was compelled to erase unjust boundaries and other assaults on human dignity by any peaceful means possible. Like Socrates and Wilberforce, Gandhi felt a strong commission to honor and uphold the law but, unlike Socrates, he was strongly motivated to oppose governmental justice when it contradicted a higher Hindu, Jain, or primal Christian standard of justice.

2. **Impact or consequences:** Gandhi knew that the consequences of each action could be immense. He deeply regretted that some of his political choices seemed to have precipitated, rather than prevented, violence. So, he became careful when considering actions that could lead to retaliation or other unintended consequences. Ultimately, his desired outcomes were peace and equitably redistributed power. He was also keenly aware that injury and incarceration, if not death, were possible consequences not only for him but possibly for his family, friends, and fellow activists. So, despite his strong longing for justice, the collective actions he proposed were always tempered by serious thought, sustained discussion, and often debate about the possible consequences.

3. **Ends and means:** As much as anyone profiled in this book, Gandhi advocated the primacy of means. Non-violence was as—if not more— important than outcomes and short-term justice. Constantly, he argued that a liberated India, if divided by civil war and mass violence, was no better than one united under imperial rule. Peaceful means, no matter how important the objective, ultimately were the real objective. Peaceful ends had to be achieved by peaceful means without exception.

4. **Tone and atmosphere:** Inner and outer peace were hand-in-glove as twin objectives. A tone of outer peace could not be achieved without interior stillness. Thus, prayer and sacred atmosphere were essential to Gandhi's tone. *Satyagraha* meant more than the absence of violence—it was also an atmosphere of honoring the sacredness of life itself. The dignity of human life called for an attitude of full-spectrum respect for all

races, castes, genders, orientations, and ages. Like justice and means, tone was sacrosanct.

5. **Motivation and higher law:** Gandhi's highest law transcended the torts of empires and legislated apartheid. Although as a barrister he loved to understand and apply human law when such laws proved moral, Gandhi frequently demonstrated that he wished to reconsider, revise, or, when forced to do so, break human laws if they seemed contrary to higher law. He studied the torts of divinity, nature, and a more dignified humanity. From childhood he had been taught that the highest law was contained within the Hindu, Jain, and Islamic sacred texts, and as he grew older, the higher law of Christianity, Judaism, and other world religions in many cases also rang true. Like Mandela, Adams, and Wilberforce, he was well trained in provincial law—but ultimately, it was sacred, universal law that propelled Gandhi, Wilberforce, Esther, and Malala more than all the others.

6. **Allegiance and loyalty:** Although it would seem that the "father of modern India" would hold no loyalty higher than his native land, in fact his highest allegiances were to his ideals and principles, and not to a nation, group, or even his own family, although he loved all three. When a member of his family demeaned an untouchable or refused to do the work of untouchables, he would frequently show loyalty to the marginalized group or equitable principle rather than to his family. If India seemed divided by conflict, his loyalty was to peace and unity, not to the leaders of rival factions, even if some were spokespersons for India. No person was above the (sacred and universal) law, so no person, not even his wife or prime minister, was given a higher loyalty than his highest ideals and divine allegiance.

7. **Values and principles:** Mohandas' oft quoted "an eye for an eye makes the world blind" implies that an important value for him was vision, not retaliation. Indeed, a Biblical principle he loved to quote was "without vision the people perish." Although his values of unity, non-violence, and non-discrimination seem well publicized, the value of vision—which implies specific, lofty goals and a unifying purpose—was equally important. The principles of "being the change we wish to see in the world" and of *satyagraha* may be Gandhi's most influential legacies. *Ahimsa* (non-violence) was taught to him as a child, while forgiveness and English court justice became more pronounced values during his higher education

and early professional career. Ethical principles, no less than tone, justice, and means, ultimately mattered more than allegiances and outcomes.

8. **Cultural context:** No matter where he was, specific cultural practices deeply disturbed and informed the Mahatma's perspective. In South Africa, the cultural traditions of apartheid mystified and angered the young lawyer, while in India many caste ceremonies and cultural traditions, including *sati* (widow burning) ignited his own fire. Culture also imparted his ongoing practice of daily prayer, a life devoted to *The Bhagavad Gita*, and his strict devotion to indigenous dress and diet. Fasting was an important part of Hindu life, but he took it to a much higher level of political impact and public visibility. Ultimately, culture was a double-edged sword that contained both unjust, enslaving traditions on the one hand, and the spiritual tools and atmosphere central to both his ends and means on the other.

9. **Implications:** Gandhi always weighed the implications of long-term peace and a unified India against possible reprisals and his own martyrdom. Ultimately, at best the implications could lead to an idealized "brotherhood of mankind" and a world of peaceful goodwill. That said, he realized that inhumane implications—widespread slaughter, his own starvation, a divided India, and perpetual inequality of race, gender, and class—were all in play. One implication Gandhi could not foresee was the long-standing, momentous influence that he would have upon vast movements of people and civil rights leaders as significant as Martin Luther King Jr. and Nelson Mandela.

10. **Proportion and balance:** On balance, Gandhi ultimately gave more weight to sacred tone, the value of peaceful means, and justice than to other considerations. Ultimately, conscience informed by his Hindu-Islamic sympathies, laced with Christian principles, was his North Star. Unlike Socrates, who placed the laws of state above his own inner laws, Gandhi perceived human law as subordinate to humane or higher law. Dating back to his early days in South Africa, Gandhi challenged national laws that he saw as unjust, and called for a more color-blind, universal law of equity and dignity. So, higher law was his highest law, and his strongest motivating factor the means by which higher law was expressed.

GANDHI'S IMPACT AND LEGACY

Mohandas Gandhi's choice of a third option proved sagacious. Soon he received all of the written assurances he had requested as the city remained calm. As a result, on that same day, September 4, 1947, biographer Coolidge reported that "tough old Suhrawardy handed Gandhi a glass of lemon juice to break the fast, kneeling at his feet with tears in his eyes."

Although the Hindu, Muslim, and Sikh assurances could not guarantee an end to world violence, Calcutta itself would remain peaceful for months to come. Possibly thousands of lives had been saved. The outcome was reported worldwide and not without penetrating impact. Moreover, Gandhi was now free to travel and plead for a farewell to arms in other cities.

The fast had lasted seventy-three hours, and the ceasefire would last far longer. However, the overall impact of Gandhi's near-death experience seemed destined to last forever. Mountbatten wrote that "*Mahatma* Gandhi will go down in history on a par with Buddha and Jesus Christ."

Although, tragically and ironically, the *Mahatma* was violently killed by an assassin's handgun in 1948, his spirit lives through the hundreds of schools, books, articles, children, films, statues, and streets that bear his name. The president of India's congress called Gandhi "the father of the Indian nation." Biographer Judith Brown wrote: "He was a man of vision and action who asked many of the profoundest questions that face humankind... It was this confrontation out of a real humanity which marks his true stature..."

Who can say how far the influence extends beyond what is recorded in history classes and biographies? How many times when activists consider a possibly violent strategy will a member of the group remind them that Gandhi showed there is an effective alternative approach?

How many hunger strikers and peaceful protestors continue to quote Gandhi in their press conferences and on their websites?

Many leaders, activists, political and spiritual leaders follow in the *Mahatma's* footsteps, teaching the vision of unity and the way of *satyagraha*.

As the decades of his life progressed, Gandhi was seen as a diminutive, bald eccentric. And yet, the smaller his body became, the larger his reputation and creative influence grew.

After working with Gandhi for decades, Jawaharlal Nehru became the first prime minister of India. He rose when Gandhi fell. But Nehru sensed that Gandhi's light could never fall when he said:

> ...his light represented something more than the immediate present. It represented the living, the eternal truths, reminding of the right path,

withdrawing us from error, taking this ancient country to freedom… A thousand years later, that light will still be seen…

Whatever his stature, Gandhi never claimed to be a perfect person. His eldest son, Harilal, who deliberately left home, drank excessively, became sexually indulgent, and was vexed by debt, reminded Gandhi of his weakness as a father.

Although his wife, Kasturba, was very loving and devoted, many unwelcome practices and guests were imposed upon her that encroached upon her boundaries. She understandably became cantankerous in her later years. Like all those living and working near her husband, she had little privacy, and she frequently suffered from a strained, stressful, and sexless marriage.

Some other family members were frazzled by the difficulties of living in a fishbowl. Often their true emotions and ranges of behavior were imprisoned by the precise Gandhi "suck it up" discipline.

Neither did the *Mahatma* claim to have been error-free in his politics. Sometimes he blamed the deaths of third parties upon his own inept strategies, timing, or tactics. At other times he questioned his political choices and retreated into contemplative sadness. Yet, he always bounced back after tragedy. "I am an incurable optimist," Mohandas claimed, which meant that incurable realists and other critics often thought him foolhardy, stubborn, or naïve.

Still, history barely recalls his family and his critics, while Gandhi himself is remembered as one of the greatest leaders or all time. Although he had compromised and chosen the third option on September 4, 1947, he was eternally uncompromising about his path of integrity.

Within and beyond his lifetime, Gandhi arguably saved millions of people and liberated millions of others, yet he never killed or authorized the killing of a single human being. Ultimately, his fast was not only from food, but also from violence and divisiveness. Gandhi modeled a third option beyond "to be or not to be." It was the option to exemplary.

GANDHI TODAY

Some years ago, I founded a group called the Association for Responsible Communication, which was eventually nominated for the Nobel Peace Prize. Led by strong, bright, youthful officers such as Barbara Coffman, Barbara Luorgos, Bruce Allyn, Will Wilkinson, and Ron Kertzner, "ARC" attracted media professionals and leaders from many countries who created consciousness-raising events.

One of the core insights within ARC was that personal change was a key to world change. For example, we realized that we had little credibility chastising world polluters during a public panel if we panelists were drinking from throwaway Styrofoam cups.

Similarly, if those of us interested in media reform wanted to rein in *The National Enquirer* and other trashy tabloids, we had no authority chastising if we ourselves were busy gossiping. So, we looked in the mirror and appreciated Emerson's famous quote: "Stop talking. Who you are thunders over you so loudly all the while, I can't hear a word you are saying?"

At the core of this understanding stood Gandhi, who has been a central figure for many organizations. How many other groups and individuals have not only quoted the *Mahatma*, but also patterned their visions, ends, and means after his? I can recall quoting, "we must be the change we wish to see in the world," more than once, and not just at ARC events. The *Mahatma* knew that if he wished the world to fast from self-righteous violence, he himself had to fast from self-centeredness. Inreach equals outreach.

The Mahatma's decision-making proceeded from this key "inner-predicts-outer" axiom. Thus, Gandhi's fast in Calcutta, like his entire life, was a giant inward arrow pointing in that outward direction.

"To be or not to be" is not really the question when the fate of others, and even of all species, hangs in the balance. The real question is "to be or not to be fully committed to inner, and thus outer, change?"

For the *Mahatma*, Mohandas Gandhi, there was only one answer.

CHAPTER 8

HARRY S. TRUMAN
(1884-1972)

THE MOST IMPORTANT ETHICAL DECISION EVER?

WHAT HARRY CONFIDED

There are those who thought it must have been the most difficult ethical decision within recorded history. Others have said that it was the most important for civilization.

Why?

In 1945 President Harry S. Truman had to decide whether or not to drop the first atomic bomb. He had been warned by his Secretary of War that nuclear weapons, if developed, used, and propagated, had the capacity to destroy civilization, if not life itself.

Moreover, once one country used nuclear weapons, others would develop them for self-protection or supremacy. Opening the nuclear door was in fact opening Pandora's Box.

But many historians have said, just as Truman said publicly, that the decision to use the atomic bomb was not difficult and was all but straightforward. By some accounts Truman had no choice other than to use atomic bombs if he wanted to end World War II. He could save many thousands of lives, if not millions, by closing the door on the boxes of two other Pandoras—Adolf Hitler and the Japanese Emperor Hirohito. Reportedly, Truman felt that by taking the nuclear path he could prevent global empires dominated by such barbarous despots. Dropping the devastating bombs was thus the lesser of two evils.

But was what he said publicly also what he thought privately?

What was his real thinking and how was the decision made? Was his dominant ethical concern about opening the door on an unknown but potentially devastating nuclear poison? Or closing the lid on fascism's coffin? Or something else which went unreported?

Behind the scenes, Truman had confided to family that the harrowing choice was not what he had told the public. Three years after his decision, Harry wrote to his sister Mary, "I ordered the atomic bomb to be dropped on Hiroshima and Nagasaki. It was a terrible decision."

His daughter Margaret wrote in a biography that "the impression that some people have that my father made a snap decision to use the bomb could not be further from the truth." She noted that in June, 1945, "Dad had been wrestling with the atom bomb ... almost continuously since his April conference with Secretary of War Stimson."

Many within Truman's circle had pointed out that no one really knew if the bomb would work. Others were uncertain of the degree of damage it would inflict.

Before making any decisions the President requested a complete report from his operations director, General Leslie Groves. Like FDR before him, this president relied upon inner circles of experts to consider both the military and humanitarian aspects of employing a thunderbolt.

Leading scientists such as Berkeley's Robert Oppenheimer and Harvard's president James Conant, not to mention Nobel Prize winners, had advised former president Roosevelt, Secretary Stimson, and Truman. Many others from the military, government, and even England's prime minister, Winston Churchill, gave input before a decision was made.

Given that so many experts were involved, why the controversy? What did Truman really think? Was he opening or closing Pandora's box? Or was he opening one box while closing another? Was this really the toughest ethical decision ever made? Or the most important? What really happened?

As with any intriguing homicide, the most interesting question might be that of motive. And with any great ethical case study, the related question must be: "What was most at stake?" Which of these values—human dignity, survival, national security, freedom, human rights, America's image, life itself, Truman's self-image and career—were the most important?

WHY MANHATTAN?

An important part of the atomic bomb story began six years earlier in August, 1939, while FDR was president. That year, the great physicist Albert Einstein departed Germany, concerned about the increasing power of the Nazis and their persecution of Jews and all political opposition.

After relocating to the United States at Princeton University, Einstein communicated to others that the Nazis had the ability to develop an extremely powerful "atomic" bomb. Soon the renowned physicist wrote President Roosevelt, Truman's predecessor, a letter warning that the Germans could develop such a weapon *first* unless other countries took the initiative.

Such information, confirmed by other scientists, catalyzed President Roosevelt into action. FDR felt he must create such a weapon before Hitler's scientists did if the second great war were to be won by the Allies.

So, that same year FDR and his secretary of war began to convene a team of military leaders and scientists who would initiate a top-secret operation. What came to be known as the Manhattan Project (since the original project headquarters was in New York City) would cost over two million dollars.

Eventually the clandestine project would employ over 125,000 people, primarily in three facilities in remote parts of New Mexico (Los Alamos), Tennessee (Oak Ridge), and the state of Washington (Hanford). Later a fourth area was required, Tinium Island, fifteen hundred miles south of Japan, so that a special bombing crew could learn how to load and deliver the enormous bombs.

By 1942, with the input of leading scientists and advisors, Roosevelt had chosen General Leslie Groves to head the project. Groves in turn selected physicist Robert Oppenheimer to choose and coordinate a team of top scientists from Princeton, Berkeley, California Institute of Technology, and elsewhere, whom he persuaded to move to the "off limits" laboratories at Los Alamos, New Mexico.

Despite his role as vice president, Truman knew virtually nothing about the Manhattan Project until he assumed the presidency himself after Roosevelt's death in April, 1945. Suddenly, the new president was privy to top secret information and dependent upon Secretary of War Stimson, General Groves, and Dr. Oppenheimer, among others, for guidance about "Manhattan."

Despite the questions of conscience he reported to his family, Truman shared Roosevelt's longing to out-step Hitler at every turn. From that standpoint he, like FDR, gave Groves and Oppenheimer a "full speed ahead" green light to do whatever was necessary to develop a "knock-out punch" to the Germans and Japanese.

The nuclear plants in Tennessee, Washington, and New Mexico continued to work non-stop to (1) develop enough suitable uranium and plutonium, (2) design multiple forms of bomb architecture, (3) solve problems such as ensuring that the bomber plane would not be destroyed by the a-bomb's radiation, and (4) discover how their own employees could be shielded at work.

By the time Truman assumed the presidency, the Allies were winning the war in Europe against Hitler. However, the new president also felt an urgency about defeating the Japanese. Truman had discovered that Hirohito's troops never surrendered, even when conquered, and they were also brutally killing and torturing American prisoners of war (POWs).

The war in the Pacific seemed destined to continue forever at the cost of hundreds of thousands of lives. So, the development of an "apex weapon," which would bring closure to years of slaughter, was more than appealing.

A RED, FLASHING LIGHT

However, there seemed to be a number of shadows surrounding the advent of a nuclear arsenal. On May 24, 1945, just one month after Truman assumed office, Secretary of War Stimson brought the president a letter from a concerned engineer, O.C. Brewster. The engineer urged the president to stop production of an atomic bomb due to the "tragedy of unrestrained competitive production of this material." Brewster had foreseen the specter of a global nuclear arms race.

Stimson himself was concerned that they might be "creating a Frankenstein." He cautioned the president: "We do not wish to outdo Hitler in atrocities."

Moreover, Oppenheimer had made it clear that there were conflicting moral views among the physicists themselves. One of his Los Alamos scientists, Joseph Rotblat, had already abandoned the project when he learned that the a-bomb was no longer needed to stop Hitler. Since the Fürher's empire was collapsing, Rotblat felt that there was no further motivation to develop a bomb before the Germans did.

Another top physicist at Los Alamos, Robert Wilson, began to convene scientists to consider the ethical and humanitarian concerns that nuclear potential had uncorked. Yet another leading physicist, Nobel Laureate James Franks, was concerned that the atomic bomb could not only spark an arms race, but that it might defy international regulations and prejudice the world against any country that stooped to deploy it.

The very man who had first envisioned a nuclear chain reaction in 1933, Hungarian physicist Leo Szilard, had tried to meet with Truman to voice similar humanitarian concerns. Szilard was referred to the incoming secretary of state, James Byrnes, and met with him without success, although Brynes said he would convey Szilard's perspective to the president.

Unconvinced that Brynes would help, Szilard later drafted a letter directly to the president urging nuclear restraint. The letter was eventually co-signed by 155 scientists working within the Manhattan Project.

Although Truman would not see the co-signed letter until after the bombing of Hiroshima, he was aware that leading scientists such as Szilard, Wilson, Franck, and Nobel genius Neils Bohr were gravely anxious about pushing

"Humpty Dumpty" off the wall. Such a devastating action would be irreversible.

Among the scientists' concerns were that (1) unleashed nuclear development would lead to "another form of holocaust," (2) there could be multiple annihilations of entire cities, (3) civilians, including children, within each city would be unwarned and burned alive, and (4) the United States' moral leadership in the world would plummet.

Opposition to "the bomb" was not merely from scientists. Initially, General George C. Marshall, chief of staff of the Army, felt reluctant and cautioned that there must at least be advance warning if such a bomb were to be used. Marshall would later go on to become secretary of defense, ambassador, and recipient of the Nobel Peace Prize.

Another general whom Truman greatly trusted, Dwight "Ike" Eisenhower, felt that such a bomb would be too devastating. Ike argued that the Japanese would soon surrender, in any event. General Curtis LeMay, who was leading the charge in the Pacific, agreed with Eisenhower.

Truman's overall military chief of staff, Admiral Leahy, was also opposed to the bomb although he proffered a different rationale. Leahy was convinced that the bomb would "never work." Indeed it had never been tested or used before and the technical, economic, and scientific hurdles facing "Manhattan" seemed formidable.

Nevertheless, the "go team"—Stimson, Graves, Oppenheimer, and others in their advisory councils—functioned as an opposing vector. What FDR had set in motion was backed by millions of dollars, thousands of workers, and dozens of experts. Despite the many shadows and the voices calling for restraint, the project accrued momentum.

COMPETING MORAL ARGUMENTS

As we have seen before, at the core of a great ethical dilemma reside substantial arguments and counter-arguments pulling the decision maker in opposite directions. While the humanitarian and "beware an arms race" arguments comprised one such vector against nuclear weapons, Truman was also well aware of strong, counter-balancing moral arguments in favor of nuclear deployment.

For example, how could he or the U.S. government be drafting millions of young men and sending them into harm's way without providing them their greatest possible protection? Could he in good conscience say to the parents of young military "boys" and POWs whom he had drafted that "I had the bomb but never used it?" Could the American government say to those who were literally dying to protect them (or us) that Japanese lives were more important than American ones?

Should the people who authored the slaughter at Pearl Harbor be spared while thousands more neighborhood boys were mercilessly killed, maimed, and tortured? Truman had seen young men who left America looking like All-American athletes return home burned beyond recognition, mentally deranged with shell shock, bearing multiple amputations, and no longer able to identify their families. Could he ignore the disabling and disfiguring harm inflicted upon his "brave sons?" A strong moral argument was made for the prevention of home slaughter and the protection of those protecting America.

What Truman knew, but could never mention to the press or the public, was his distrust of the Russians. What if they developed the bomb first? Communism was feared nearly as much as fascism.

Truman's classified information revealed that the Manhattan Project had been infiltrated by Russian informers. Indeed, even Oppenheimer, despite his wealth, cultured background, and academic credentials (Harvard, Cambridge, Berkeley, and Cal Tech), looked suspicious to the FBI: "Oppie" and one of his girlfriends had been loosely associated with left wing groups some years earlier.

Fear and distrust circulated in high places. What if there were critical information leaks? What if another tyrant, Russian leader Joseph Stalin, who was just as bloodthirsty as Hitler and Hirohito, was already developing the bomb? Harry Truman was deeply concerned about who would have nuclear supremacy after, and not just during, the war. Dropping the bomb would send a message from the U.S. to the Soviets, not just to the Japanese.

Other arguments were advanced in favor of nuclear development. Would not the presence of nuclear weapons serve as a deterrent to future world wars? Who would possibly risk war if there were atomic weapons on both sides? Could not nuclear power potentially generate electricity and be employed in other positive ways?

There was also the reality that the Japanese seemed determined to fight to the last man standing. Various American generals and War Department officials had estimated that the United States might lose anywhere from 100,000 to 700,000 more troops while the Japanese doggedly held onto every inch of home soil. And many Russian troops would also be at risk, since Russia was expected to declare war upon Japan within days.

Meanwhile, American and other prisoners of war were being starved to death, tortured, and burnt alive by Japanese army officers. Every day there were reports and letters about POW's who were beheaded, wounded, and mentally abused.

A perpetual stream of U.S. casualties were flown back to military bases for amputations, emergency surgery, and treatment for mental disorders. Many would never fully recover… nor would their parents, spouses, or children. Almost everyone Truman knew had relatives, often sons, grandsons, or nephews, at risk. Many of these soldiers had grief-stricken or fearful wives and children of their own.

Female casualties, although fewer by comparison, were tragically on the rise. The Army WACs, Navy WAVES, and Air Force WASPs, not to mention nurses and support personnel within all of the war theaters, were reported missing, severely wounded, and killed each month.

The anxious and grief-stricken letters from parents and spouses who had heard or feared the worst were numerous and heart-wrenching. Truman read these with a lump in his throat. How could the president sleep at night with these casualties, both real and pending, on his conscience?

Then there were the economic factors. Ultimately, over two billion dollars would be invested in nuclear development and related salaries and activities. For Roosevelt, it was only two million during the early days of the Manhattan Project. Truman knew that FDR would have used the bomb in a minute if only to show that he had "not wasted two million of our tax payers' dollars." What would the public say about a far larger sum?

Nor did Truman want Japan to have any lingering power after the war. Since 1931 Japan had been ravaging Asia. During that time, they had slaughtered one hundred and fifty times the number of people who would later perish in Hiroshima and Nagasaki. Japan had proven to be an horrific imperialist invader that left a crimson trail of slaughter, pillage, rape, and abuse behind it.

Since Japan had never been defeated, their leaders carried an aura of invincibility and a self-righteous, supposedly divine mandate to dominate others. Thus, in the eyes of the Allies, the Japanese, no less than the Third Reich, would be an ongoing threat to world peace and stability if they were not completely annihilated.

Unlike the many hated wars throughout history, World War II was a "popular war" to rid the world of evil, invasive tyrants and genocide. Did not such ends justify such means? Should not barbarians themselves be barbequed? Shouldn't they be shocked into submission by the ultimate force, since no other approach had worked?

These were strong arguments for unleashing the beast of atomic weaponry. But the arguments against were also extremely compelling.

THE NUCLEAR FAMILY

Despite the full force of these arguments, the real costs of nuclear initiatives could not be measured in dollars or even in lives. The clairvoyants and visionaries predicted a world in which there would be a new type of "nuclear family," one that included terrorists, tyrants, and "crazies" who would steal or bake homemade nuclear weapons and start the last world war. Even a small group of "safe" countries, each armed with the bomb, could prove perilous. And what if rogue agents, psychopaths, or militants seeking genocide or revenge, could not be defused by the James Bonds of the world?

Truman knew that any decision would be irreversible. Once the United States dropped a bomb, he would not have the moral authority to say that other countries could not do so.

Moreover, such weapons could create a climate of fear—fear of Armageddon, of military control over science, of communist dominance, of an unending arms race, of destruction of the environment, of nuclear leaks and accidents, and of widespread annihilation.

After the first atomic bomb was dropped, the Japanese would protest that America had violated articles 22 and 23 of the Hague Convention by using "cruel weapons." Thus, the a-bomb was not only unethical in the eyes of many, but was illegal according to international agreements. However, the question of breaking human laws was not the only one posed by the situation: to millions of religious believers there was also the question of breaking God's or nature's laws. Scientists had long been accused of playing God by tampering with the natural world. In this case, the proof of violating nature was that all Hell would break lose.

Essentially, physicists were reverse engineering what a greater engineer—God—had created, and many believers felt that certainly there would be a price to pay. Even many atheists felt that tampering with the laws of nature was imprudent, if not forbidden, by nature itself.

Nuclear arms would also change the tone of human affairs. Author Felix Morley spoke of a lowering of human standards, the abolition of spirituality and peace, and the advent of what he labeled "a return to nothingness." Symbolically, such "nothingness bombs" would become indiscriminate killers such that nothing would survive.

Due to their enormous footprint, or blast range, these weapons could not distinguish between military targets and the thousands of civilians, including children, who surrounded them miles away. Their aggregate use resembled genocide if not omnicide.

Indeed, no one could have anticipated the bombs' actual impact. After the bombing of Hiroshima, the measurable results were far greater than had been anticipated. The first bomb generated a heat of approximately 300,000 degrees Fahrenheit at the explosion epicenter. The resulting heat on the earth's surface would have initially measured about 5,400 degrees. It is estimated that over 80,000 people were killed within one half second, just as if they had been hurled into the sun itself. Thousands more—including children—burned to death in a few seconds or minutes, or gradually perished from radiation poison. Over 70,000 structures were destroyed, including every building within a two mile radius of the core explosion. Only a fraction of these were military targets, and 80% of the victims were civilians. The blast was equivalent to 20,000 tons of dynamite, not the 1,000 tons originally reported to Truman and Stimson.

Eyewitness accounts reported survivors whose burnt flesh was barely hanging from their muscles and bones. Some were trying to push their intestines back into their bodies while others staggered slowly and painfully, like zombies. Heads and other body parts were everywhere. All survivors resembled the homeless in search of some source of healing, food, drink, and orientation.

Photos of people with their faces melted away, without ears, and burnt beyond recognition confirmed survivor tales. Hospitals working with exhausted skeleton crews and no electricity or plumbing were filled with twitching bodies, vomit, feces, and urine. The few surviving, overwhelmed doctors were mystified by patients who wandered into hospitals with "Disease X" some weeks following the bombing. Curiously, X-victims looked unburned on the outside, yet they would soon collapse from internal erosion due to radiation poisoning. For this disease there was no cure, nor were the exhausted, over-taxed doctors and nurses immune to the afterglow of radiation.

When making his decision, Truman had not been advised of the nature and extent of such desecration. Nor could he have been informed, since only a handful of scientists knew what radiation poisoning was like, and none knew it would be unleashed with such potency and scale.

Likewise, the president was unaware that Hiroshima was far more than just a military target, although it was indeed a communication and distribution center for the Japanese army. Truman was never told that the bomb's impact would be primarily upon civilians, who would suffer in unprecedented numbers and ways.

Those who had briefed both Truman and Stimson had greatly underestimated the clout and treachery of their "young Frankenstein." But, they had told him enough to cause him to later share with his family that it was a difficult and dreaded decision.

A LONG PARADE OF OBSTACLES

In addition to moral cross-currents, Truman, FDR, and the Project faced many practical and interpersonal hurdles in developing nuclear research. There had been the academic politics surrounding which scientists and labs—Princeton, Columbia, Chicago, Berkeley, etc.—would be selected and involved? Among the elite scientists who were recruited, many were Nobel laureates and *prima donnas* whom Oppenheim (who had not won the Nobel) would have to manage and appease. Convincing such scientists to be sequestered at top-secret, remote facilities without comfort and travel was not always easy or possible. And since nuclear physics was a new field with few experts, their staff and equipment operators would often need to be fully trained on the job.

No one could be fully trusted. General Groves learned to compartmentalize knowledge such that staff knew only about their own small pieces of the puzzle. Intelligence was gathered about questionable staffers. It was impossible to know who might secretly be talking with Groves' intelligence core, or with the FBI, or with the Germans, Japanese, or Russians. Innumerable codes, pseudonyms, and disinformation campaigns had to be employed at Oak Ridge and other hands-on sites, which added to the consternation and confusion of many.

Moreover, testing such a bomb was not without its own challenges. Beyond the possibility that it would be a dud were the questions of where and how such tests could be conducted locally without detection and without irreparable harm to people and nature. Nor could the unknown short and long-term effects of "dirty molecules" circulating in the atmosphere be predicted.

All in all, Presidents Roosevelt and Truman, and the Project, faced many unknowns, speed bumps, pressures, and counter-pressures. An ethical case study in which a choice between Hirohito's and Hitler's holocaust on the one hand, and the hastening of a world-scale nuclear holocaust on the other, may indeed be a candidate for the most important decision human leaders have ever made.

But was it the most difficult?

THE FINAL CHAIN REACTION

At the core of unleashing nuclear power is a process called a chain reaction. A series of linked (hence the word "chain") events are each caused by the one preceding it, and then each causes the one which follows… like a row of falling dominoes.

The final events of World War II in 1945 also seemed like a chain reaction of human interactivity. On July 16, an atom bomb was first experimentally and successfully exploded in what was called the "Trinity Test" in the desert of New Mexico. Soon thereafter, Truman received word that the bomb was ready for use in Japan.

By all appearances he had already made his decision. On July 21, the president approved the order to drop one, if not two, bombs, if the Japanese did not surrender.

However, he would honor the humanitarian arguments of the many who advised him by giving the Japanese an explicit warning. On July 26, the Allied leadership asked the Japanese for "unconditional surrender." They cautioned that the only alternative was "prompt and utter destruction" of Japan. It is frequently forgotten that the Japanese military was clearly warned prior to the dropping of the bomb, and that they were given the opportunity to cease fighting and thus prevent the nuclear attack. However, no warning could properly have prepared any country for what was to follow, even if the words "atomic bomb" had been included within the text.

On July 27, the Japanese replied that they would not surrender. That message precipitated the next link in the chain. On August 6, President Truman's order was implemented. In agreement with the unanimous recommendation of the key committees involved in nuclear use and strategy— and following consideration of the input from Winston Churchill, Secretary of War Stimson, Robert Oppenheimer, and General Groves—the first uranium atomic bomb used in warfare was dropped upon Hiroshima.

Not only could a bright light be seen from miles away, but smoke rose 40,000 feet into the air in the shape of a mushroom cloud. Within two days Russia declared war upon the Japanese, who still did not surrender, triggering another step in the chain.

On August 9, the United States dropped a second bomb, in this case plutonium, upon the ship-building port called Nagasaki. Since the primary target was clouded over that day, Nagasaki was bombed as an alternative, back-up target. Such is the luck of war.

The combination of these three events on August 6, 8, and 9 catalyzed the final World War II event: Japan's surrender to the Allies on August 14. Emperor Hirohito, whose voice had never been heard before by his people, broadcast news of the surrender to the surviving Japanese on August 15.

Truman, Churchill, and Stalin had accomplished their goals of defeating Nazi Germany and its Japanese and Italian allies. But the human, environmental, emotional, and economic costs were unprecedented and overwhelming. At that time, the devastating story of Hitler's holocaust camps, Hirohito's POW camps, and the long-term effects of two atomic bombs had not yet been discovered and revealed to the outside world.

Within this rapid-fire "chain" schema, Truman's seemingly quick decision to authorize the atom bombs on July 21 appeared to be a snap judgment. But as his daughter and many records testify, he had pondered the matter for months, and waited until he read the Trinity Test results and received the input of many advisors before proceeding. Truman was also hoping against hope that the Japanese, who had already been mercilessly bombed and decimated, would surrender.

By the day that he received the Trinity Test results, time was of the essence. But what was the real reason for the bombing? Was it his apprehension about a Russian-made bomb, as some historians have surmised? Or was there another story which has never been told?

CAPTAIN TRUMAN'S ETHICS

In fact, Harry Truman had faced similar ethical choices to the pivotal one of his presidency, and he was no stranger to world-wide military confrontation. Almost three decades earlier, in World War I, Captain Harry Truman of the U.S. army had faced two enemies: the Germans, and his commanding officer, Colonel Karl D. Klemm—both in the Argonne region of France.

By 1916 it had been a nasty, colossal war. In the Meuse-Argonne offensive, in which Truman held command of Battery D of the 129th Field Artillery Regiment, there were over 117,000 casualties on the American side alone.

Everywhere there was the smell of rats and decaying human flesh. In the ubiquitous trenches, where mud was omnipresent, black humor had it that the menu was "mud for breakfast, dirt for lunch, and mud cakes for dinner." Although officers like Harry received more comforts than their men, most thought that they shared the same address: Hell.

Amidst much carnage and chaos, it was obedience to military orders that provided the only organization and sanity. Failure to follow orders came with the possibility of severe discipline, including a court martial, which would mean facing a grueling trial conducted by superior officers. The penalties exacted during court martials in most countries were not lenient: years in prison, dishonorable discharge—even death by firing squad.

Harry's immediate superior, Colonel Klemm, was a crazed, Prussian style disciplinarian in the eyes of his soldiers. A fanatically exacting martinet, Klemm not only expected all orders to be followed *ad absurdum*, but he was also harsh and irrational whenever humane short-cuts were taken. Klemm had hurled endless angry threats and imposed severe penalties.

At one point Colonel Klemm ordered perilously exhausted troops to run double-time (twice as fast) up a hill after marathon marching. Truman pulled his own men off the road to rest and Klemm was furious. One of Captain Truman's sergeants had twisted his ankle and could no longer march. Harry allowed him to ride his own horse to avoid greater injury or possible isolation from the group. However, allowing an enlisted man to ride an officer's horse was against orders. Klemm verbally attacked both the sergeant and Captain Truman.

It was neither the first nor the last time Colonel Klemm would threaten Harry with a court martial. Indeed, it was usually Truman who talked Klemm out of court martialing powerless enlisted men.

Later during his fighting within the Argonne region, Truman was faced with a serious ethical dilemma. A German army artillery group was advancing into a position that could compromise dozens of American lives. Captain Truman's orders were to fire only upon enemies within his sector... and these German's were clearly, if minimally, outside of his jurisdiction. The precise standing orders were to fire at Germans facing and threatening Harry's 35th U.S. army division. This visible enemy unit was poised to fire upon the 28th division, not Harry's 35th.

Truman knew he was on the hot seat with Klemm, and that at some point the court martial threat might become real. But he also knew that comrades in the 28th division were about to be cruelly butchered, and he could be their protector. What to do?

Captain Truman had no time to consult volumes of Aristotle and Kant ... nor could he remember them. And he could not phone a mentor or minister in his home town in Missouri. It was now or never, and yet he had been trained never to disobey orders.

Many soldiers had been court martialed and then shot, demoted, or imprisoned not only for desertion but also for disobedience. Once again, he wondered what to do.

Truman would save lives.

He would defy orders to attack the German bullies now and risk facing another bully, Colonel Klemm, later.

Truman's artillery crew was accurate and the German battery was soon nullified. Many American lives were saved and to his own men, the captain was a hero.

Soon the outraged Colonel Klemm was on the field telephone, angrily threatening a court martial. Fortunately, the heating up of combat and the cooling down of Klemm's temper allowed the threat of the moment to eventually drop.

Truman had seen too many dead, injured, paralyzed, and traumatized American boys to turn his back upon the 28th division. And he had seen too many troops whose spirits were broken by caustic, if not psychotic, officers, to blindly support Klemm.

The captain had also learned the value of superior weaponry. After arriving in France, the first gun he was taught to fire was the French .75 millimeter rapid-fire rifled cannon. The French called it "the marvel weapon," and would later say it was "the weapon that won the war." The canon was so accurate and fast, it could kill far more soldiers per hour than any comparable device.

Even then, Harry was no stranger to cruel weapons. The first field order he received was to fire a gas barrage at the Germans. While he seldom saw the impact of his shelling, it is likely that he killed others with the poison gas commonly used by both sides—and witnessed their deaths. Indeed, he had recently learned to use his own gas mask. Young Truman knew he would not be spared by enemies who found gas weapons too cruel. Cruelty was a fact of war.

Hardened soldiers learned that the term "cruel weapon" was a redundant misnomer, since any weapon could be brutal. Thousands of men died slow, agonizing deaths, whether by rifle or cannon shot, or by suffocation due to gas inhalation. Others died quickly, in ways that left no corpses for their mothers to mourn over.

With the development of each new major weapon, people could be killed in greater numbers and at faster rates, and yet still more would die slow, agonizing deaths. Those who survived would learn to live with amputations, chronic suffering, and mental illness.

FROM CAPTAIN TO PRESIDENT

When Truman was later faced with deploying the atom bomb, there was really nothing new about the decision. Thousands would die instantly, and thousands more would die slow agonizing deaths or be burnt alive—just as with the fire bombs which ravaged Tokyo and other cities earlier that year—and just as with the French .75 millimeter and with poison gas.

The World War I flame throwers he had witnessed first hand had also badly disfigured men as they burnt them to crisps. And the accidental killing of thousands of civilians—or collateral damage—had long been a savage fact of war. There was no escaping cruel weapons nor being burned alive in warfare.

Innocent children could not be spared either. The American bombings of German cities, and the German bombings of London ... and on and on ... had become standard operating procedure. Was the atom bomb or poison gas any more terrible than the treatment of enemies and their families by Attila the Hun? Or by the Romans, who had crucified thousands? Or by ordinary soldiers worldwide who for thousands of years had been maiming, raping, and torturing their enemies and their innocent families?

Were not Hitler's Nazis and Hirohito's Pearl Harbor squadrons nasty assailants that needed to be neutralized? After all, the Japanese had lured American POW's into trenches, then doused them with kerosene, and barbequed them alive. They had beheaded other POWs, and forced wounded and diseased men to march mercilessly, for miles, to their deaths. From an Asian perspective, Japanese troops had been the "Nazis of the East" who inflicted intense torture, rape, executions, and conquest on much of the Asian continent. Violent and painful atrocities by the Japanese were the rule, not the exception.

Must not Truman, who wrote his beloved Bess about the "dying boys who must be saved," do for his men in World War II, what he had done for them in World War I? Could he not grant them the same mercy he had personally experienced in 1918—the end of a war of endless waste and horror?

He well remembered the great sense of relief that had come on November 11, 1918, when he and his surviving troops reveled and drank long into the night at war's end. And he remembered standing up to a tyrannical regime by using superior weapons to get the job done... He was particularly proud of saving the lives of almost all of the so-called boys in his own command.

Thus, for Harry, the ethical decisions of war had been faced and made long ago. The atomic bomb was only a matter of scale. Or was it? Many highly intelligent people who had also experienced the ravages of war had deep reservations about nuclear weapons, and many tried to place pressure upon the president.

World War II was larger and longer than World War I. In a parallel fashion, atomic bombs were larger and more menacing than other bombs. But in the final analysis they were new, superior weapons by which some would die instantly, others would die slow, agonizing deaths, and still others would be disabled for life, just like every weapon—from stones, to swords, to mines—used in battle throughout history.

Despite the painful tragedy derived from all weapons and all wars, Truman had to annihilate cruel demagogues who would not surrender. And he could do so with the shock of a new, superior weapon. He knew he could save hundreds of thousands of lives—American, Canadian, Australian, Japanese, New

161

Zealand, Korean, Russian—and others who would likely be killed in months or years to come. It was a familiar story from the last World War, only with increased scope and new leading characters.

And yet, he knew that nuclear physicists themselves were divided about what to do. He also knew that he would reap what he sowed, and nuclear weapons might be unleashed upon the United States.

After Truman's decision, apologists for his choice to use atom bombs would paraphrase Mill's "greatest good for the greatest number" ethical principle. They would say that two moderate size Japanese cities were destroyed so that far more lives and land could be saved. The aggressive empires, Germany and Japan, had been subdued so that, as President Wilson had once said, the world would be "safe for democracy." Young Truman had been impressed by Wilson's rallying cries and enlisted in the army accordingly. Truman valued not only the greatest good for the greatest number, but a planet "safe for democracy" as an apex ideal.

However...

THE NATURE OF CHARACTER

Harry Truman never needed to enlist to fight in World War I. He was a farmer, the sole male in a family in which his mother and sister were in his care, and two years older than the mandatory age of conscription. Harry was legally blind and had to cheat on his eye exam to enlist in the army. Any one of these restrictions could have exempted him from military enrollment. His service to his country, if not to humanity, as soldier and as statesman, was thus voluntary if not exemplary.

Ironically, Colonel Klemm went on to commit suicide while Captain Truman went on to become president. Hitler, as well as many German and Japanese military leaders, also committed suicide. Ultimately, the bullies took their own lives after taking so many others.

From Truman's perspective, justice had prevailed. For the president, the lesser tragedy of utilizing cruel weapons was surpassed by the greater victory of peace in a world that was safe for democracy, allowing millions of people to return to ordinary lives with extraordinary relief.

Most importantly, Truman hoped he could live to a ripe old age in peace, knowing that he had made the right ethical decision. He later told a college audience "I made the only decision I ever knew how to make. I did what I thought was right." And yet he had confided to others that it was unclear to him what was right until he had consulted not only his experts but also his conscience.

THE ETHICAL RELATIVISM OF WAR AND PEACE

The former captain Truman had developed a sense of what was right from inside the rules of war. But are there not other rules outside of military protocol? Military training instills an ethics pertaining to whom and how to kill. However, many philosophies and religions have questioned whether one should ever kill or even harm in the first place.

Are ethics role specific? Is murder justified if one wears a uniform and declares war? A military chaplain is not supposed to kill or even bear arms, but what if he and his colleagues are attacked in battle and other lives are at stake? A doctor is supposed to "do no harm," but what if he is a military doctor following orders or under attack?

Should a wartime president follow different rules regarding the annihilation of millions of civilians than a peacetime president? Who has the final say on whether these ethical choices depend upon role, law, conditions, culture, or all of the above?

Such questions bring us back to a consideration of...

THE TEN FACTORS

1. **Notions of fairness and justice:** It is notable that during wartime, concepts of international fairness fade quickly, such that "all's fair in love and war" often prevails. Truman was reminded that there was nothing fair about Pearl Harbor when he was told that dropping nuclear bombs upon Japanese civilians would be unfair. For this president, justice was about redressing the extreme injustice of Tojo and of Hitler, not about creating a level playing field for all warring parties. As such, it might be seen as insular or concave justice—just as Japan and Germany perceived a self-serving convex justice. Neither side could see the entire picture without distortion. Neither could adopt the perspective of the Hague International Court of Justice as a neutral referee. Hence, each would see the enemy as unjust, and seek to render corrective justice without concern for over-arching notions of fairness.

2. **Impact or consequences:** Undoubtedly the consequences of this decision could be monumental. A world war might finally end. A new nuclear era would begin. The precedent of such warfare could precipitate

the further development and use of nuclear weapons by numerous other countries or parties. Thousands, if not millions, of innocent victims could be killed or wounded for life. On the other hand, the lives of thousands of soldiers, sailors, and potential victims of other bombings might be spared. Whichever choice Truman made, the consequences would be immense.

3. **Ends and means:** As much as any factor, considerations of ends vs. means informed this decision. Paradoxically, the winning argument seems to suggest that the more violent the means, the more peaceful the ends. Ultimately, when all factors were considered, Truman valued the ends— world peace and American national security—more than the means that in this case irrevocably opened Pandora's Box. In this regard he was more of a pragmatist and survivalist than a moralist.

4. **Tone and atmosphere:** Already the genocidal, all but misanthropic tone of Hitler, Mussolini, and Hirohito seemed the nadir of civilization. But Truman did not think it necessary to model a higher tone. Rather, he and his advisors reasoned it best to fight fire with fire, a fire so intense and inhumane, it was seen as lowering the human incivility index even more. Atmosphere was not nearly as important as outcome.

5. **Motivation and higher law:** Truman offended many of his fellow Baptists by publicly using four-letter words. He did not seem particularly compelled by a strong vertical loyalty in the way that say Gandhi, Queen Esther, and Wilberforce did. Motivated largely by national security and patriotism, he felt most compelled by the goals of winning and saving those lives to which he felt strong affinity. After all, he had been sworn in to serve and protect the American people, not Rachel Carson's near infinite web of life. Whether as Captain Truman or President Truman, he felt strongly motivated to guard his own tribe and the free world.

6. **Allegiance and loyalty:** A former army captain, Truman identified with his role as commander-in-chief and thus felt a strong loyalty to American troops, including the youngest and most vulnerable G.I.s in harm's way. Frequently conferring with Churchill, he also wished to protect and defend loyal allies, as well as the families of all of these. Truman had also inherited particular goals, strategies, and projects such as "Manhattan" from Franklin Roosevelt. As a politician, veteran, former haberdasher and judge, he had a strong allegiance to the Democratic party, U.S. business, the military, and mainstream America. Loyalties to mankind seemed more abstract and distant, although he felt that eliminating dictators was indeed of service to mankind, not just to America.

7. **Values and principles:** Making the world safe for democracy was a principle for which Harry was willing to die in World War I, and which he remained determined to protect at all costs in World War II. Although he valued humane practices, he knew that in war he valued winning and protection of his own country above all else. The type of ethical fair-mindedness which Truman valued most was one which protected the vulnerable underdog against oppressors such as Clemm, Hitler, and Tojo. Ultimately, Truman valued effectiveness more than most ideals. The outcome of World War II for Americans was more important than the international laws of the Hague.

8. **Cultural context:** Clearly Truman's upbringing within the heartland Bible belt, the U.S. Army, and the Democratic party, created a cultural outlook through which he identified with the little guy (he stood 5' 8"), the Caucasian, the Christian, and the patriot. He knew nothing first hand of Japanese traditions, religion, values, and mores. It was natural for him to assume both cultural and political superiority over what he deemed a demagogic, if not demonic, "Oriental" regime. From the current perspective, his attitude, like that of most Americans at the time, was highly racist against the Japanese. Living in a cocoon culture makes it very difficult for military rivals to seek understanding and empathy toward the foe, who is inherently "other." It is worth asking whether a culture with a much stronger understanding of and respect for Japanese people and their traditions could have pulled such a large trigger? Similarly, had the Japanese military leaders known and respected many American women, children, men, and values, could they have bombed Pearl Harbor?

9. **Implications:** In a worst-case scenario, the implications of the nuclear precedent were devastating. The end of the free world—if not civilization itself—were possibilities if the bomb was developed and used *carte blanche*, whether by tyrants, terrorists, or Americans. But the best-case scenario was strongly appealing: no country would wage war if there was the possibility of nuclear retaliation. Clearly, Harry's decision was not just about the outcome of an epic war: Truman was also "playing for all the marbles" within the context of human history. The implications of his decision were perhaps the greatest of all cases, because the survival of humanity and indeed many other species were fully at stake.

10. **Proportion and balance:** On the whole, while Truman weighed many of these factors, he was focused most upon the consequences, outcome, and casualties of the war in the Pacific. Whatever the risks regarding Japanese

civilian tragedy, his own reputation, humanitarian concerns, and international laws about cruel weapons, his strongest allegiance was to his own people, allies, and the principle of keeping the world safe for democracy. The fear of prolonging, if not losing, the war was deeply embedded. Pragmatic military values strongly outweighed those of strict moralists, environmentalists, and concerned nuclear physicists. On balance short-term victory, no matter what the moral and humanitarian costs, trumped long-term risk. All things considered, the ends justified the means.

THE NUCLEAR LEGACY

Of course, Truman's endorsement of a nuclear initiative led to a transformed, more dangerous world. The precedent for using nuclear power did indeed lead to an arms race, to meltdown crises at nuclear plants such as Chernobyl and Three Mile Island, to the ongoing threat of nuclear war and nuclear terrorism, to incidents such as Kennedy's confrontation with Khrushchev as discussed in chapter one, and much more.

Once the perils of Hiroshima and Nagasaki were publicly reported, controversy and protest increased. In 1946, a major article in the *New Yorker* exposed and questioned nuclear fall-out of many kinds. Physicist Neils Bohr continued his campaign by forcefully writing to the United Nations in 1950. By 1955, two other great thinkers, Bertrand Russell and Albert Einstein, created a manifesto against nuclear war that led to the first Pugwash conference.

After being elected president, General Dwight Eisenhower addressed the United Nations and called for "atoms for peace," nuclear limits, and sanity. Later, many voices, including American Secretary of State Henry Kissinger and Russia's head of state Mikhail Gorbachev, pressed for a reduction and roll back in the U.S.–Soviet nuclear arms race.

By the 1960s, protests against nuclear war and power plants became commonplace, and the use of nuclear power is still hotly debated. More recently, North Korea and Iraq triggered global concern about hidden weapons of mass destruction, or WMDs.

Meanwhile, India and Pakistan continue their own private neighborly arms race. The fear of nuclear terrorism has catalyzed the creation of huge security budgets and specialized personnel. Pandora's box has indeed been opened.

Moreover, nuclear safety has been a major concern as recently as 2018. In Hawaii, the genuine scare of an oncoming missile was prompted by human error. Leaked stories about missiles that were almost fired, nuclear explosives mistakenly shipped to public facilities, ongoing cheating scandals and drug abuse by "rocketeers" (those who operate nuclear silos), and reports about outdated, broken nuclear equipment are all too frequent.

In more open societies several of these leaks have been publicized. But in closed, highly censored societies, it is impossible to know which human and computer errors have caused other types of leaks.

Books, plays, and films (*Fail Safe, Dr. Strangelove, On the Beach*, among others) have depicted the potential folly of nuclear weapons in human hands. Despite the assurances of experts and generals, there has been chronic uncertainly about whether we are just one human error—or one psychotic dictator—or one vindictive terrorist—away from apocalyptic closure.

TRUMAN'S LEGACY

Truman's decision that may have in fact prevented nuclear apocalypse. As with the Cuban Missile Crisis, the very presence of nuclear weapons may have ironically safeguarded the planet.

Who is to say how many of us would be alive if World War II had lasted longer, or if Truman had taken a different turn? Would another country have dropped an atom bomb if the U.S. had not?

Had he been a man of the 21st century, or one who could see through Japanese eyes, Truman might have acted differently. He would not have behaved so ethnocentrically and insensitively to Japanese horror. However, Harry Truman was a sheltered farm boy of the mid-20th century. He spent his youth surrounded by fellow Midwesterners who placed God, home, family, democracy, and country atop their Americanized totem pole. Seen in that patriotic, "All-American" context, and in the shadow of Captain Harry Truman, the artillery division military hero of World War I, it is not surprising that the president felt he had done the right thing.

WHY TRUMAN?

Harry S. Truman is not included in this book because he chose to use nuclear weapons. Rather, he was chosen partially because he was willing to face Klemm's court martial to save dozens of lives, and later willing to face the court martial of world opinion to possibly save millions. He is included primarily herein because he concurrently faced formidable dictators and an awesome ethical decision, one that forever changed war, peace, and the shadow over humanity.

While the largest decision he—or indeed, anyone—ever made remains a controversial one, Truman's use of the bomb may have paradoxically prevented its future use. To this day, it has been deployed by neither dictators nor terrorists.

If the Japanese had won the war, Harry S. Truman might have been brought before the world court and tried for crimes against humanity anyway. Clearly America and every other country at war had violated the Hague international laws about cruel weapons or about the treatment of prisoners and civilians. This too had haunted his conscience.

However, from the perspective of the victors, Truman was a true patriot who saved his men from torture far more cruel—and saved humanity from wars far more cruel—than can be imagined.

NUCLEAR ETHICS IN THE CLASSROOM

Although I have never been asked by students if I favor nuclear war, I have been asked in the classroom how we can prevent one. This question leads to important discussions about the various channels of diplomacy, about whether the United Nations can be effective, about reciprocal disarmament treaties, and related topics.

But the haunting question about whether nuclear war can be prevented also leads to a corridor of discussion few students expect. "In addition to all other factors we have discussed," I reply, "there is another *a priori* consideration which I find important. Please give this some thought."

Then I continue.

"Do you think I can credibly advocate for nuclear peace if my personal, inner nucleus is at war? If we are nuclear reactors, can we effectively eliminate nuclear reactors? I am not being cute."

Often the room falls silent.

Not wishing to impose a mindset and be doctrinaire, I add one more thought—one which affirms that the primary goal of the academy is independent thinking, and not nuking students with rigid orthodoxy from on high.

"Something to think about? Class dismissed."

CHAPTER 9

RACHEL CARSON:
(1907-1964)

AGAINST THE TIDE?

A bed should be a reward, but hers felt more like a bed of nails. It aggravated aches and worries that had accrued throughout the day. The more she twisted to find a pleasant sleep position that March 1962 evening, the less comfortable Rachel felt.

Her decision was an agonizing one, and not only in terms of moral conflict. Every decision took precious energy away from a distressed body in agony—one suffering from the cumulative pain of chemotherapy, a mastectomy, heart attack, sinusitis, arthritis, ulcer, diseased eyes, angina, and an irreversibly spreading cancer. The prolonged stress of each critical decision added to the workload of a failing body, which had recently collapsed when she was shopping.

Due to her dimming vision caused by inflammation of the iris, her slippers appeared to be two large amoebas on the floor. She could not decide which shoulder to favor, since the sharp jabs to her back and chest came unexpectedly, then persistently, to either side.

Not knowing which way to turn was symbolic of the many decisions Rachel constantly faced. Each day she asked herself which public appearance, if any, could she manage? Could she travel to receive an honorary degree, or visit a studio for an interview? Which of her mountains of letters should and could be personally answered?

What, if anything, could she eat and keep down today?

There was also the deeper moral dilemma, more stressful to the heart than body. When her niece, Marjorie, had died in 1957, Rachel, almost fifty, had adopted Marjorie's five-year-old son Roger. Since Roger had already lost one mother, how could Rachel permit a boy, now eleven, to lose another—his sole parent—just six years later?

Roger could not be abandoned a second time. Every hour with him was precious. It seemed that each new public event in her life might prove to be the last—one that would orphan Roger... again. Already her periods of nausea and near blackouts felt like barriers between her and Roger, not to mention everyone else.

On this late autumn day in 1963, the pressing decision was whether to continue her commitment to be interviewed by Eric Sevareid on *CBS Reports*—or not. Both her body and her advisers had recommended that she cancel. While it had the potential to be the most influential and critical interview of her life, it would also be the most draining. She feared it could be the final nail in her coffin.

There were convincing reasons to be interviewed. In a best-case scenario this major national news program, focused upon her crusade against pesticide overkill, could have enough outreach to discredit the critics and corporations destroying millions of small creatures—and Carson's reputation.

Rachel also felt positively about CBS host Eric Sevareid, whose values seemed close to her own. His producer, Jay McMullen, had proven to be a potent investigative journalist and *CBS Reports* had a substantial national following.

Furthermore, Rachel's publisher, Paul Brooks, discovered that CBS's Fred Friendly, who had originally asked for the galleys of Rachel's latest book in April, was the same Fred Friendly who produced Edward R. Murrow. She was aware of Murrow's televised tilting with goliaths such as the Pentagon and Senator Joseph McCarthy (chapter 10). She too was facing gargantuan bullies.

Thus, *CBS Reports* was a likely ally in exposing, if not yoking, huge chemical companies. Sevareid could definitely help increase public awareness of the harmful underbelly of toxic pesticides such as DDT and dieldrin that she had been investigating as a scientist.

Moreover, contract negotiations with CBS had already concluded in August. Could Rachel back out now, even if she cited her chronic ill health? For all these reasons, it seemed wise to carry through.

And yet…

To Rachel, this interview carried enormous risks. She was concerned about a making visual public appearance that would be seen nationwide. Carson had conveyed deep feelings of discomfort to her closest friend and paramour, Dorothy Freeman: "I just hope I don't look and sound like an utter idiot." The combined impact of the chemotherapy, rapidly spreading cancer, numerous medications, mastectomy, ulcer, tumors, other illnesses, and the stress of facing so many critics and opponents, triggered unpredictable bouts of nausea, mood swings, and frequent exhaustion.

Despite her exceptional intelligence, she could no longer predict when she would be intelligible—and in this case she would be speaking to her largest audience. The veteran scientist remembered times when dizziness had led to her silence and struggle for words.

Moreover, there was another wrinkle—her wrinkles themselves. These could not be seen on radio, nor by the readers of her books. But television? The toll of her health attrition and prolonged public controversy had accelerated her visible aging.

And she was advised by her publicist not to wear make-up on TV. Lipstick looked black on a black-and-white screen, so it was verboten. But no make-up at all would leave her naked and ghoulish. And wouldn't she have to wear a wig?

She was concerned that at fifty-five, she might look seventy on television.

To her intimates she had emphasized that she wished to keep her growing cancer condition completely private. "Gossip about an author in the news goes like wildfire" she had anxiously written her beloved Dorothy. Rachel had been recently sent to a heart specialist, who discovered that she had a rare form of angina. He said that she should no longer tax her heart by using staircases. Indeed, she had confided that she could not even lift a cat or open the blinds without fear of going too far. Great restraint was essential. Her recent black-out and fall while shopping next to a record rack was proof in point.

So how would such a decimated zombie look to the educated eye? Rachel knew the camera would not lie. Wouldn't a huge audience watching *CBS Reports* quickly grasp her secret? She had even heard from a friend that, after Sevareid and McMullen met with her, Sevareid told McMullen, "Jay, you've got a dead leading lady."

On some days Rachel had already felt death in the air. She had discovered two new tumors on her collarbone and neck that would need attention and diagnosis. Just one month earlier, she had written her beloved Dorothy: "it seemed as though time was standing still and there might be no tomorrow."

Her undoubtedly terminal illness was her first secret. But there were reasons she could not disclose why the spreading cancer had to be only a family matter. There were even secrets about her secret she could not reveal to anyone except Dorothy.

Then there was that other secret, the one she could never discuss. No one else could ever know—possibly not even Dorothy. It was far too painful.

TV OR NOT TV?

Jay McMullen's reputation for slow, methodical work was also gnawing at her. Rachel had been warned that his intrusive camera crew would virtually live in her house, possibly for days. Wouldn't unwelcome houseguests with bright lights and heavy equipment, not to mention incessant bustle and conversation, destroy her only atmosphere for rest, if not recuperation? And what about Roger and his homework... and privacy?

Already CBS had delayed and delayed again the interview. Rachel and her publicist worried that McMullen was being lobbied by the other side. Might her critics be trying to indefinitely postpone or kill the production? Was CBS going to cave in? Could she tolerate another postponement? By the time they invaded her house, she might be on her deathbed, or worse. Every day she felt more decimated.

Equally stressful was the discovery that the *CBS Reports* interview would not be a tribute to "Miss Carson," as she was called. Rather, it would seem like a debate created by point–counterpoint editing. Not only would Rachel's perspective be presented, but also the views of her staunchest critic, Robert White-Stevens, the "anti-Carson." Moreover, the U.S. surgeon general, and leaders from the FDA and U.S. Public Health Service, who were convinced that Carson was an alarmist, would also be interviewed. She would need to be on top of her game to accurately withstand, if not overshadow, so many apologists for corporate greed and complicit government policy.

As she rolled from shoulder to shoulder to relieve pain, Rachel wondered how she could possibly shoulder more responsibility. Her doctor had recommended far less stress. This was far more.

Although she, White-Stevens, and the others would be filmed at different times and locations, Rachel knew that the multiple interviews would be synthesized into a single program. As a result, she would be facing chronic adversaries in an editing plan over which she had no control. If the shot sequence proved favorable, she might seem to be refuting, even nullifying White-Stevens' best arguments. But alternatively, the TV editing could give her critics the last word. If so, her research and position might look dubious, if not ridiculous.

Moreover, other opponents would be watching the program, poised to pounce upon her every sluggish slip-up and drug-induced error. Poison pens would fuel the PR crusades of powerful chemical companies, the tabloid press, and misguided experts, some of whom she had once admired. Well meaning but poorly informed journalists and professors would be chomping at the bit for engaging copy to feed newspapers, academic journals, and magazines. After all, she was not just a controversial environmentalist, she was a female scientist. Tragically for Rachel, many of her critics and colleagues thought "female scientist" was an oxymoron—and a punch line.

And what if the tabloid media exposed that other secret, the one that would open Pandora's box, the one she must never reveal? Or, what if they revealed the hidden reasons for her first secret—her rapidly declining health.

As she pondered all this, Rachel suffered from the fear that each new pain could trigger her collapse, and that each might be evidence that the cancer had spread yet again. Even as she tried to rise to go to the bathroom, there was fear of falling and incessant gasping for breath.

It took forever just to turn without aggravation. And then it took forever all over again to pull herself off the bed and into an unbalanced, limping walk that grew slower every week.

The mental pain was no less severe. Again and again she wondered—what would happen to Roger? And Dorothy? And who could lead her cause, one that might save voiceless millions?

Yet the timing seemed right, if not for her body, then for the world. The public was being highly sensitized to radiation poisoning. The fallout after Hiroshima and Nagasaki, the horrid, unintended effects of H-bomb testing upon Japanese fishermen near the Bikini military zone, the backlash to gypsy moth spraying in the Northeast and fire ant treatments in the South, and many other cases, were raising awareness of the wide-ranging impact of human poisons.

Moreover the effects of that poisoning, damage, and decay were turning up hundreds—even thousands—of miles from the sources of radiation testing and insect treatment. Winds blowing toxic air, ships carrying tainted fish, steaks carved from cows that had digested sprayed grass would show up two or even ten time zones away. People who ate contaminated fish would visit doctors thousands of miles from the source of the toxins and learn little of their actual conditions.

So toxic effects seemed widespread, inter-connected, and unpredictable. It was prime time to make a case that pesticide overkill had many parallels with nuclear fall-out, and that the worst was yet to come.

The Nobel Prize-winning scientist Linus Pauling had presented a demand for the end of nuclear testing to the United Nations. It had been signed by over eighty thousand scientists from forty-nine countries. Beyond all the current lethal impacts of radiation poisoning, these scientists were concerned about the birth defects of future generations. Carson could see deadly similarities in the long-term impact of spraying.

The extent of the aggregate collateral damage of toxic sprays was not yet reported. For example, Carson was convinced that dieldrin was twenty times more toxic than the dreaded DDT, and would impart irreparable damage. But most sectors of the public knew little about the effects of either pesticide. Who would blow the whistle, if not Rachel?

Thus, there were strong conflicting pressures upon Miss Carson. While she strongly wished to protect her loved ones and her wilting body, she also deeply felt she must educate and protect the public, if not reverse the course of ecocide. What could she do?

ANATOMY OF A DILEMMA

How had all this started? What events had precipitated this damned-if-I-do-damned-if-I-don't decision? And just what were the secrets she was protecting?

Rachel had been running a marathon uphill ever since she could remember, and life kept inserting frequent roadblocks. As early as 1927, the young undergraduate at Chatham College had been discouraged from majoring in the sciences. She had been warned that there were no science jobs for women.

This message was reinforced constantly despite the exceptional encouragement of one mentor, who would help her for the next decade. Thanks to that Professor, Mary Scott Skinker, Rachel became a biology major and an honors graduate, but she was consistently advised by others that the hard sciences were for the truly rational, clinical, and highly intelligent male Ph.D.'s. Women who liked biology could gravitate toward the soft side of the animal and plant kingdoms by focusing upon nature study, writing poetry about the outdoors, and teaching lower level courses to younger students... but, Marie Curie to the contrary, the laboratories were reserved for men.

Wherever she looked, Carson heard the same discriminatory language— "no jobs for women"—including from Elmer Higgins, the acting director of the U.S. Bureau of Fisheries. However, her combined persistence and intelligence led Rachel to eventual employment there. Even after she was hired, however, the qualified researcher was not permitted to conduct experiments. Instead, her job would be to synthesize and report the studies of others.

Often, Carson had to work harder than her peers to be the first (or only) woman on a project, or on a research boat leaving port for oceanographic testing. At times, she was criticized for her work only after it was discovered that it had not been written by a man.

Even the positive events of 1930 presented fresh hurdles. The good news was that, with Skinker's help, she had obtained a full scholarship toward a master's degree in marine zoology from John's Hopkins University. Consequently, the bad news was that she would stand out like bagpipes in an orchestra as a woman in the male-dominated classrooms. She was often the butt of their jokes.

Her rivals were all competing to eventually replace the graybeards in their fields. But where could Rachel obtain a beard? After overcoming chronic and frustrating discrimination, she obtained her master's in 1932.

Once again, despite previous success against the odds, the 1930s, pocked by the Great Depression, proved unfriendly. After commencement, she knocked on doors that remained closed not only to women, but to everyone. Despite her master's degree from a prominent university, she was not deemed "leadership material" to all the male leaders whom she did not resemble.

So, Rachel turned to writing, and penned successful radio scripts for the Bureau of Fisheries in 1935. Within two years she had also published in the prestigious *Atlantic Monthly*.

Still, Carson faced ongoing setbacks. When her father died in 1935, she was only twenty-eight, and the family was too poor to travel back to Pennsylvania for his funeral. Just two years later, her sister died of pneumonia. Almost every year that she achieved professional success, Rachel was also broken-hearted by personal tragedy. Every family death was premature, and all the more difficult to bear.

Her other sister and only brother both suffered failed marriages. Consequently, these siblings and their children moved in with Rachel and her mother, Maria. Naturally, the Carsons seldom experienced privacy, and almost always felt domestic tensions and crowding.

As her academic critics were quick to emphasize, the young scholar was unable to complete her Ph.D. With up to five family members depending upon Rachel financially during the Depression, she had neither the means nor the time to reach closure on time-consuming graduate studies. It seemed that every step forward was followed by two backward.

Even Rachel's early publishing success turned quickly to failure. While sales for her first book, *Under the Sea Wind*, seemed destined to soar, they were torpedoed by the 1941 attack on Pearl Harbor just two weeks after publication. Interest in new books about ocean creatures capsized as the nation braced for war.

This bittersweet, emotional seesaw continued throughout World War II. During the 1940s she rose within the Bureau of Fisheries, from assistant to the chief of the Office of Information, to the editor-in-chief of all of the bureau's wildlife publications. Yet in 1948, her beloved teacher, mentor, and close friend, Mary Scott Skinker, died prematurely of cancer. Again, Rachel lost heart.

Throughout the 1950s the young scholar continued to experience far more than her share of tragedies. On the one hand, this would be her breakthrough decade, because her "biography of the ocean," *The Sea Around Us*, would win a National Book Award in 1951. On the other hand, it was also the decade of her radical mastectomy, sinusitis, ulcer, arthritis, and severe pneumonia.

While *Under the Sea Wind* was republished as an acclaimed bestseller in 1952, concurrently Rachel's niece Marjorie became pregnant and moved in with her.

Not only were Marjorie and the baby in need of incessant care, but Rachel discovered firsthand how pregnancies out of wedlock were stigmatized. The Carson family members, including their young breadwinner, soon shared in the pain of ostracism.

By 1955 the long-awaited publication of *Edge of the Sea* reinforced Rachel's reputation as a gifted and compelling author. She was commended for artfully revealing otherwise submerged narratives. In this case, she uncovered the hidden, fascinating life of creatures that could live both beneath the high and above the low tides at the ocean's edge. Overall, Miss Carson had created a comprehensive trilogy of the seas, earning her world-class literary status.

But all was not as well above as under the sea. Rachel was aghast that the balance of terrestrial nature was being profoundly disturbed by human hubris. For example, she heard repeated reports of attempts to rid crops of insects with toxic sprays that simultaneously polluted the land, killed wildlife, and contaminated people.

She felt she could lend her voice and expertise to halting such dangerous processes. So, in 1957, Carson became involved in what was soon called the *Long Island Gypsy Moth* case. Supporting environmentalists and alarmed New Yorkers, Rachel endorsed their petition to delimit the widespread over-use of dangerous pesticides. However, to her surprise, the judge refused to stop the spraying and seemed to be in the pocket of major corporations. The petition, like Rachel herself, was snubbed.

Greater tragedy struck that same year when Rachel's niece, Marjorie, died quickly and prematurely during hospitalization, leaving young Roger orphaned. Although almost fifty years old, Rachel adopted Roger who was only five. Already taxed by decades of chronic caregiving and illness, her body seemed much older. At one point, she confided to Dorothy that she "felt one hundred years old." Yet Roger became Rachel's first love, albeit a crippling responsibility who was "as lively as seventeen crickets."

The most severe blow to Carson's personal and professional life came just one year later in 1958, when she lost her mother, Maria, to a stroke. Over the years Carson's mother and home-keeper had also become her personal secretary. The loss was devastating to Rachel who held her mother's hand before, during, and after her passing. Maria had been her first and most beloved mentor as a close observer of nature.

FACING INNER AND OUTER DEMONS

By 1960, Carson's greatest ordeal had begun. Diagnosed with cancer, the oceanographer faced nauseating chemotherapy. Ironically, her scientific logic held that strong toxins could not be used to eliminate pests without contaminating the web of life in which they are embedded. Similarly, she herself could not use chemotherapy to eliminate the pests in her own body without also damaging the surrounding organs that sustained her.

Thus, the treatments depleted her energy and kept her bedridden. Sometimes they also aggravated her duodenal ulcer, sinusitis, or her other aches. At one point there was also a swelling of the sternum, pains in the back, neck, armpits, and then further spreading of what would become chronic pain.

Unfortunately, her cancer diagnosis arrived too late. In an age when doctors reported a wife's illness to her husband, Rachel's doctor had withheld information from her for over nine months. She had no husband, and so her doctor remained silent about an important diagnosis. To be fair, her biopsy had allegedly tested negative. But in fact one of her tumors was malignant and thus was misreported, as her doctor soon discovered. Disappointed in the withholding of information, she changed to another doctor, whose wife would die of breast cancer within the next year. The tea leaves did not look promising.

Over time, other complications appeared. One tumor flared up during chemotherapy. A staph infection soon depleted all her energy. Even a hospital bed had to be moved into her home in Maryland, where she become bedridden. Once Rachel later regained partial mobility, she would be accompanied by a pronounced limp, a walker, or a wheelchair at all times.

Roger and those who visited her at home or in the hospital would be shocked and sometimes heartbroken. Colleagues were also frustrated by her delayed meetings and now meaningless deadlines. Some days her chemotherapy made her so nauseous that she could not even think about work.

The cancer also produced a psychological anxiety. She confided in Dorothy that "every little pain seems like a hobgoblin and one lives in a little private hell until the thing is examined."

Rachel had also overheard how cancer patients were regarded by others. At an event she attended, colleagues were talking about Senator Maureen Newberger's cancer surgery in hushed tones. Some commented "she can't last," not realizing that Rachel, who was seated close to them, had a similar condition.

SILENCE THUNDERS

As was evident in the 1957 *Long Island Gypsy Moth* court case, Rachel had become aware of pesticide problems long before she wrote her tour de force best-seller, *Silent Spring*. Indeed, by 1958, she had attempted to convince the celebrated *New Yorker* writer, E.B. White, to write about the problem. Despite his enthusiasm for the content, he was already overcommitted. So, White suggested that Carson herself write the article.

This incentive, coupled with Rachel's own concerns and conscience, led her to make several phone calls to publishers in April 1958, about a possible book on the "human control of nature." Although her surface concern was about specific herbicides and insect sprays, her deeper horror was that humanity could now reshape, if not misshape, the environment and thus the natural balance of life. Such arrogance seemed appalling and worthy of a large—and published—red flag.

By 1960 she had plunged more fully into writing the exposé. Carson knew that over two hundred different chemical formulas were being employed to manufacture 638 million pounds of pesticide within an industry that garnered $250 million per year. To her view, that was outlandish.

Yet she worried about how far to go when writing such a book. After all, it would have seemed like throwing down the gauntlet to chemical companies and government agencies. On the other hand, the public needed know that their children, pets, wildlife, and they themselves were being poisoned on a grand, if gradual, scale.

Her commitment to pesticide research became taxing. Each hidden fact often led to two more. And each professional source often led to two more of whom at least one refused to speak with her. Sometimes each day working alone led to two more days recovering from chemotherapy and other speed bumps.

Some of the documents she needed were under corporate lock and key, and their guardians were often warned not to cooperate. Still, she persevered with the persistence of a mosquito... and several officials wanted to treat her like one.

Carson was soon able to reach an arrangement with the *New Yorker* to prepublish chapters of the book as articles. In two-month intervals, a chain of important events occurred. In April 1962, CBS producer Fred Friendly asked for galleys of the book-in-progress with hopes of a major Carson interview. In June, publication of serialized chapters of *Silent Spring* began in the *New Yorker*. By August, many key allies and other positive megaphones were given advance copies of the text. Only one month later, in September 1962, the most controversial non-fiction book of its era—and, according to some reviewers, also the most important—*Silent Spring*, was published.

As both author and publisher feared, the book was met by fierce opposition from vested interests. Although the sea trilogy had been received with high acclaim, a narrative about toxins sprayed on plants, people, and animals touched a nerve.

Fearing distribution of the book, major chemical companies such as Dow and Monsanto sought to frighten Carson and her publisher to halt publication. They requested advanced copies, threatened lawsuits, created PR campaigns to discredit her research, and attempted to undermine her professional reputation.

The *New Yorker* was also aggressively threatened by corporate power plays. Ironically, some of the very companies that threatened lawsuits were soon sued themselves by poisoned citizens and employees.

CARSON THE COMMUNIST?

By 1962, Carson's research was so controversial that the FBI was searching to see if she had ties to the Communist Party. Why would scientific research be so threatening to the government? What exactly had Miss Carson discovered?

Rachel felt that the public needed to be properly informed not only about corporate ecocide, but also about the equally culpable and sometimes gullible government agencies that protected the status quo. The FBI thus concluded that Rachel was a double threat. Both Wall Street and Washington were at risk.

The feds were right to suspect that Carson distrusted large corporations. Ever since her childhood, her parents had expressed concern about the damage to nature done by heavy industry. They pointed to the grey-filled sky in neighboring Pittsburgh and held their noses. Young Rachel never forgot.

At a deeper level she reminded everyone that the U.S. government was not in control—nature was. "Hoover's boys" and the chemistry alliance feared someone challenging not just the profits of corporate America, but also the dominance of government, corporations, and others who felt in charge.

The supremacy of science itself was also in question. During the early 1960s, the public already had been persuaded that other scientific blunders were in evidence. Americans became aware of the tragic birth defects caused by insufficient testing of thalidomide. The hazardous drug had just been taken off the market in 1961 after substantial public protest.

Americans were also increasingly aware of the ongoing problems of radiation poisoning evident at Hiroshima (chapter 8). Even the grand symbol of

America, the bald eagle, was becoming sterile due to human error. What if another major mistake had already occurred involving pesticide overuse?

Such scientific errors could prove immense. Specifically, Miss Carson had noted that insufficiently tested, unbridled use of killer chemicals pointed toward these devastating facts and implications:

1) Spraying insects and plants sometimes breeds stronger strains of insects that are immune to the spray.

2) When used improperly, the sprays can kill or cripple other species in the line of fire, including birds, rabbits, squirrels, livestock, pets, and even humans.

3) The toxins in such chemicals eventually travel throughout the food chain and damage other species. For example, DDT sprayed on alfalfa, which is then eaten by cows, can migrate to humans via the cows' milk, butter, cream, cheese, and meat.

4) Powerful chemical companies generated large profits from the sale of pesticides and herbicides. In some cases, greedy executives created large PR campaigns about the positive impacts of pesticides. Little had been publicized about the negative consequences.

5) Humans exposed to excessive chemical toxins, whether the residue in water and foods, or direct use of the chemicals, faced increasing health risks including possible leukemia and other forms of cancer.

6) Some sprays simply did not work, although their side effects might be substantial.

7) Hidden effects might extend far beyond the area sprayed. For example, residue that soaked into submerged water tables, reservoirs, sewage drains, and rivers could travel to the ocean and kill fish and other seafood consumed by humans, or might migrate directly to the water supplies of towns and cities.

8) The sprays often killed what humans considered the "good insects" too. When spiders, Venus fly traps, and other predators were killed, their prey multiplied.

9) The residual effects of long-term use were yet unknown. To the extent that toxins infiltrated DNA and other genetic material, birth defects and other future failures could arise and multiply.

10) Some of the deaths to animals, if not humans, seemed extremely painful. There were eyewitness reports of twitching birds and rabbits, among others, breathing heavily and making heart-wrenching sounds.

11) A general lack of high-quality scientific testing by neutral parties meant that other unintended consequences could likely appear.

While each of these problems proved formidable, Carson's greatest concern was with the attitude behind it all. The then increasingly popular scientific creed stated that humans should subdue nature rather than cooperate with it. Thus, she was not only challenging corporate, scientific, and regulatory America, but also the collective ego and entitlement of Western society writ large.

She concluded that chemical companies must pull back, way back, to allow time for independent scientists to conduct neutral studies while the government determined appropriate regulations. But who within the upper echelons of science would listen to her, a "woman scientist" without a Ph.D., who was seemingly protecting, if not promoting, disease-infested insects?

Moreover conducting research on pesticides and herbicides had proven vexing. While Carson's early work was hard to fund due to her gender, her 1960's research was even more difficult, since many colleagues feared being associated with a perceived whistle-blower.

In fact once, she decided to write *Silent Spring*, some previously friendly sources no longer replied. Others would only speak if they were promised anonymity. It distressed her that many contacts were worried about possible recriminations from lawyers and publicists representing the heavyweights.

POISON PEN FALL-OUT

After *Silent Spring* was published in 1962, many critics deliberately misrepresented, and then attacked, the research. Based upon previous experience, Carson sensed that other dirty tricks were being planned by corporations at risk. For example, she had discovered that a national association of chemical companies had budgeted half a million dollars to distribute counter-attack literature. One company alone budgeted an additional quarter million. Monsanto soon published a parody of *Silent Spring* that envisioned (rather than a world saturated with pesticides) a desolate, bug-infested world of famine without pesticides.

Despite such toxic opposition, *Silent Spring* proved enormously successful in sales and translations, yet the Carson smear campaign continued throughout 1963. Even more painful than the expected tabloid defamation were attacks by former jilted colleagues such as Ed Diamond. He wrote in the *Saturday Evening Post* that Carson wanted to bring the planet "back to a dark age of plague and epidemic." Even *Time* magazine warned that *Silent Spring* was "partly unsound."

Predictably, those who were threatened most tried every angle of attack. Still driving under the influence of the McCarthy era, several American so-called "patriots" proclaimed that the radical Miss Carson was probably a Communist trying to deplete America's food cabinet by down-sizing the supply of pest-safe crops.

To male chauvinists she was a spinster. Noting how "emotionally unstable" women were, one attack dog asked: "what is she so worked up over genetics for?" To mainstream traditionalists, she was portrayed as part of a fringe, "backpacky" culture of "bird-lovers" and a leader of the "cult for the balance of nature."

Male scientists reasserted that Carson, like other women, was more easily misled by emotions than facts. Misunderstanding Carson's position, one heckler wrote: "isn't it just like a woman to be afraid of a few little bugs?"

Adding to her angst were the attacks that came from respectable professional publications. In *Chemical and Engineering News* she was lumped together with fringe groups such as "natural foods faddists" and "organic eaters" in a putdown which made them all seem ignorant of real science. Other articles in *Nutrition Reviews, Science,* and *American Scientist* ignored Carson's true credentials and noted her "absence of a diploma" and unscientific, "visceral appeals."

Freely and frequently linked with "food quacks" and unrealistic extremists, Carson was dubbed a pseudo-scientist, amateur, and demoted from scientist to "science journalist" in various publications. Visually, in photos such as those in *Life* magazine, she was pictured with her cat in matronly poses, rather than in her lab coat like her male counterparts.

Often her adversaries had not read *Silent Spring* or, if they had, they made false or inflated claims. Then there was another wave of attempts to link her to "red" plots to deplete safe American food. After all, who would want to feed their children vegetables that had not been sprayed to prevent disease? Somehow "Carson the Commie" would also be to blame for eventual nationwide starvation.

The cumulative impact of all these arrows of criticism in her chest was inexorable pain. In her research, she had begun to link pesticide use to the increased risk of cancer. So when Rachel was first told that she had breast cancer, she wondered if what they had really found inside her chest were bullet holes from her critics—or pesticides from her adversaries.

NATURE'S SAINT JOAN

By 1963, Rachel had experienced (in Dickens' language), "the best of times" and "the worst of times." For example, abundant praise and damnation of her work sprang simultaneously from high places. Although every public appearance felt like a dagger in her back, each was also another nail in a much larger coffin, one that was slowly closing upon the pseudo-regulated pesticide companies.

Due to her haunted conscience, Rachel Carson felt a strong compulsion to reach the largest possible audience through *CBS Reports*. Earlier she had written her confidant and paramour, Dorothy, that "knowing what I do, there would be no future peace for me if I kept silent."

Rachel knew that it would be insufficient to simply complain, so she proposed alternative, more natural ways to limit the damage caused by insects. She felt she could appeal to the government and public with these alternatives she presented within her writing and media appearances. Although not a crusader by nature, Rachel was labeled the "St. Joan of the environment" for her persistent advocacy.

Each step that she had taken, whether publishing chapters in the *New Yorker*, giving interviews to NBC and the *New York Times*, accepting high-profile awards and honorary degrees, or working with the President's Science Advisory Committee, had added increasing pressure to examine overuse and abuse. Each was another speed bump on the wild road to eliminate pesticide overkill.

But each was also another power drain on Rachel's heart. And the impact was not just upon Rachel Carson, the biologist, but also upon "Mom," Roger's mother; upon "dear Rachel", Dorothy's best friend; upon Rachel Carson, progressive women's new role model; upon "St. Rachel," the voice for the voiceless; and upon "Miss Carson," as the president called her—nature's protector.

Fighting possible collapse, she doubted that she should also continue to fight the leviathan. She had told Dorothy that the CBS decision could be her undoing. Strong vectors pulled her in opposite directions, and she felt deeply divided about the marathon-like interview.

Seen from one angle, she was no stranger to adversity. Far more than a survivor, she was a victor and trailblazer. Though she had lost some battles, she never lost sight of why she fought. And Rachel had also triumphed.

From another angle, her most formidable opponent was not Robert White-Stevens, but rather the status quo. The "scientific" premises of reigning experts seemed like sound arguments to a naïve public. The number-one premise held that pesticides killed the carriers of disease. Premise number two stated that far more people could be fed when pests were eliminated. Finally, a third premise proclaimed that pesticides protected the livelihoods of farmers and related professions such as grocers and truckers.

Still other arguments maintained that pesticides helped the economy and the medical profession. They protected children in developing countries ravaged by epidemics. Pesticide production provided jobs, research grants, and in many cases sizable incomes for thousands of employees—scientists, manufacturers, sprayers, crop-dusters, PR firms, etc.—affiliated with chemical companies.

Rachel was up against not only the paid hecklers and gadflies, but also the conventional wisdom that pesticides helped people, were tested by neutral scientists, and were regulated by informed government agencies.

All of these factors weighed upon Miss Carson as she contemplated her next step. In the back of her head were the secret fears, the ones never discussed, the ones that felt like a razor next to her heart.

THE UNDISCLOSED FEARS

What were they?

There was one fear she could not express to anyone, except possibly to Dorothy. However, the subject matter might deeply disturb her friend, so Rachel was uncertain whether to confide in her or take it to the grave, forever undisclosed.

It was the fear of being found out. In later decades it would be called the fear of being "outed." For Rachel to have a close woman friend in the early 1960s was acceptable, even commendable, if it were the right woman. But what if that woman proved to be more than a friend? In 1963, being identified as a middle-aged lesbian having an affair could quickly play into the hands of her critics and the tabloids.

Such exposure could also have pressured, or even ended, the great sweetness that she and Dorothy had known. Just as the publicity about Marie Curie's affair (chapter 6) had ended Curie's association with Langevin, a publicized affair with a woman, especially a married woman, could have deeply damaged and possibly terminated her only and cherished romance.

Such a scandal would also have inflamed the misogyny already aimed at Carson. And what impact would it have had upon Roger? Whatever the nobility of her cause, above all Carson was compelled to protect the people closest to her—Dorothy and Roger. But if she could be undermined by runaway gossip writ large in the tabloids, what would come of her forward strides for the species she loved?

Her critics had already launched a parade of put-downs— "old maid," "tomboy," "tree-hugger," "bitch," "spinster," and "Miss Quixote," to name a few. Would they then add all the codewords for "lesbian" and "adulterer," if not the words themselves? Added to that would have been the story of Dorothy's emasculated and cuckolded husband, who was in fact Rachel's close friend. Carson's chemical industry adversaries would love the smell of another type of chemistry—an affair, especially one with kinky implications.

Once that secret was revealed, what would Roger have been called by his classmates? Could he ever have understood? Her life was already on the verge of being dangerously exposed with no place to hide. Why should she have moved further toward, rather than away from, the public spotlight?

After all, Dorothy could never be exposed: she had been Rachel's sweet spot in life and her great escape. She needed the greatest protection. Dorothy and her husband Stan had met Rachel in 1953, when Carson purchased a summer home in Maine on an island close to their own residence. Although Rachel quickly befriended Stan, it was Dorothy who proved to be her "cosmic mate." They shared a deep love of nature walks, poetry, and soul-bearing conversations. At the end of 1953, their correspondence had grown from chatty news to professions of love and the planning of secret getaways.

By 1954, the two consistently referred to each other as "darling" in an increasingly deep correspondence, which included "apples," their codeword for letters within letters. Inside each envelope was a newsy letter they could share with family and friends, and a far more discrete second letter that each read alone. These confidential epistles intensified a passionate romance.

On February 6, Rachel wrote Dorothy such a strong declaration of love that, when looking back, Rachel and Dorothy chose that day as their anniversary. Soon they proceeded into full spectrum involvement—multiple long-distance phone calls, frequent "apples," and another escape rendezvous while Stan was travelling.

If Rachel's visits to her doctors were the agony, then her visits to be alone with Dorothy were the ecstasy. She had never been happier.

However, no explicitly sexual comments appeared in their intimate writing. Such decorum may have been due to their personalities, social taboos, discernment, or mutual emphasis upon the strong platonic and romantic sides of their relationship. In any event, there was no tangible way to prove or disprove the extent of their erotic involvement. So, a case could be made that they were merely platonic, naturalist soulmates, like Emerson and Thoreau.

Still, Rachel was well aware of how their friendship would appear. Smart journalists or lawyers could have shown evidence of an affair, including hotel records of long-awaited trysts in private settings, hushed phone calls, lengthy time alone in bedrooms, written euphemisms ("you know what I mean," "our special time," etc.) in their correspondence, and of course the secretive nature of the "apples." The press, town gossips, and Rachel's critics could have easily launched an obscene scandal that would have ended Rachel's career, Dorothy's marriage, and their romance.

The second unmentionable fear loomed just as large—the implications of her cancer to her critics. Would a patient, whose health and lucidity were waning, have had any scientific credibility? Would greybeards in lab jackets have considered her to be no longer sound of mind, and thereby unfit to conduct research?

She also knew that some adversaries would twist things and cry "conflict of interest." How could someone with cancer be neutral when positing that pesticides are a cause of cancer? Wasn't she really just lashing out at those who, at least in her mind, had caused her illness? Wasn't her research tainted by both feebleness of mind and impure motive? How could she be an objective professional in such a state?

No wonder she had asked members of her family to lie when journalists asked about her health. No wonder she was even more anxious that the cancer was spreading, and undoubtedly irreversible. No wonder she would not like a camera crew staying in her home—so close to her real condition—so close to Roger—so close to Dorothy's apples—and within earshot of phone calls from doctors and Dorothy.

Worry about these secrets ate away at Rachel.

And yet... she was just one living being. There were literally millions of other beings who were being tortured and killed by pesticides. Who would speak for them, if not Rachel? Would not humanity itself be at greater risk if more and more humans ingested toxic crops, water, and meat?

On balance, she could sum up the situation quickly. Roger and Dorothy were extremely important, as was her credibility and health. But could they really compare to humanity and the web of life?

What to do?

THE WIND AT HER BACK

Whatever the "slings and arrows of outrageous fortune" she, like Hamlet, faced at her front, Carson also felt support at her back. Her mother, Maria, who lived with her until death, had been alternatively her caregiver, housekeeper, secretary, comforter, and advocate. Mary Scott Skinker, Carson's college biology teacher, strongly influenced her to become a scientist and to follow her to Johns Hopkins University's graduate school. There both women had succeeded within an almost entirely male academic discipline. Both Maria and Mary played key roles as mentors who cultivated Carson's early appreciation for the micro-kingdoms of zoology, botany, and biology.

While Miss Carson found occasional inspiration in the works of writers like Henry Williamson and naturalists like William Jefferies, she gained her daily backing from strong teammates such as her publicist and manager, Marie Rodell, and of course her closest intimate, Dorothy Freeman. The catalyst for *Silent Spring* was Olga Huckins, a friend who was outraged about the pesticide-induced deaths of the birds in her Massachusetts nature sanctuary. Noting that these birds and other animals had suffered painful convulsions, Olga wrote both her newspaper and Rachel with dire concern.

There were many other "Olgas," whether within the Sierra Clubs, or working on farms, parks, and campuses, who would write Rachel letters of encouragement, news, and appreciation. These letters often reduced her suffering, as Rachel saved them to read just before heading to her "bed of nails" late at night.

Beyond such human allies, Carson had another source of backing—nature itself. She loved prolonged visits to the ocean, developed deep communion with her cats, and studied each sea creature as if it were a personal friend—always returning living specimens from the oceanside to exactly where she found them.

Although not overtly religious, Carson had Presbyterian roots that bequeathed to her a sense of a larger designed order that scientists were beginning to call "ecology." She saw such ordered beauty as important and wrote:

> I believe natural beauty has a necessary place in the spiritual development of any individual and society. Whenever we destroy beauty or substitute something man-made and artificial for a natural feature of the earth, we have retarded man's spiritual growth.

Embedded within such a statement was a sense that Carson not only had (primarily masculine) adversaries in front of her, and a feminine wind at her back, but she also was motivated by an inner spiritual gulf stream.

One aspect of her interior values might be seen as an environmental aesthetic, closely linked to Schweitzer's "reverence for life." Indeed, *Silent Spring* is dedicated to Schweitzer. Carson knew that Albert went out of his way to avoid stepping on insects and would not tear even one leaf from a tree. He thought of such reverence as an expression of the "ultimate ethic," for which he had searched many years.

AN ETHICS OF LIFE AND OF CARE

At the heart of Schweitzer's ethic was a respect for the volition, or will, to live inherent in all beings. Behind Carson's purpose is this same guiding principle that life itself—not money, not power, not fame, not ideology—is both *a priori* and a priority.

Such an ethic might be seen as antecedent to Nel Nodding's ethics of care. Unlike the previous, more abstract ethical systems of Aristotle, Kant, and Mill, twenty-first century feminists such as Noddings, Carol Gilligan, and others have honored the importance of life, and the need to care for it with compassion. Of great importance to Noddings is the primacy of relationship— the person caring and the person cared for take on a flesh-and-blood importance, which is given more emphasis than abstract notions of justice or truth.

For Carson this care extended to all forms of life, not merely to human beings. Two primary reasons for this are that: 1) in Schweitzer's terms, each living being has intrinsic worth, and 2) even if human beings are deemed the only or most important life, human existence depends upon the well being of animals, insects, and plants. Hence it becomes necessary to care about all life and life's home, the planet itself.

INDIGENOUS ETHICS AND MILL RECONSIDERED

Nothing about Carson's ethic would have surprised most indigenous peoples. For example, many Native American nations felt you should not kill an animal or tree until there would be a use for all of it. The idea of shooting game for sport or just for the antlers, pelt, or scent of an animal (as in perfume manufacturing) seemed wasteful and disrespectful. Most early indigenous tribes worldwide shared a strong communion with life. When it became necessary to kill a fellow creature, they might first thank the animal, or often ask its permission.

While Rachel did not go to this extreme, her mother and life itself had taught her long ago that each miniature life form was sentient, likely sensitive to pain, and above all a teammate in the web of life. An ethic featuring environmental care, protection, and stewardship was essential.

Such an inclusive vision requires that John Stuart Mill's ethical thinking be seen in a new light. Should Mill (and his thought partner, Jeremy Bentham) have asked, in this situation, "what is the greatest good for the greatest number?" one would have to ask in return, "number of what?" When taken into account, the number of birds, fish, insects, squirrels, pets, and all else, changes Mill's math ratio considerably. The utilitarian English philosopher also argued that one must consider not only numbers, but also the intensity, fruitfulness, and other factors associated with each ethical decision. Surely, the intensity of a painful death from excessive pesticide spray and the fruitfulness of a healthy planet are worth more than the happiness that relatively few elite human beings derive from corporate profits.

Moreover, there is the ethical question of justice. While the great thinkers on this topic, such as Abraham Lincoln in the White House and John Rawls on Harvard's campus, championed important arguments for the fair treatment of each adult, one must also ask what voice children, animals, insects, and plants must have in decisions which concern their welfare?

Adult human beings in many countries presumably have the right to vote for or against those who uphold or ignore environmental policies. But what voting rights or voice do cows have when their food is poisoned? Or ducks coated by oil slicks? Or trees when their entire families are felled for human profit? Or children exposed to carcinogenic DDT at the beach, or lead paint in their homes?

Rachel Carson wished to give voice to the voiceless. In that light, her appearance on CBS would not deprive Roger of a mother so much as speak out for all the children like him and protect their future against a poisoned planet. If numbers mattered, and if intensity and fruitfulness counted, and if life in all its variety mattered, Carson knew she was speaking for a sizable, vital, and crucial silent majority.

AND THE WINNER IS...

When all was said and done, and when all the factors had been considered, Rachel Carson knew what she had to do. All along, "nature's Joan of Arc" sensed that, if she could function and speak intelligibly during the interview, and if she had sufficient strength, then she was obligated to continue her mission. Once she decided to write *Silent Spring*, Carson had known she could not escape the consequences of tilting with corporate windmills.

Of course, at many moments she would have preferred to be by the sea with her specimens, playing a game with Roger, or resting in bed. However, her pain grew from one body location to many others in all but heart-stopping fashion—indeed, her heart had stopped before. So no activity, even one by the sea, was an escape from discomfort.

Whatever the roadblocks, Carson's integrity compelled her to speak truth into the chamber of deception. She knew she should try to complete the race, even if her tank was running on empty.

Each day the decision had to be faced anew, but as for this day...

Rachel Carson would speak for the speechless on *CBS Reports*, even if she had to be constantly seated to stand tall. Her personal voice of conscience and persistence had won the inner duel.

Despite the men and bright lights living under her roof, the CBS prolonged interview went as well as could be expected. The program, still visible in video excerpts online, has since been viewed by millions. The initial audience perception was mostly that Rachel was more genuine, level-headed, and convincing than those opponents who seemed like corporate hit men or histrionic henchmen. To more discerning members of the television audience, Robert White-Stephens seemed a melodramatic, fear-mongering extremist. And Harvard graduate President John F. Kennedy, who had been alerted to view the program, which featured both scientists like Carson and obvious "guns for hire" for the corporations on the program, took note.

Another nail had been driven.

Although she would die just five months later, this one true scientist at the tip of the arrow had affected enormous penetration. Within three years the U.S. Environmental Protection Agency was created, "within the expanded shadow of Rachel Carson." Many years later, Earth Day, *An Inconvenient Truth*, the banning of DDT, numerous laws such as the Environmental Protection Act, and many environmental foundations, clubs, and agencies also now live within that shadow.

THE INTERVIEW AND THE INNER VIEW

On April 3, 1963, *CBS Reports* was seen by Americans nationwide. Rachel ultimately triumphed, and another screw had been driven into the coffin of corporate ecocide.

Yet Rachel had paid the price. Her inner view was quite different than the interview. She wrote Dorothy that for the entire two days of filming she was in "a state of exhaustion." Afraid that she could not control her body, she seldom moved it and unknowingly spoke with what she later called "an unnaturally husky voice."

As always, there were also hostile critics launching yet another wave of flaming arrows. She knew that no good deed would go unpunished, and as predicted, harassing calls to CBS and nasty letters to Rachel were in full supply.

Still viewed frequently online to this day, *CBS Reports* became a classic that has now been screened by millions. Her decision and testimony helped to change the world. Of course, Carson gave credit to others, such as the team of women at her back—her mother Maria, her lover Dorothy, her mentor Mary Skinker, her publicist and manager Marie Rodell, and the catalyst for *Silent Spring*, Olga Hutchins.

There were also leading men in Rachel's life, whom she knew only from their writings. Naturalists like William Jefferies and Henry Williamson provided published inspiration that she loved to read.

One other man in particular, whom she greatly admired, had catalyzed the Carson philosophy. She would give him her highest honor—*Silent Spring* is dedicated to Albert Schweitzer.

THE TEN FACTORS

1. **Notions of fairness and justice:** In Carson's expanded democracy, justice is not only for corporations or even for humanity, but for all life. For her, it was not as if each species or living form should vote, but rather a recognition that they all count and are essential to our overall survival. So, the elimination of one species is not only unjust to that species but also to all the others. Hence, notions of justice are radically altered by Carson, and point toward an ethic that might be called *environmental justice* or *full-spectrum fairness*.

2. **Impact or consequences:** In a worst-case scenario, ignoring environmental justice means omnicide, or the end of all life. While Carson was not an extremist, she realized that at the very least, the consequences meant serious harm to many, if not all species. She realized that the limited use of pesticides might also have positive short-term consequences, and that these needed to be weighed against the long-term ramifications of untested side effects and unintended problems for future generations. Ultimately, she felt that tighter regulation and better research were needed to reduce the ratio of negative to positive consequences. Although other factors mattered to Carson, it was the dire outcomes produced by unlimited pesticides that catalyzed her action. The prevention of future environmental damage was of utmost importance.

3. **Ends and means:** Television was hardly Carson's preferred means of publicity. It was reductive, edited by others, often superficial or sensational, and foreign to her style. Nevertheless, reaching the largest

possible audience was important, since that meant preventing as many fatalities and harmful side effects as possible. She would have preferred utilizing scholarly journals and scientific books for the public, but television was tempting due to its universal audience, including the illiterate, semi-literate, youth, and those with minimal time. And if she did not use TV, she knew her critics would. In this case, the ends seemed more important than belittling the lowest common denominator of means. She also had to consider if total self-sacrifice was the means by which her message could be conveyed. Was the end worth martyrdom? Could not others deliver her message for her? Still, all of her means were honest and transparent (except for the hiding of her health condition), so the question of ends and means was not her most important one.

4. **Tone and atmosphere:** Ironically, it was the lower tone of relatively uncultured commercial television which would allow Carson's higher tone to stand out in contrast to her critics. Other, more caustic voices would look over-the-top compared to the reasoned, balanced, yet obviously concerned humanist. Tone was important to Carson, who did not wish to be associated with violent extremists or an atmosphere of vilification. While she had an answer for her critics, she did not wish to stoop to their lower tone of acerbic putdowns backed by bogus evidence. Although atmosphere, including Schweitzer's "reverence for life," was important, it was not as critical as for Wilberforce and Gandhi, whose religious practices made a sacred atmosphere of inner prayer crucial to their approach. Nevertheless, she wished to be credible, scientific, and balanced. Such a tone was ultimately more convincing than that of her critics.

5. **Motivation and higher law:** The sanctity of all life was a great source of inspiration for Carson. Her motivation was to preserve the higher law of nature rather than the short-sighted human legal systems often supporting corporate avarice and government complicity. To a scientist, natural laws, such as those unveiled by Newton and Einstein, will continue to work consistently, unlike human laws which are transitory and relative to culture. Her motivation was to bring human law and regulation into harmony with natural or higher law. The human attempt to control natural law was abhorrent to Carson, who knew that such efforts would backfire. Honoring the higher law of nature was essential.

6. **Allegiance and loyalty:** Although many loyalties (to scientific peers, to children, to Roger, to Dorothy, to citizens, to future generations, etc.)

were involved, Carson felt an equally strong allegiance to other species, and thus to life writ large. At many points in her life, she was torn between career and family, especially the victims of tragedy, poverty, and separation in her immediate family. She wrote quietly of her strong loyalty to her alleged lover, Dorothy, and spoke openly of her loyalty to her son and her mother. But ultimately, her highest allegiance was to another mother... Earth.

7. **Values and principles:** Survival does not seem to be a noble value like dignity, truth, and freedom, but without it the others are unachievable. Ultimately, Carson had to weigh her own survival against that of many species. Darwin's principle of "survival of the fittest" would win out if she could not stay fit to champion the survival of the voiceless. Principles such as "live to fight another day" opposed those such as "the greatest good for the greatest number," and she had to choose between almost clichéd principles such as "women and children first" and "all men are created equal." Ultimately, it was not only the survival of the species that she championed, but the well-being of their inter-dependent ecology. Wasn't the preservation of this natural fabric more valuable than her own life and closeness with those she loved most? The most important principle might indeed have been "the greatest good for the greatest number" of living beings.

8. **Cultural context:** Unlike in India, where cows were sacred, and unlike in those indigenous tribes that honor insects, Carson lived within a culture that increasingly promoted human dominance over, not cooperation with, nature. It was a society that often devalued the views of female professionals and was increasingly focused upon quick fixes rather than protecting the next four generations as among Native American nations. During her life, no institution had risen to greater power than the multinational corporation, and there was an increasingly incestuous relationship between powerful companies and the ill-named "watchdog" government. Within such a culture, Carson had far fewer powerful supporters and more hurdles than she would have had she lived with the Amish or Aborigines. The avaricious corporate culture sought to be omnipotent.

9. **Implications:** The long-term impact of Carson's decision would be immense. If one pro-social activist could attract serious television attention, others could do so as well. Possibly pollution, and not only that of pesticides and herbicides, could be countered, if not contained and

minimized. And if one scientist could successfully brave the ostracism of the larger professional community, a precedent would be set for other honest scientists to follow. Even larger implications were that imbalanced and interrupted natural cycles could be restored if others followed in her footsteps. Insect, animal, and human health could return to homeostasis, and a far safer planet would thrive. Moreover, whistleblowers could become heroes, rather than *persona non grata*, if they persistently and patiently followed a moral compass and presented reliable evidence.

10. **Proportion and balance:** How much weight could Carson give to each of these factors? As a mother, lover, daughter, friend, scientist, and moral leader, her loyalties to those frequently seen in her world loomed large. "But what about those who are unseen?" she asked herself. Is not more loyalty owed to those without representation in Congress or a vote in human affairs? What of the twitching, fading birds drinking water poisoned by DDT? What of the deformed, diseased children breastfed by mothers who fed on cows that had feasted on pesticide-covered grass? Did not this invisible world and their generations yet to come deserve more attention than life forms already fading, such as Carson herself? Was any one family worth more than the family named "posterity?" Was the human species more important than other species, or more essential to survival? On balance, she had to give weight not to one factor or species, but rather to what already provided a natural distribution of weight to all species—equipoise. Hence, the most substantial factors for Rachel Carson were environmental justice, honoring natural (cf. higher) law, and Schweitzer's "reverence for life."

A LEGEND AND A LEGACY

Rachel Carson became the most respected and influential physical scientist of her era. While still alive, she became legendary for masterfully telling the stories of small creatures to large audiences. The *New York Times* wrote: "once or twice in a generation does the world get a physical scientist with literary genius."

Among her awards and honors were top recognition from Guggenheim, Westinghouse, *National Geographic*, Saxton, and receipt of the Albert Schweitzer Medal. Supreme Court Justice William Douglas called *Silent Spring* the "most important chronicle of this century for the human race." Senator Abraham Ribicoff, who chaired the subcommittee hearings at which Carson testified, broke with protocol and asked her to autograph his copy of *Silent Spring* not after, but during their sessions.

Ultimately, President Kennedy acknowledged Miss Carson by creating a Scientific Advisory Committee that initially examined and later endorsed her thinking. Shortly after Carson's death, Senator Rubicoff said, "today we mourn the passing of a great lady. All of mankind is in her debt."

Forty years after *Time* magazine panned *Silent Spring*, it would name her one of it's "100 Most Influential People of the 20th Century" along with fellow scientists Albert Einstein and Jonas Salk. Meanwhile, *Silent Spring* continued to be translated into eighteen languages and published worldwide.

Inducted into the American Academy of Arts and Letters, Carson also became the first woman to receive the Audubon Medal. Immortalized by a U.S. postage stamp and by the Rachel Carson Wildlife Refuge in Maine, she became first a controversial and later a saluted household name far beyond the 1960s.

The venerated scientist had been dead for sixteen years when, in 1980, President Carter awarded her America's top honor, the Presidential Medal of Freedom. Although the names of her critics have long been forgotten, Rachel Carson lives on in spirit in her widely available sea trilogy and in *Silent Spring*. You may also sit next to her at Wood's Hole, Massachusetts where, as a seated statue, she eternally writes her books while gazing toward the ocean.

Carson's spirit also lives on in what is now called the feminist "care ethic" and in an over-arching environmental ethos. Wherever there are those saving the whales, opposing nuclear power plants, and protecting endangered species, they can hear Rachel Carson's voice in the wind. She serves as a constant reminder to such advocacy minorities that "one and the truth are a majority."

Due to the courageous and agonizing decision she made that chilly night in March, Rachel Carson's actual voice lives on in *CBS Reports*, and is frequently heard on YouTube and beyond. Carson's books also populate libraries worldwide and are now mandatory reading in many classes.

Her impact could later be seen in the naming of babies and the renaming of roads and schools. But most of all, beyond all of these human tributes, her influence lives on every not-so-silent spring—and winter, fall, and summer—in the lives of millions seen and unseen all around us.

IMPLICATIONS FOR OUR LIVES

When I traveled to Maine to visit the outdoor Rachel Carson National Wildlife Refuge, I started to mindlessly apply bug spray on my unprotected arms and legs. The nature trails appeared to lead into a possible haven for mosquitoes and horseflies, and I sensed that I would be a likely target. So, I sprayed vigorously without thinking.

But then I began to question my actions. Was I spraying too much? Should I wait to spray, and do so only when I hear, feel, or see flying insects? Should I have bought the natural repellant advertised in health food stores?

At one point I thought, "maybe there won't be insects today and I am overreacting." So I wondered, "am I poisoning my own breathing air and killing other bugs who don't bite?"

Ultimately, I asked: "What would Rachel Carson do?"

The irony of my location at the Carson Refuge was not lost upon me. Although the bug spray smelled pungent and I felt I was poisoning my fresh air supply, I realized I had been socialized to accept the process of excessive spraying as a necessary evil. At that point I began to question what I was doing. I realized that I had not been thinking, I had simply engaged in what people do.

I was also compelled to realize that, although Rachel Carson did not feel comfortable being asked to preach and proselytize, she was very much at home inviting her audience to think. And there I was—a human being who had never met her—thinking about the ethical implications of a seemingly minute ethical decision—one with life-and-death consequences for miniscule yet essential habitants within nature.

Ethical practice is not always about blowing a whistle and standing tall for a cause at gunpoint. It is often involved with simply thinking further and more deeply about how much to say... or spray.

Great ethicists do not just live on only in our libraries, statues, and memorials. They live on in our consciousness. They, and Rachel Carson among them, still pose the question: "How deeply and wisely are we thinking?"

Miss Carson, as she was called by President Kennedy, lives on in today's ethos of environmental reform, in the lives of whistle-blowers who swim against the tide, and in the thousands of women and girls working and striving in scientific fields to make the world a better place. Rachel's courageous voice still ripples through our collective consciousness over YouTube archives of *CBS Reports*, across the pages of her literary classics, and most importantly in the lives of all creatures, large and small, that constitute the great web of life.

CHAPTER 10

EDWARD R. MURROW
(1908-1965)

THE CAMERA IS MIGHTIER THAN THE SWORD

"Do you think I'm doing the right thing?" Edward R. Murrow had asked his reporter, Eddie Scott. In March 1954, Murrow faced a daunting ethical dilemma. He had reached the point of no return.

To anyone at a distance, little seemed amiss with these two drink-devouring colleagues, both named Ed. But from Eddie Scott's close-up view across the table, he could see Ed Murrow's twitching hands as Murrow repeatedly coughed.

Alternatively ingesting alcohol and smoke, Murrow explained that he had been walking the streets of Manhattan for hours trying to sort it all out. Premature, dark ducts under his forty-six-year-old eyes were the product of years of international travel, incessant deadlines, censorship disputes, and sleepless hours jay-walking city streets.

"What if Ed Murrow and CBS–TV are about to irresponsibly destroy the reputation and career of a U.S. senator and his family?" Murrow asked Scott.

"And what if that senator is about to irresponsibly destroy the reputation of CBS, Edward R. Murrow, and his family?" Scott replied.

Television had only recently accrued enough viewers and hypnotic power to deliver a deathblow to a human subject. As a man of conscience, Murrow was concerned that he could destroy a U.S. senator, his young family, and the public's trust in CBS to be objective.

A crumpled napkin was lifted to his mouth to arrest the chronic hacking. Years of chain-smoking had led to one fit after another.

Murrow's tired eyes swept the dimly lit restaurant to see if he could be overheard by anyone who might be an informer to "the three H's"—Hoover, the Hearst Papers, or HUAC—the dreaded House Un-American Activities Committee. In an age of paranoia, everyone was suspect of being either a communist "red" or an informer. Even the bartender and waiter were scrutinized.

Ed firmly reminded Eddie Scott that if their program, *See It Now*, looked like a smear campaign against the senator, they would be enraging a major Republican leader backed by the president of the United States, as well as an effective propaganda machine. Both knew that "Tail-Gunner Joe," the nickname given to Wisconsin Senator Joseph McCarthy, was an attack shark who seldom lashed out at just one victim.

For example, when "the HUAC boys" had successfully convicted the State Department's rising star, Alger Hiss, of being a communist in 1950, they had also implicated the Secretary of State, the State Department, and thus the U.S. government. Similarly, the Wisconsin demagogue had also reprimanded the senate at large, major universities, and Hollywood when accusing individual senators, professors, and media celebrities of being red or "pink" (i.e. soft on communism).

Unknowingly wrenching his napkin, Murrow concluded that any attack on Ed and Eddie would also target CBS writ large, and thus indict their producer, Fred Friendly. Also guilty by association would be their sponsor, Alcoa Aluminum; several CBS affiliate stations nationwide; their families; and independent-minded journalists and free speech advocates elsewhere. Both men knew that Joseph McCarthy would employ what Ed called a "personal Gestapo" of vicious lawyers, tabloid barracudas, FBI informers, HUAC (House Un-American Activities Committee) prosecutors, and feared right-wing "patriotic" publications, *Red Channels* and *Counter-Attack*, that outed and listed "secret communists."

Murrow also confessed to Eddie his concerns about his family. Death threats and hate mail had repeatedly reached him and CBS. "Janet's going to be away. So I am asking the in-laws to watch Casey," he anxiously relayed to Scott point-blank.

Murrow expanded that his eight-year-old son, Casey, was now branded "a dirty commie" by his elementary school classmates. These students were too young to know what they were talking about, but his son was nevertheless ostracized, afraid, and confused. Had his dad suddenly become America's enemy? Murrow started to iterate that Casey must be watched at all…

Before he could finish, the hacker's cough violently interrupted, followed by an ominous wheezing. Quite concerned, Scott noted that special uniformed officers had already been hired to safeguard the lobby of CBS. He wondered if Murrow would be hiring a bodyguard.

"Not yet," Ed replied, "but Casey will need to be constantly chauffeured and chaperoned. I've gotten used to the death threats toward me, but one came yesterday addressed to me, Janet, and Casey. Eddie, you can't get used to death threats addressed to your wife and child."

THE BEGINNING OF THE END

How had all this started? As early as October 27, 1947, Murrow experienced déjà vu when he witnessed House Un-American Activities Committee (HUAC) proceedings. The veteran journalist immediately broadcast: "...this reporter approaches the matter with rather fresh memories of friends in Austria, Germany, and Italy who died or went into exile because they refused to admit the right of their government to determine what they should say, read, write or think."

Murrow was clearly concerned about First Amendment violations, if not outright fascism in the United States. Behind closed doors, FBI director J. Edgar Hoover took notice of Murrow's editorial.

At that time, Hollywood "red" (i.e. communist) screen writers were also being publicly prosecuted by the same House Committee (HUAC). In response, Murrow again editorialized that HUAC had crossed a line violating citizen rights of free speech and free association. Hoover's FBI then began a more comprehensive background check on Murrow. To Hoover, being an *anti-anti*-Communist was just as red as being a card-carrying member of the Communist Party. Murrow seemed decidedly un-American.

By 1948, the razor-sharp pendulum of anti-Communism swung closer to Murrow's chest. A close friend and European correspondent, George Polk, was found on May 16th floating in the shallows of a Greek harbor with a bullet hole in his head, his hands and feet tied. His body was found bobbing up and down eight days after Polk was reported missing.

Only seven months later Laurence Duggan, an admired friend and the son of Murrow's former mentor, was found dead on the sidewalks of Manhattan beside his smashed glasses. He had jumped or fallen from his office sixteen floors above, where an overshoe for his right foot was found. Duggan's blood-drenched left foot was wearing the other one. Laurence's wife and four children were shell-shocked and heartbroken.

These 1948 deaths devastated Murrow and he was outraged that both were blamed on "the communists." Although Polk was allegedly executed by Greek communists, Murrow and others suspected a cover-up with red scapegoats.

Similarly, Duggan's suicide was blamed upon his close association with communists who had just been exposed by HUAC. However, upon closer examination, the House Un-American Activities Committee realized that Lawrence Duggan might have been innocent of any charges. A zealous up-and-coming HUAC lawyer and congressman named Richard Nixon soon acknowledged that there had been what he called "misunderstandings."

But Laurence Duggan had already taken his life, so Murrow quickly galvanized high level officials to make statements protecting Duggan's reputation. Nixon looked slick, if not suspect, to Murrow. Although others were saying that 1948 was Murrow's "best year ever" due to his trophy room full of new awards, this was also his year of agony about both political and personal tragedy.

Murrow told friends he was thinking about speaking out against the bullies within the United States. But would that be responsible journalism? Would that be career suicide?

On March 13, 1949, Edward R. Murrow was flummoxed by the courtroom antics of Senator Joseph McCarthy in the Senate Caucus Room. Seated within the press section, Ed watched an obese, aggressive, and over-heated Senator ruthlessly throw accusations at Secretary of State Acheson about protecting communists within the State Department. McCarthy seemed to relish self-righteous condescension toward esteemed statesmen and decorated war heroes.

Ed could not believe that the hatemongering, sinister senator, with the high-pitched, irritable laughter, had seized a venerated congressional podium and turned it into a nationally televised bully pulpit. The journalist had now found his own public enemy number one, the same Senator from Wisconsin who reminded him of recent European dictators. Ed quickly wrote a friend that "the whole McCarthy business is squalid beyond words."

By 1950, Murrow had seen enough of the HUAC and McCarthy "witch trials," and wrote that in a democracy even witches and accused witches were protected by the Bill of Rights. He watched anxiously as CBS colleagues such as Howard K. Smith and Alexander Kendrick were named in *Red Channels*, a book fingering 151 broadcasters suspected of having ties to communism. He managed to save both of their careers, but all three—Kendrick, Smith, and Murrow—knew they were being closely watched.

With the advent of the half-hour news program *See It Now* in 1951, Ed Murrow and his producer, Fred Friendly, feared that they would become targets of HUAC as they observed the red purge from front-row seats. Soon CBS news staff had to be protected from smear campaigns in *Counter Attack*, the newsletter affiliated with *Red Channels*. Still other colleagues angrily contested the need to sign a loyalty oath that disclaimed any proximity to the Communist Party.

An old friend and CBS employee, Deirdre Mason, anxiously asked to see Ed for advice about the loyalty oath. She had been dismissed from working on a show until she signed. Other reputed colleagues including Bill Downs, Don Hollenbeck, and Howard K. Smith all told Ed they were counting on him to strongly oppose the mandatory pledge. And yet the oath became a harsh reality. No one was exempt.

When Murrow first interviewed McCarthy on *See It Now* in 1952, he felt the angry pit bull's teeth. Instead of answering Murrow's questions about the rights of those testifying to the committee, McCarthy ignored him and lashed out at fellow Senator William Benton of Connecticut.

The talented CBS reporter Bill Downs began urging Murrow not once but chronically to "do something about McCarthy." By 1953, Downs had become so relentless that Bill's wife, Roz, could predict when Downs would be lobbying Ed and would give Murrow a head's up. Although Downs launched the largest McCarthy salvo to Murrow, he was hardly alone.

Meanwhile, there were also others shouting, "do something about Murrow!" In 1953, media outlets owned by H.L. Hunt, the wealthy oilman in Texas, broadcast rants about Murrow's so-called "tainted leanings." A Dallas broadcaster said that Murrow would be revealed as "the Alger Hiss of broadcasting."

Not far away, another Hunt-affiliated radio commentator in Houston falsely exposed Murrow as one of the "directors of the Moscow summer school." It was common knowledge that H.L. Hunt also bankrolled McCarthy.

Although he knew that these sensational Texas broadcasts were deliberately presented without context, Murrow felt the HUAC-sharpened blade inching even closer. He had become Poe's central character in "The Pit and the Pendulum."

THE SURINE INCIDENT

While he sensed that a Pearl Harbor-type sneak attack would be aimed at him, Murrow never guessed it would be an indirect ambush of Wershba by Surine. On November 17, 1953, while Murrow's CBS reporter Joe Wershba was covering hearings in Washington, D. C., he was shocked to see McCarthy's lead investigator, Donald Surine, blocking his path like a linebacker as he left the hearing room.

Surine was licking his lips to show Wershba two photostats of pages from a 1935 Hearst newspaper in Pittsburgh, which supposedly proved that Ed Murrow had been on the Soviet payroll. Before showcasing the article, Surine ranted that he was unhappy with Murrow's recent *See It Now* episode about Milo Radulovich, a reserve officer on trial by the U.S. Army.

Surine was livid. He could not believe that Murrow had made it seem that "Radwich" was wrongly framed because his relatives had allegedly been involved with left wing activity and publications.

The Radulovich episode of *See It Now* had indeed warned against both guilt by association and ignoring legal due process. Although McCarthy's concern was security leaks, Murrow's concern was McCarthy. Surine rattled his saber about "Radwich" for what seemed like eternity, and then absconded with Wershba upstairs into what appeared to be McCarthy's office.

Joe Wershba knew that the shadowy Surine had been accused of doctoring documents in the past and could not be trusted. Nevertheless the stories looked genuine and seemed sufficient to tarnish, if not torpedo, Murrow when presented in a false light. Just before Murrow's reporter could scramble away to find his sound man, Surine added one last thinly veiled threat. Taunting Wershba, he shouted, "isn't it something that Murrow's brother is an officer in the Air Force?"

Once Murrow heard from Wershba about Surine's shades-of-blackmail, he realized McCarthy was sending a strong message: "Back off or we will nail you… and your brother." All around him, friends had been vivisected and humiliated. Would Murrow and family be next?

Ed would be sent other warning signals too when the State Department refused to offer him a passport unless he signed the loyalty oath. Even his body had sent him signals when he recently collapsed after a *See It Now* episode in Korea. Given his congenital pulmonary condition exacerbated by deadline pressures and chain-smoking, Murrow had also collapsed at other moments of peak stress in his life. So, he faced another kind of enemy within, and realized that major confrontations with goliaths like McCarthy could leave him literally breathless.

Once he had seen the photostats that Wershba delivered from Surine, Murrow's resolve intensified. He considered creating a McCarthy episode, if not an exposé, on *See It Now*. Surine's ambush had backfired.

On November 24th, just one week after the Surine episode, Murrow asked Friendly how much McCarthy footage had been archived. He was especially interested in finding documentation of a speech given by "Jeering Joe" in Wheeling, West Virginia. When none seemed available, Murrow requested that an audiotape be located.

Ed remained uncertain of McCarthy's next steps. Was Surine signaling an imminent Murrow inquisition? Or was he only telling *See It Now* to keep quiet about HUAC? Either way, Murrow knew that the best defense was an effective offense. It was high noon at the O.K. Corral. In the absence of any moral leadership, shouldn't Murrow play sheriff?

WHAT ABOUT CBS?

By January 1954, Ed Murrow and Fred Friendly were determined to create their McCarthy exposé soon. The idea was met with mixed feelings when broached with higher-ups and legal minds.

While his boss and friend William Paley initially sent word that he was supporting Murrow in January, by February Paley indicated privately that he had reservations about an episode spearing McCarthy. He did not wish to screen it.

Fred Friendly could not find one CBS executive willing to discuss or preview the program. It was as if everyone on the higher floors wished to distance themselves, so that if there were recriminations from HUAC, they could say later that they had no idea what *See It Now* had been preparing.

Nevertheless, both Paley and CBS president Frank Stanton made clear that the odd couple, Friendly and Murrow, should move quickly in order to beat McCarthy to the punch. *See It Now* should also offer Joe equal time for rebuttal in a later episode before McCarthy could demand it himself.

It soon became apparent that *See It Now* had also been abandoned by CBS's publicity arm. The word that came down from above was that if they wanted advertising, Fred and Ed would personally and atypically have to pay the *New York Times* $1500 for the announcement. Furthermore, any such ad could not carry the CBS logo or any trace of the corporation and their sponsor.

CBS executives then notified the FBI that a controversial episode about the Senator would air on Tuesday night. To Ed and his producer, such behavior indicated that "the suits" were doing all they could to protect only themselves, not Friendly, not Murrow, and not the *See It Now* staff. Were Ed, Friendly, and their crew being set up as the fall guys?

So, when Ed Murrow asked Eddie Scott if it was right to proceed with this program, he did not just mean morally right as a responsible journalist and American. He was also asking if he was doing the right thing ethically if he wished to be accountable to their endangered families, their skittish employer, a vulnerable crew, and all who might be targets of retaliation.

ROBIN HOOD THE RED

By the outset of 1954, the Red Scare hysteria became so extreme that even the legendary figure Robin Hood was under attack as a communist. Would the schools take all Robin Hood literature out of the library because he stole from the rich to give to the poor? Many journalists, parents, and educators were aghast.

A friend of Murrow's who could relate to Robin Hood's plight had been blacklisted. He asked Ed to be a witness in a libel suit against *Red Channels*. Knowing he would be at greater risk, Murrow nevertheless replied: "Just tell me the time and place."

Meanwhile, McCarthy was publicly roasting another decorated war hero, General Ralph Zwicker, for promoting an army dentist whose crime was pleading the Fifth Amendment. Murrow was keen to protect many such witch trial victims, and built episodes of *See It Now* around similar persons of interest, including a Catholic priest, a Pentagon worker named Annie Lee Moss, and leaders of the ACLU. Once again, Murrow asked Friendly to review and enlarge their stash of McCarthy film.

During the last week of February 1954, an internal rift in the Republican party surfaced. There were growing signs of inner opposition to McCarthy's methods. Murrow read this as a favorable tea leaf and a crack in McCarthy's armor. Despite his inner debate, Ed discretely told his crew that the McCarthy episode was on for March 9th.

Work on the program soon reached a fever pitch, with Murrow overseeing far more details than usual. The production crew felt an intent surveillance during every editing session. Busyness abounded as the team struggled to splice just the right combinations of shots, to fact-check and then double-check, and to rethink where Ed would add commentary.

They took informal shifts, then slept only briefly and occasionally to keep pace. At some points, Murrow asked for triple-checking, since one small error could prove to be their Achilles tendon.

Ed was secretly elated on Saturday, March 6th, when Democratic leader Adlai Stevenson publicly forecast on radio and TV that a divided Republican Party, half McCarthy and half Eisenhower, could not produce national unity. It was another chink in the armor of the black knight, and it was foreshadowing that Murrow's "D-Day" should be planned.

A VEXING DECISION

Nevertheless, Murrow was having second thoughts when he went for drinks with Scott. His wife Janet had said she felt a spine-tingling chill when she realized Ed would take on McCarthy. And it was Janet who would suffer the most if "Tail-Gunner Joe" not only hyped Ed's 1930's administrative affairs with the Russians, but also exposed his other affairs with actress Marlene Dietrich, socialite Pamela (Digby) Churchill, and possibly others.

What fish stories would Hoover, Hearst, HUAC, and especially the hawkish senator embroider with those rumors? Ed feared that J. Edgar would invite him behind closed doors to field questions about racy photographs.

CBS was also importing a sharp legal mind to vet its own employees and to help identify, if not terminate, any who looked pink enough to endanger the company. Little could Ed know that colleagues would be pressured to leave CBS, and even commit suicide, within the next three months. When he eyeballed the armed guards now stationed in the CBS lobby, he was also reminded that the network was receiving menacing calls demanding Murrow's scalp and targeting top-floor execs.

He knew from firsthand experience that not all death threats were crank calls, and he knew that throughout history many of those who were assassinated had received death threats just days or weeks before. For eight-year-old Casey, who had no understanding of world politics, the threats were from some of his former classmates at school, who could no longer socialize with him. Their parents had forbidden them. Ed had no answer for third-grade blackballing and bullying, or for vicious letters with no return addresses written to his wife and son.

By March 1954, the hate mail was not only being sent to Murrow's home address but even to his hideaway in the country. Not all of these vitriolic attacks were anonymous. Newspaper and magazine ink would soon flow like venom denouncing Murrow's "commie" background, loss of credibility, and supposed disloyalty.

In light of all this, Ed was not sure that he was the right hitman for this job. He was a journalist, not a character assassin. Even the president and secretary of state would not publicly confront the rogue senator. What would happen if a broadcaster did so? Indeed, there was a clause in his CBS contract pledging that he would be scrupulously neutral. Journalists were hired and paid to report, not to engage in reckless bias and personal vendettas.

Both Eds knew that they had two more episodes of *See It Now* in their back pocket ready for broadcast. So, they were not necessarily forced to tilt with the McCarthy windmill. Why not play it safe and air something less controversial?

A decision had to be made by the following night about whether to broadcast that Tuesday. If they went with the McCarthy episode, they would have to rapidly chisel their rough cut—which contained three hours of footage—down to thirty minutes.

Ed surveyed the restaurant again for possible eavesdroppers. His prolonged cough turned to oxygen-starved wheezing before subsiding. Eddie was not quick to reply. After all, Scott had recently seen the fire in McCarthy's eyes when he angrily told their CBS crew to stop filming him. Eddie had also been held by the police while on a location shoot for Murrow. Moreover, Scott was previously employed by the left-leaning program *PM*, a flashing yellow light that no Hoover-boy would miss. The reply to Murrow's question would not be an easy one... for Eddie Scott nor for Ed Murrow.

CONFLICTING ETHICAL FORCES...

Murrow knew that a large number of ethical principles were being violated by the Senator—innocent until proven guilty, freedom of speech, the right to face one's accuser, the right use of power and public office, the right to reply, academic freedom, guilt by evidence rather than by association, loyalty by choice and not by mandatory oath, equal rights before the law, and many more. But he also knew that he himself was treading dangerously close to a number of professional ethical transgressions regarding fair and balanced reporting; accountability to employer, sponsor, stockholders, and audience; the rights of the accused; objectivity above bias; defamation of character and libel, among others.

In short, Murrow could easily violate the standards of journalistic integrity. He would be seen as using his own trusted platform as a bully pulpit to bully a bully. Could two wrongs—those of McCarthy and those of Murrow—make a right?

There were also the ethics of consequences. If Murrow, despite noble ambitions, were to lose the battle, how many others would be destroyed with him?

This query raised another pragmatic question: "Could he win the bout?" In the boxing world, non-partisan odds makers in Las Vegas might have handicapped a Murrow-McCarthy fight as even money. The showdown would have been intense, since both were undefeated heavyweights.

IN THIS CORNER...

If they fought, then in one corner of the ring Murrow would be a formidable, undefeated challenger. The most honored broadcaster of his era, Ed had obtained celebrity status as a radio reporter who broadcast galvanic firsthand accounts of World War II bombing raids, concentration camps, and air battles. When the journalist returned home from Europe after the war, his was a beloved voice that millions of Americans recognized and applauded.

Success had been Ed's eternal middle name. At his high school, he was valedictorian, debate champion, cheerleader, basketball stand-out, and an attraction to the girls. At Washington State University, Ed became a dashing ROTC colonel and was elected president of the impressive, well-funded National Student Federation of America. Suddenly, he was a student with an office in New York City and the assistant to a leader within a vast educational organization.

Soon he had interviewed first-class artists, such as the poet Rabindranath Tagore, and thinkers such as physicist Albert Einstein. Despite the racial tension in Atlanta in 1930, Murrow successfully integrated a student convention there covered by the *New York Times*. Before he was thirty, Ed would become head of the European News Bureau for CBS Radio.

New York Times media critic Jack Gould hailed him as the man who brought substance to television. By the forties, the revered journalist was on a first-name basis with Churchill, FDR, Eisenhower, and many media celebrities.

Never had Murrow been afraid to be a lone voice against a leviathan. His ancestry featured Abolitionists in a slave state, Quakers residing among evangelicals, Yankee supporters living within the Confederacy, and a handful of Republicans living among legions of Democrats.

Risking everything, some of his relatives had even smuggled slaves to freedom. The family patriarch, John Murrow, had chosen a half-Indian wife in an era in which miscegenation was heavily ostracized—if not terminated by vigilante-style lynching.

In short, being independent, fearless, iconoclastic, and outspoken for social justice was part of the family business. Ed would later say, "I've always been on the side of the heretics against those who burned them." His strong Calvinist-cum-Quaker values meant that doing right, even if doing so alone, was better than doing well financially and being popular.

Ed was quick to challenge the conventional wisdom and slow to accept the status quo. He was a hard man to stare down. Edward R. Murrow was unafraid to exemplify the adage, "one and the truth are a majority."

He knew that the camera could be mightier than the sword. As an American undefeated hero and icon, he was a proven heavyweight.

AND IN THIS CORNER...

However, "knock-out king" Joe McCarthy was opposite him in the ring. Joe had not only handily won his senatorial election, but he was predicted to someday win the presidential one. His approval rating with the American people had never been higher, and there were many who felt he was overshadowing President Eisenhower.

The precocious McCarthy was the youngest person elected as a circuit judge in Wisconsin, and, when first elected to Congress in 1946, also the youngest man in the United States Senate. By this moment in 1954, he had already become chair of the Senate's Committee on Government Operations and been re-elected to his office for a second term. Both as president of his law school class at Marquette and as a Marine lieutenant, Joe aggressively tackled obstacles and opponents with the fearless *semper fi* tenacity of the Marine Corps.

No one had ever taken on so many concurrent battles with such formidable foes. By January 1954 it looked like McCarthy could deliver knock-out blows against alleged communists in higher education, the State Department, Hollywood, the Senate, and even the U.S. Army.

Moreover, he never fought alone. "Tail-Gunner Joe" seemed to have the backing of the president, his cabinet, Congress (especially its most menacing committee—HUAC), Hoover's hidden army of investigators and informers, toxic tabloid tainters, anti-communist millionaire patrons, and a wolf pack of hungry, aspiring-copycat lawyers including Roy Cohn, Donald Surine, and Richard Nixon. Anti-communist groups such as the American Business Consultants and their publications also effectively dug up and magnified dirt on anyone whom the senator found suspect.

McCarthy had also enlisted two more deadly allies named patriotism and fear. Who would wish to challenge a true patriot with a high conviction rate and lethal track record? If he could place State Department officials such as Alger Hiss and successful Hollywood artists such as Dalton Trumbo behind bars, why would anyone oppose McCarthy? The twin fears of defeat and stigmatism had silenced most American political pugilists.

There would be no referee in the ring with McCarthy to call blows below the belt. He had broken the rules of decorum and due process repeatedly, and no umpire had stepped in to penalize him or stop the fight. Instead, other heavyweights and a large audience seemed to be cheering him on.

MURROW WAS NOT THE FAVORITE

To the non-partisan handicappers, this could have been anyone's fight, and Murrow had no guarantee of success. The consequences were potentially disastrous. He felt bound to consider any possible casualties.

Yet, at a higher level, Murrow saw himself aligned with the eternal values of fairness, freedom, truth, and justice. If he backed away from such values to protect his son from death threats today, what kind of world would his son inherit tomorrow? McCarthyism projected a future in which hearsay would replace evidence, might would make right, and fear could rule a nation.

Nevertheless, Murrow was working in a country where the press had inherited two conflicting roles—that of the neutral messenger never taking sides, and that of the watchdog investigating and taking sides against corruption and power abuse—all while fully protected by the First Amendment. How could he reconcile both roles?

Ed wondered if he was truly a watchdog. Was he the great white knight saving the round table and fair young virgins? Or was he the lead kamikaze pointing his squadron toward the S.S. McCarthy?

THE DECISION

Ed could not postpone the decision. The program had to air—or not—within seventy-two hours, and the decision was needed within twenty-four. The ad for the program had already been placed in the *Times*. His *See It Now* crew, like McCarthy's piranhas, were poised for action.

Neither the headache, nor the cough, nor the deadline would go away. Time had run out. Eddie again surveyed the shadowy room for shadowy people. He was finally ready to reply.

Eddie Scott told Ed Murrow that he was indeed doing the right and courageous thing. But Murrow, who half smiled, was unconvinced.

He thanked Eddie, quickly confirmed their timetable, exited the restaurant, and continued to wrestle the questions. Walking the streets of Manhattan again, he would talk to himself about what McCarthy might and might not do if checked or left unchecked. He weighed Scott's verdict just as he had listened to Friendly, Paley, Stanton, CBS's legal team, and others. But he knew the decision was now fully his.

If Murrow waited for someone else to step to the plate, or for "Jeerin' Joe" to eventually self-destruct, how many other innocents would be publicly disemboweled in the meantime? Good timing was essential, and, if Murrow was reading the stars correctly, the senator's credibility and support base were dimming. Eisenhower and Nixon, further embarrassed by McCarthy's excesses, seemed to be distancing themselves from a runaway train.

The best moment to strike would be when McCarthy was most vulnerable. If Ed did not attack first, McCarthy would likely broil him. If that happened, Ed would become too overwhelmed facing HUAC, Hearst, and Hoover, not to mention McCarthy's scorpions, to mount any kind of campaign against the Moloch.

AT HOME WITH CASEY

Anxious about his son, Ed scampered home to make sure Janet's parents were there to keep the boy safe. Janet was visiting friends in Jamaica, so Ed feared more than ever for Casey. Long after everyone in the house was asleep, the houseguests would be awakened by Ed, who could be heard pacing the floor below.

Murrow could not be contained by four walls and soon extended his pacing to the New York streets again. He was rethinking the most pressing factors. It seemed that the threat from McCarthy's aide, Donald Surine, was the last straw. Weren't Joe's jackals signaling an imminent attack? Yet seeing Casey again after yet another death threat had increased his resolve to protect his and other families at all costs. Why endanger innocent people?

It was now or never, and possibly do or die.

Day was breaking over Manhattan and Ed had been walking the lamp-lit streets for hours. He was exhausted, but he had made an irreversible decision.

Muzzling a cough, he opened the shadowed door at CBS into the first ray of light. His coat was quickly unbuttoned and thrown across a chair. Facing an empty typewriter, the veteran seized a blank piece of paper knowing exactly what he would type.

Murrow could not turn back... or turn his back upon others.

On Tuesday, March 9, 1954, at 10:30 p.m., *See It Now* would expose the junior senator from Wisconsin.

NIETZSCHE AND SOCRATES

In Friedrich Nietzsche's *The Will to Power*, fragments of the great German philosopher's thought were assembled to describe "perspectivism." This term suggests that individuals and groups develop their perspectives not based upon truth or faith, but rather to maximize their effectiveness and power.

An example of this would be that the eyes of wolves have evolved in the front of their heads to more accurately see and pursue their prey. Conversely, rabbits have developed eyes in the sides of their heads to better view predators approaching from many angles. Thus, their perspectives are strategic and empowering, not accidental.

Applying this insight to human beings, Nietzsche cited the example of the ancient Romans developing a might makes right, survival of the fittest perspective to justify their rule by cruelty and conquest. But Nietzsche also noted that the Christians, who were persecuted by the Romans, claimed a higher moral virtue known as "turning the other cheek." For Christians, their reward was in the afterlife so, even if they were sacrificed by the Romans on earth, they would gain the greater moral ground through eternal happiness and selfless martyrdom.

Hence, in Nietzsche's terms, each group developed a philosophy or theology that allowed them to defeat the other, whether physically or morally. In other words, they obtained power via perspective. Within the Roman perspective, you must win through physical power—hence the Romans were powerful victors in their own eyes. However, within the Christian perspective, power is gained by surrendering to a higher power, no matter what one's status or longevity on earth. Within this logic, the Christian perspective sees itself as being aligned with the ultimate and greater power.

Murrow knew that he was engaged in a game of perspectivism, not between Christians and Romans, but between patriots (now synonymous with anti-communists) and truth-tellers protecting individual freedoms. For the journalist, the power of the First Amendment would allow the pen (or the camera) to be mightier than the sword. But for McCarthy, the pen that undermines the state needed to be sheathed or destroyed in the interest of a collective power called "national security."

Joseph McCarthy's perspective demanded an ethic by which loyalty creates collective power. Thus disloyalty—in thought, speech, affiliation—was unethical. Disloyalty undermined collective power. For Murrow, blind, unthinking loyalty that led to the persecution of the supposedly disloyal undermined the power of freedom and true democracy.

So, if he were to face McCarthy, it would be a battle of perspectivism, each man trying to control the frame or the agenda by which ethical behavior was viewed. Each was insisting upon a perspective by which the other should be measured. In thinking through his plan of attack, Murrow had to be careful not to play into a perspective by which he could be viewed as disloyal, and at the same time advance the perspective that human dignity or, in civic terms, the Bill of Rights, mattered more than conformist adherence to an unbending dogma.

Socrates (chapter 3) had made similar claims that truth-telling and thinking mattered more than blind subservience to convention. The men of Athens who sentenced Socrates to death were also concerned about the health of their city-state. Some of Socrates' most independent disciples had unleashed great destruction to civil society and breeched the Athenian equivalent of national security. For both the Athenians and McCarthy, the freedom to think had its limits when it catalyzed the freedom to harm. In McCarthy's view, the very prospect of communist expansion predicted social harm.

Both Socrates and Nietzsche raised the prospect that true power and freedom derive from an independent perspective, individual vision, and self-determined action. But the ethicist must struggle with where the boundary lies between such individual power, freedom, and rights—and social stability. Murrow knew that McCarthy would continue to champion the perspective that social stability must be defended at all costs.

It was Murrow's job to demonstrate that some costs were unethical, inhumane, and unacceptable. He had to foster a perspective upholding above all honesty, humanity, and the constitutional rights of citizens. Each perspective, McCarthy's and Murrow's, was potentially appealing depending upon how it was presented and documented. So, Murrow knew he must win the battle of perspectives.

THE ETHICS OF "OBJECTIVITY"

To gain this upper hand, however, Ed also knew that he would not be viewed as neutral or objective. Thus, his inner struggle was about the ethics of fairness and impartiality, and about his accountability to the public and their trust. If he presented only the perspective prioritizing human rights, he would be unfair to McCarthy and to the perspective prioritizing American loyalty and national security.

As a veteran journalist, Murrow knew that no newsman could avoid the perception of bias. Even a broadcaster who gave equal time to the left and the right might seem right-biased to those on the left and vice versa to those on the right. Nevertheless, he knew that the best journalists seemed to avoid the appearance of bias despite the reality of human fallibility and subconscious preference.

The watchdog ethic placed social justice at the top of the value hierarchy. If corporations had already invested millions of dollars in PR campaigns that concealed their corruption, why should an investigative journalist strive for balance rather than simply exposing the cover-up? The PR side had already been told, so revealing the cover-up side provided balance in an overall sense.

Moreover, an ethics of social justice potentially gave more weight to the voiceless, poor, and victims of abuse than to their oppressors. Should a chronic liar or dictator be given a press megaphone? Would Murrow give equal time to Hitler when covering the war? Not if his life depended upon it—and for many years, it did.

Both ethical systems—those upholding the neutral messenger and those championing the watchdog—were part of the American media legacy. The public, however, did not usually think this through. If a journalist took a position, he or she seemed biased, even when playing the role of public protector. So, the act of exposing McCarthy's tactics would seem to some as partisan, biased, and unfair—and thus unethical—and like poor journalism. Yet it would seem courageous, counterbalancing, socially just, and thus ethical—and like great journalism—to others.

Such conflicting values and ethics rested at the heart of Murrow's own inner debate. If he used his program as a watchdog, he could bring the full weight of television's power to attack a destructive megalomaniac. But if he set such a precedent, what would prevent copycats from using television to destroy the reputation of other individuals, even those who were virtuous? Wasn't it wrong for the messenger to also become the judge and jury?

On the other hand, the watchdog could not become a lapdog. Who would protect the people from deception and abuse if not the fourth estate? Should not any citizen use any legitimate tool to prevent the entrenchment of star chamber persecution within one's own country? How could any responsible journalist or citizen let elected officials establish bullying as an acceptable public practice? If the usual American justice referees were frightened by McCarthy's red-smearing, who else could preserve the rights to a free trial, to face one's accuser, to freedom of speech, to innocence until proven guilty by manifest evidence?

COMPETING ETHICAL STANDARDS

Given these two ethical standards at play, what was Murrow's proper role as a public media professional? If he were making a documentary about the Holocaust ten years earlier, he certainly would not have bent over backwards to grant the S.S. camp wardens equal time. Should the Holocaust's negatives be balanced by a glowing perspective flaunting the "positive" case for genocide?

Murrow thought not, but Joe McCarthy was not Adolf Hitler, despite the alarming parallels between Hitler's early days and the increasingly impassioned antics of the junior senator.

So, Murrow was inwardly divided between his loyalties as a citizen and as a journalist; as a watchdog and as a messenger; and as a human being facing reprisals and a paid corporate employee responsible for accurate programming in the public interest.

THE AFTERMATH AND AFTERGLOW

Murrow and Friendly decided to let Joseph McCarthy hang himself with his own rope. Minimizing voice-over comments, their *See It Now* episode emphasized news clips and other recordings of the senator in which he contradicted himself, presented half-truths, besmirched proven patriots, spoke in error, and revealed bizarre quirks of personality. For many watching the program, McCarthy came across as a mix of fanatic, persecutor, con-man, and fool.

However, some of the more conservative viewers were incensed, and accused Murrow of being one-sided, unpatriotic, irresponsible, and even a "commie-lover." CBS and the program's sponsor, Alcoa, the makers of aluminum foil, once again received threatening letters requesting that he be fired or forced to apologize.

Nevertheless, the response was overwhelmingly in support of Fred Friendly and his host, Ed Murrow. By noon the next day, over ten thousand phone calls had been received by CBS. Eventually over seventy-five thousand letters and cards arrived—a record number for any television program. The response was ten to one in favor of Murrow.

He was immediately hailed by hundreds of average Americans on the streets of New York and by calls and telegrams from notables such as Supreme Court Justice William O. Douglas and actress Lauren Bacall, who was vacationing in Europe. When Ed first emerged from CBS, two colleagues had to call a cab to usher him away from the madding, mobbing crowd keen to praise, if not crush him.

Friendly had well remembered that William Paley and Frank Stanton had insisted that *See It Now* provide McCarthy with equal time to answer Murrow's charges. Murrow made this offer of equal time clear within his opening commentary on March 9th.

The irate Senator availed himself by providing a full thirty-minute counterblast on *See It Now*, April 6, 1954. This time the response was only two to one in favor of Murrow—a sizable jump in support for McCarthy.

But on the whole, CBS and Murrow were the substantial winners, whether by ten to one initially or by two to one a month later. When all the calls and letters were totaled from the two programs, Murrow and Friendly garnered over four-fifths of the votes.

Later, Murrow's immediate boss, CBS president Frank Stanton, ushered Friendly into his office to present some findings of related research. One-third of *See It Now* viewers had become convinced by McCarthy during the second program that Murrow had a pink—if not red—identity. Thus, Ed's fears about becoming tarnished were well justified.

Even when McCarthy died three years later, CBS, Friendly, and Murrow received hate mail accusing them of viciously precipitating the senator's early demise. In June 1954, longtime friend and colleague Don Hollenbeck, who had been relentlessly red-baited by the Hearst press, gassed himself inside his closed apartment. Only forty-nine years old, Hollenbeck was found snow white and supine two hours later. The *See It Now* victory would thereby remain bittersweet.

Throughout the spring and summer of 1954, the McCarthy clan continued to smear and intimidate Murrow's friends and employers. Pressured by voices within and without, *See it Now* sponsor, Alcoa Aluminum, eventually dropped the program. Notwithstanding the adversarial pushback, Murrow and Friendly knew that a fatal blow had been delivered. They watched as the dragon, although still breathing fire, began to flail and fail.

THE TEN FACTORS

1. **Notions of fairness and justice:** Long before and after Ed's birth, the Murrow family was known for championing the underdog and the outsider. Above all, Ed was committed to protecting individual and minority rights and making certain that all parties had a fair trial. The Constitution, Bill of Rights, and First Amendment had to be honored and fully upheld, and wherever they did not apply, common sense notions of justice needed to prevail. Murrow had witnessed the absence of justice firsthand in fascist countries and was passionate about protecting justice in America from such a fate.

2. **Impact or consequences:** By 1954, Murrow had already found the impact of McCarthyism to be tragic, and if left unchecked, it had the potential to become catastrophic. While the consequences of his action might have been lethal for his career and possibly his institution, Murrow's inaction could have led to far more serious consequences for America and democracy. The suicides, career homicides, and fear storm directly linked to McCarthyism might have reached epidemic proportions. No matter what the risk to his family, these consequences for democracy seemed more dire.

3. **Ends and means:** To use his television program as a bully pulpit meant treating his human subjects as a means, not an end. Murrow struggled with the issue of turning human beings into editorial fodder and wondered if any disrespect that he showed McCarthy might set a poor precedent for television. Targeting others could have backfired such that he would be treated in the same way. To Murrow, Friendly, and their employers, their means, not only their ends, were of great importance.

215

4. **Tone and atmosphere:** Part of Murrow's concern about the Red Scare was its tone of incriminating innuendo and slam-dunk slander. However much he disagreed with McCarthy, the polished broadcaster wished to model the language of dignity and discretion rather than the rhetoric of smear campaigns and propaganda. Although the Murrow–McCarthy conflict was about specific issues and democratic procedures, for Murrow it was also a about graceful style, open-minded atmosphere, and the tone of civil discourse.

5. **Motivation and higher law:** While a product of the Judeo-Christian ethic and an independent moralist, Murrow did not publicly appeal so much to a transhuman law as to fully honoring human law and rights without exception. Motivated first and foremost by an American "melting pot" sense of civic non-discrimination, his goal was to use journalism as a tool to protect human liberties and the democratic process. Quietly in the background was the heavy religious instruction that his parents and other Quaker Friends had implanted into his conscience, perhaps the largest organ of his body. Ultimately, the higher law for Murrow was tied more to social justice and humanism than to religion.

6. **Allegiance and loyalty:** Murrow's allegiance to his family, colleagues, employers, sponsor, and friends made him strongly consider his and their protection. However, his allegiance to his profession, viewers, and country, if not to the free world of democratic nations, caused him to deeply ponder exposing McCarthy(ism). These conflicting loyalties were further complicated by the ambivalence that his national president (Eisenhower) and his corporate boss (Paley) felt toward McCarthy the senator vs. McCarthy the vigilante. Ultimately, Murrow's allegiances, like theirs, were divided.

7. **Values and principles:** The combined influence of Murrow's family, college, and professional mentors had taught him to value accuracy, fair-mindedness, rationality, and equity above all. Murrow valued Voltaire's principle, "I may not agree with what you say, but I will defend to the death your right to say it," a principle which seemed strongly at odds with Red Scare tactics that suppressed free speech. The conflicting vectors of national security vs. personal liberties effected a natural tension in the decision Murrow must make. Ultimately, however, the value of national security seemed to have become an untenable pretense for the senator's ethically challenged grand-standing.

Against the advice of those who valued his safety, Murrow had flown with the troops into the heart of harm's way to demonstrate his patriotism. While Ed saw himself as a red-blooded American, McCarthy had a different definition of "red." In the end, Murrow and McCarthy valued two different conceptions of patriotism.

8. **Cultural context:** It is hard for twenty-first century Americans to understand the chilling cultural climate of the 1950's that made the U.S. feel like a different country. At that time, any statements critiquing the U.S. government and any history of association with liberal organizations made an individual a person of interest, no matter how patriotic and loyal he or she might have been—even as a military or national leader. According to McCarthy, communists were supposed to have cleverly infiltrated all aspects of the government and social institutions. So, within such a culture of suspicion, it became impossible to know who served vs. who spied. This fear-based culture made Murrow's decision both more difficult and more imperative.

9. **Implications:** To Ed, the implications were profound. He had seen firsthand how a seemingly benign country such as Germany, Italy, or Japan could turn malignant and malevolent due to ambitious, manipulative leadership. He felt the popularity and power of McCarthy could have been an early warning signal that the U.S. might also become corrupted and overwhelmed by false prophets. Other implications, such as the safety of his family and peers, were important concerns, but ultimately a threat to family and colleagues could not compete with the threat to an entire nation and way of life. Although he could hardly see all of the implications of his decision, Murrow sensed that they were vast and carried the potential to alter the path of nations, critical thinking, human liberty, and independent journalism.

10. **Proportion and balance:** Considering all of these factors, Murrow gave great weight to the conflicting loyalties he had to evaluate, and to the possible consequences to his career, peers, employer, and family. Principles and values also deeply mattered, and the greatest of these was Murrow's sense of justice. Bullying implied ignoring equal treatment for all, and Murrow was even more incensed that unchecked bulldozing could come by the hand of a publicly elected official. While many other factors mattered, he struggled the most with: 1) competing loyalties, 2) justice, and 3) the long-term implications for individual liberties within a democratic society.

A TERMINAL PAS DE DEUX

Whatever the controversy surrounding both episodes of *See It Now*, Murrow had emerged once again, as he did after World War II, as a public hero. Conversely, "Tail-Gunner Joe" went into a smoky tailspin, and on December 2, 1954, was censured by the U.S. Senate by a vote of sixty-seven to twenty-two.

In 1957, Joseph McCarthy died alone, tragically destroyed by alcoholism. His name would be forever associated with the Red Scare paranoia and persecution which, donning the label "McCarthyism," became America's black eye of the 1950s.

Murrow, on the other hand, despite ongoing opposition by a caustic minority, sky-rocketed to greater fame and celebrity. Before his death in 1967, the Queen of England named Murrow to be Knight Commander of the British Order. His boss, William Paley, smiled broadly when Murrow and CBS received the Freedom House Award.

Despite an FBI "Murrow file" that had grown to over one thousand pages by the 1960s, President Lyndon Johnson presented Murrow with the prestigious Presidential Medal of Freedom in 1964. Ed was also awarded the Distinguished Flying Cross for his heroism in World War II.

The "general" among veteran journalists greatly enlarged his collection of Peabody, Emmy, DuPont, and other major awards and prizes. Eventually his wife, Janet, commented that he had so many that he did not know where to put them.

Despite unfavorable coverage of Murrow in Hearst and anti-communist publications, the senior journalist was consistently hailed by the most important and visible ones. *Time* magazine stated that he "...was a network unto himself... the king of broadcast news." *Variety* added that he was "practically a national hero," and that his 1954 *See It Now* program on McCarthy was "the performance of his life." Jack Gould, the media critic for *The New York Times*, called Murrow "the man who gave TV a spine."

Edward R. Murrow's death was front-page news in hundreds of newspapers. Among those who attended his funeral were Robert Kennedy, Walter Cronkite, Adlai Stevenson, William Paley, and a host of other notables. Over thirteen hundred guests packed inside the memorial arena, while hundreds more lined Madison Avenue outside. Major documentary tributes were broadcast by CBS, the BBC, and other major media worldwide.

For two men who became interlocked within a historical snapshot, it was, to paraphrase Dickens, the worst of deaths and the best of deaths. While both faced painful illness, McCarthy knew that his work and reputation had descended to rock bottom, while Murrow had ascended to stardom and obtained the image of a national savior that McCarthy had coveted.

Although Edward R. Murrow's final years were checkered with unhappiness due to government and corporate politics, and especially due to the loss of a smoke-stained, cancer-infested lung, he was praised and pursued by leaders worldwide, who viewed him as a bright beacon of broadcasting and civil liberty.

Until years after his broadcast, Ed remained uncertain whether he had won the ethics battle regarding two wrongs making a right. Had his ends truly justified his means. Yet from his perspective, and those he admired most, he had indeed won larger moral victories for human rights; for protecting a high tone and atmosphere in public life; and for values he had championed—fairness, civility, freedom, justice, and human dignity.

Edward R. Murrow, unlike Joseph McCarthy, could finally rest in peace. Like Eddie Scott and millions who had watched and heard him, he now knew with certainty the answer to his vexing ethical quandary. It was a question that, albeit deliberately voiced to Eddie Scott, was subconsciously addressed to himself: "Ed, do you think I am doing the right thing?"

CHAPTER 11

NELSON MANDELA:
(1918- 2013)

SPEAKING TRUTH TO POWER

Tormented by a frightening image, Madiba had tossed and turned all night. Sleeping was impossible with Kerr's floating face staring him down. Was he lost in a nightmare? Or was this a premonition of his meeting with that face tomorrow?

Madiba knew he needed sleep, yet on this humid, windless night in 1939, even rest was impossible. Only twenty-one years old, the young student was involved in a stand-off with his South African university principal. Madiba knew his response to Principal Alexander Kerr's intimidating ultimatum was required the next day—and to make matters worse, no one else would witness their confrontation.

Kerr's face was so vivid that Madiba was confused. Was he already at the meeting? The face danced and scowled like a warrior's mask, but he could hear no words. No smells, no sounds, no tastes, no lights—just a bouncing, haunting countenance taunting him throughout the night. It had to be a horrible dream—and yet he could feel himself shift weight. Wasn't he awake?

Adding to the young student's terror, K. D.'s face appeared next. Kaiser Daliwanga Matanzima, nicknamed K.D., had advised Madiba to stand up to Principal Kerr. K.D. Matanzima was Thembu royalty and could not be ignored. Ever since Madiba had arrived at Fort Hare University, K.D.—an upperclassman and relative—had taken him under his wing and become his mentor.

Matanzima had served on the very student council to which Madiba had just been elected. K.D. knew the turf and the players. Madiba trusted his perspective and bowed to his regal tribal legacy. To have the upperclassman's approval meant everything.

Still, Madiba wondered if he was hallucinating. Or else a nightmare had carried over into that strange limbo world between sleep and awakening. Alexander Kerr's forbidding face would not disappear. And now K.D. was glaring on the other side. Madiba was caught in between.

The risks were high. If the young student followed his conscience and Matanzima's advice, Madiba would likely be expelled from Fort Hare

221

University. It was the only residential center of higher education for black students in South Africa. His future education and career would be doomed.

Madiba's opposition was formidable. Alexander Kerr, who had been educated at the University of Edinburgh, had virtually founded Fort Hare. During the 1930's, Kerr was the white authority who held the future of most black students in his hands.

Yet one never opposed Thembu regal leadership. Madiba and Matanzima were linked by blood, although K.D. was much higher in the royal hierarchy. Neither authority, Kerr nor K.D., could be disrespected.

No wonder the young student's body twisted as the dancing, elusive Kerr mask glared. Time stood still… but not the face. Then K.D. appeared again. Like the mask itself, Madiba's fear enlarged. If he turned to look away, K.D.'s face re-appeared.

Were both faces chasing him? It was the perfect nightmare.

Only three days prior, the young African had been elected to become a member of the Student Representative Council, the most important leadership position among Fort Hare students. Principal Kerr insisted that Madiba honor the election and serve the Council. But, like most of his classmates, the second-year student felt that the voting was illegitimate. After all, an overwhelming majority had previously voted to boycott the election as an attempt to effect campus reform.

To honor the substantial majority, those students who were elected chose to resign. However, Kerr doggedly and cleverly called for a re-election at dinner, so that everyone would have full opportunity to vote. Once again, during the dinner re-election, five-sixths of the student population honored the boycott by refusing to vote. But, the twenty-five students who voted once again chose Madiba, among others.

Madiba could not honor such a small vote, one that worked in opposition to the boycott. He felt a strong accountability to his peers, who had given him their trust. They were acting in solidarity and he could not betray them. After all, Madiba himself, like the vast majority, had voted in favor of the boycott, and he had made it clear to other students that this was his position. Madiba knew he should resign despite Principal Kerr's insistence to the contrary.

He did so.

Then, without warning, Kerr had called Madiba into his office only yesterday. The message was clear. If he insisted upon resigning, he would likely be expelled from Fort Hare University. Kerr gave him one night to think it over before they would privately meet again the following day.

Madiba was aggravated by the inflexible, autocratic approach that Principal Kerr had taken once again. He later wrote in his autobiography: "I resented his absolute power over my fate. I should have every right to resign from the SRC if I wished. This injustice rankled, and at the moment I saw Dr. Kerr less as a benefactor than as a not-altogether-benign dictator."

Madiba's mind worked overtime to find an escape hatch.

None appeared.

In his dreamlike vision, Kerr blocked one exit, while K.D. the other.

THE LAY OF THE LAND

Dr. Kerr held all of the cards. First, he called Madiba "Nelson," reminding him of the English name, Nelson Mandela, which he had been given when he first entered school. The name was always a reminder that he was in an anglophone universe governed by South African law, college rules, and Dr. Kerr's rigid decisions. Moreover, Kerr had already reminded students of his power by ignoring the student boycott, restaging elections, and summoning "Mr. Nelson Mandela" to his office—twice.

So, it was a matter of principle vs. principal. Madiba had grown accustomed to being called Nelson. But he was unaccustomed to stressful decisions in which he must choose between survival and loyalty to peers, mentor, and conscience. As an adult, it was his first truly vexing ethical decision.

Accountability mattered a great deal to Mr. Mandela. If he could not be counted upon to represent his colleagues and to stand by his position, would he not be seen as a doormat? Or even worse, as a lackey or puppet in Kerr's hands? Certainly, one reason for the student boycott was that the representatives did not wish to be a rubber stamp.

Although he had heard yesterday that some of his peers were fantasizing about whom they might sleep with, Madiba was more concerned about whether he could sleep with himself. Indeed, he later wrote that he had a "restless night" weighing whether to do what was "morally right," and thus to "sabotage [his] academic career."

Madiba tried another position that might prove more conducive to sleep, but the dancing mask and K.D.'s image ignored the efforts of his body and paraded before his mind. He still had no answer.

WHO WAS MADIBA?

Madiba was a tribal name he had taken on by preference, but at his birth in 1918, his father had named him Rolihlahla Malibhunga Mandela in his homeland on the East Cape of South Africa. Rolihlahla literally means "pulling the branch of a tree" or "troublemaker." He was later jokingly asked if his father was clairvoyant.

Madiba's father had been a chief of the Thembu people. Then he was stripped of his title, lands, and most of his livestock by a white magistrate for insubordination when Madiba was just one year old. Madiba's mother, Nosekeni Fanny, was one of the chief's four wives, who raised livestock, children, and crops. Unlike her husband, Fanny converted to Christianity, so Madiba learned to be a shepherd, farmer, and Christian from his mother. From his father, he adopted a chiefly dignity, pride in the Thembu legacy, and stubbornness in the face of authority.

Rolihlahla inherited his royal blood from both parents. Madiba's mother descended from the royal house of kings and his father from the regal house of counselors to the kings. Influenced by two Christian brothers whom she respected, Madiba's mother determined to send Rolihlahla to a Methodist school. He would be the first member of their large family to be educated.

It was in 1925 in a one-room Methodist schoolhouse that Mandela was given an English name, Nelson, due in part to the reluctance of the white teachers to learn African names. Under his mother's influence, Nelson was baptized in the Methodist church and attended services.

His father prematurely passed away from a lung disease when Nelson was only nine. Thanks to his father's foresight, Nelson was raised as the ward of a powerful regent, Jongintaba Dalindyebo, a friend of the family, who had promised to give the boy a full education. From Jongintaba, Madiba also learned the leadership skills of a great chief, including the ability to build consensus, listen thoughtfully, and incorporate all points of view.

In 1936, Madiba also passed through a painful but meaningful circumcision rite de passage with twenty-five other young men. After the agonizing slicing of his foreskin with a spear, he shouted, "I am a man!" He then buried his foreskin and adopted his new manhood name, "Dalibunga," meaning "founder of the council."

As he evolved into a good scholar, Madiba completed a three-year program in just two years at the Clarkebury Wesleyan school, and then attended Healdtown School in Fort Beaufort, a days' trip from home. Both schools were as British as they were Christian. Singing "God Save the Queen" each day and marching to church in boys' and girls' lines was a constant reminder of the colonial mold in which the students were being cast.

But none of these secondary schools could compare to Fort Hare University, the pinnacle of educational opportunity for a black South African. Madiba later said that for tribal Africans such as himself, Fort Hare was "like Oxford and Cambridge, Harvard and Yale, all rolled into one." The rustic boy was proud to be accepted to the prestigious ticket to the elite. Moreover, among the students who knew the lines of tribal royalty, both Mandela and K.D. were treated like princes.

However, at first Madiba was in over his head. He looked and talked like a country boy who could hardly match wits with a great Shakespearean scholar like Alexander Kerr. Still, he and his guardian were very proud that he was at Fort Hare and he soon sampled as much as possible—a variety of courses, soccer, dancing, church, student government, and even the drama club, in which he portrayed John Wilkes-Booth, the assassin of Abraham Lincoln.

For some time, Madiba and K.D. became almost inseparable in sports, entertainment, and even teaching Sunday School. Soon Mandela won his first student political battle. The freshmen had been excluded from their house committee. Nelson succeeded in not only winning them a seat at the committee table, but actually giving them control of the committee. Thanks to his assertiveness, the freshmen now had the right to assign chores to upperclassman in a rare reversal of power.

But his second foray into student politics, the current nomination and election to the Student Representative Council, had proven far more dangerous. He quickly found himself caught between K.D. and Kerr, family and friends, dancing mask and mentor, classmates and career, present and future, principle and principal.

WEIGHING IMPORTANT LOYALTIES

Loyalty to his peers and the boycott were crucial to Nelson. He later wrote about not giving in to his "own selfish interests." But Madiba also knew these "selfish" interests also included the unselfish honoring of his family. His mother had sacrificed much so that he might have a better life. Should she be punished for what would seem to her like mere student politics?

Should the most important thing, both to him and to her—his education—be terminated over an issue that might later seem minor? After all, part of the boycott was about improving student food—hardly the most important issue in the larger world of extreme racism, poverty, disease, illiteracy, and violence.

When the nine-year-old Nelson had lost his father, it was his mother who had brought him to live with the regent despite her own loss. So, Madiba's greatest ambition was to use the money that a Fort Hare education would afford him to build a far better home for his mother and sisters.

He had his eye on a civil service job, the highest position available to the students of Fort Hare. That would bring him enough privilege and money to restore his family's place in society, for they had never forgotten the sting of his father being stripped of position, property, and reputation.

Mandela's newly adopted father, the Thembu regent, had been his protector and benefactor who invested many years and shillings in Nelson. Would it not be a major act of betrayal of both his guardian and mother to leave college? Madiba had also made a commitment to honor the policies of Fort Hare. Was he also betraying the university?

CROSSING CULTURES

Part of Mandela's frustration came from being socialized into British institutions. He had been raised in the climate of African *Ubuntu*, a community spirit fostering exceptional cooperation and care. Years later, Archbishop Desmond Tutu would define *Ubuntu* as "gentleness, compassion, hospitality; openness... vulnerability... and knowing you are bound up with others in the bundle of life." To Mandela's view, *Ubuntu* should be extended to everyone, including students. It was inconceivable that some of the white leaders he had met, like Principal Kerr, seemed so stern, bureaucratic, and hollow.

Yet somehow, learning to be "cultured" in the British aristocratic sense seemed important to many students. Mandela later wrote, "we were being told by our teachers 'Now you are at Fort Hare, you are going to be a leader of your people.' This was what was being drummed upon us, and of course in those days to have a degree as a black man was something that was very important."

The regent also held this view. In Madiba's words, his guardian was "very proud that he had a son, a member of the family clan, who was at Fort Hare"

It was even argued that the Xhosa people (of whom the Thembu were one subset) were a good match for Fort Hare given their penchant for argument and reasoning, unlike their northern Zulu neighbors, noted instead for military prowess as warriors. Madiba exhibited this Xhosa aptitude for debate and logic. He had a strong interest in law and, despite his inclination to become a civil servant, K.D. encouraged him to become a lawyer.

On the whole, Madiba thought that much could be gained by mastering another culture's perspective and skills. Nor was he opposed to Christianity like his father and many other relatives. He later reflected that two institutions had greatly supported impoverished Africans, the missionary churches and the chieftains. Despite corrupt exceptions, both church and chief had reached out to provide charity, education, and stability wherever possible.

All things considered, whatever the seeming tyranny of Alexander Kerr, a diploma from Fort Hare and a bi-cultural fluency in South Africa could be a springboard to success. Being expelled from Fort Hare would be high tragedy.

Madiba could not forget that he was first Thembu; then Xhosa; and finally South African. Family and tribal allegiances trumped colonial incentives, and yet British culture was a foothold toward becoming part of the cultured black elite.

FACING THE FACE OF AUTHORITY

The sleepless night was over. He looked like he had slept in his clothing. Hastily, he changed into his best suit. The floor was creaking beneath him and he wondered if it was an ominous warning. One eyelid seemed puffy and both eyes looked bloodshot as evidence of sleep deprivation.

Although he had wrestled with himself all night long, Madiba still was undecided. Anxiety, rather than the answer, ruled. The appointment was only ten minutes away.

Madiba still felt his accountability to his Fort Hare classmates, to justice, and to his conscience. But Nelson sensed that his own academic survival, his previous agreement to follow Fort Hare's rules, and his loyalty to family exerted an equally strong pressure.

So, it was not just K.D. vs. Kerr or principle vs. principal. It was also Madiba vs. Nelson. Two accents—one Thembu and one British—spoke from within.

It was now only five minutes before the meeting. He anxiously straightened his tie on his way to Kerr's office.

What to do?

The sleepless night had made matters worse. Could he actually focus upon what he would say to the dancing mask? How could he be articulate and assured?

His palms seemed clammy. His heart was racing. Nervous and even jumpy, Madiba did all he could to summon his persuasive powers.

The door to Kerr's office felt far heavier than he remembered. Opening it was like pushing one of those heavy luggage pushcarts.

Kerr did not look friendly. The two kept their distance as the perfectly groomed principal motioned to an empty chair. It was only when Kerr quickly asked Madiba a direct question that he made up his mind. "Nelson Mandela, will you now see things my way for the good of Fort Hare University?" Kerr queried.

Risking all prospects of being an educated man of good reputation, Nelson winced and summoned the courage:

"Principal Kerr. I must resign from my position.

Madiba went on to explain that he could not in good conscience capitulate to the request of Dr. Kerr, no matter what the penalty. The disturbed student was both relieved that he had finally resolved the matter and anxious about Kerr's pending reply.

Madiba's heart was pounding. He could no longer meet Kerr's eyes. An hour of angst passed within a moment of silence.

"Mandela, you will not be immediately expelled," Kerr replied. "You should complete your exams." The principal gave the impression that he had already decided Mandela's fate.

Madiba was momentarily relieved. He would not have to tell his parents the worst any time soon, but he could tell that Kerr had more to say.

"However, if you expect to return to Fort Hare in the fall, you will have to do so as an elected member of the SRC." Kerr proclaimed.

So this was the compromise. Mandela had been given a stay of execution over the summer to further consider his decision, but the alternatives were black and white in more ways than one. If he wanted his education at Fort Hare, he would have to surrender to Kerr and serve as part of a student puppet regime.

Although in great distress, Madiba knew this was not a worst-case scenario. In effect, it was a compromise he had been seeking, but could not find. He could say to his classmates that he stood tall and he would not need to tell his family anything. Kerr had made his position clear, but there would be time for Madiba to reconsider and possibly withhold the situation from his family. Perhaps even some miracle, or an act of solidarity by students, would force Kerr to change his mind.

FROM PRECEDENT TO PRESIDENT

Such a compromise between victory and defeat would become a pattern that would follow Madiba for decades. Although threatened with execution years later, he would always be spared by some compromise fate, such as imprisonment or postponement of a verdict.

Moreover, Nelson's choice at Fort Hare would also anticipate another lifelong pattern. He would take a bold action that would be met initially by rigid opposition. But then incremental social change and eventual full-scale *perestroika* would follow. His reply to Alexander Kerr would be the first small step in a great march to freedom.

Nelson had no way of knowing that he was setting a precedent for future self sacrifice and ethical decision-making. Neither could he have guessed that within forty years he would be known worldwide as the controversial, imprisoned freedom fighter for racial equality—Nelson Mandela—nor that within fifty-five years he would be the Nobel Peace Prize winner and president of South Africa.

Madiba had no means to predict that he would help to liberate others from the harsh era of apartheid known in his home country. Little did he realize that the consequences of his Fort Hare decision would bring many more sleepless nights, increasingly severe penalties, and penultimate rewards.

ENDLESS IMPACT UPON OTHERS

Not only were Madiba's mother and guardian shocked and saddened by his decision, but the regent tried to encourage Mandela to return to Fort Hare and apologize to Principal Kerr. Madiba would not.

This precedent of placing family in the path of danger and dishonor would sew the seeds of a recurring pattern. When he became a leader within the African National Congress (ANC), he opened the door to not only his own family, but also many other spouses and children of anti-apartheid activists, being harassed and jailed.

Later, when Nelson was imprisoned for twenty-seven years, his house was burned to the ground and his second wife, Winnie, was first threatened and later incarcerated. Winnie was eventually evicted from her home, kidnapped by the police, and driven to be dumped with her belongings in a distant town dominated by white conservatives. Unable to speak their language, or buy or rent property, she was an exile within her own country.

Winnie's harassment not only deeply saddened Madiba, but also led to great frustration—as a remote prisoner, he could not defend her. He usually heard about her torment weeks or months after the fact, so he was never able to contact her during the emergency, let alone come to her rescue.

Mandela also felt heartbroken when he could not attend either his mother's or his son's funerals during his later imprisonment. Looking back, he wrote, "when your life is the struggle, as mine was, there is little room left for family. This has always been my greatest regret, and the most painful aspect of the choice I made." Damaging his family's reputation by being expelled from Fort Hare was thus the first of many family heartaches. Nelson knew there might be possible recriminations against his tribal father and mother if he was labeled a rebel by Kerr. Like Madiba, they too could be stigmatized, if not ostracized.

Nelson's loved ones would suffer in other ways. During his notorious years in jail on Robben Island, Madiba was only granted a single, supervised thirty-minute family visit every six months. His children seldom saw their father. The mail to and from his family was always censored and sometimes the guards told him it was lost or delayed. Occasionally, a letter had been so completely censored that it looked like a sieve and he could read only a few words.

With such poor communication, Mandela could never be certain of the status of Winnie and other relatives. Would his own actions calling for reform within his prison further jeopardize their safety? They too had received death threats similar to his.

Backlash came not only from the government, but also from hateful extremists who took matters into their own hands. Vigilante justice and violence were widespread, so for many of Nelson's colleagues this was no longer a matter of being evicted from college, but rather from one's home, job, health, or even being evicted from life itself.

THE GREATER GOOD; THE GREATER GOALS

In future years, Madiba's risks would increase due to a military state of emergency in Africa. In a parallel way, his goals toward the greater good would also increase. Nelson Mandela and his colleagues would no longer be championing the rights of hundreds of students. Rather, they saw themselves as representing millions of Africans. They would also make alliances of solidarity with oppressed people worldwide.

Over time, Mandela's goals became clear-cut. First, he wanted to end apartheid in South Africa, and then to free those in jail who had sought to oppose apartheid. Next, he aimed to create a multi-racial South African government with voting privileges for all, and proceed to advocate and practice tolerance and respect for minorities, whether white, black, or "colored." Finally, he wished to bring about reconciliation and forgiveness for injustices of the past, and to champion a humane and dignified *Ubuntu* society led by accountable servant-leaders. This vision was widely publicized.

Obtaining these goals, however, would be costly. Although his trial by fire with Kerr would last only one day, his first public trial would last five years (1956-61), and his second brought a five-year jail term. He would eventually be sentenced to life imprisonment and ultimately serve twenty-seven years in jail, many of which involved long days of hard labor. For years, Mandela and several colleagues faced the likelihood of the death penalty for treason.

Equally problematic was Mandela's ongoing harassment. All black Africans experienced the constraints of strict segregation and slave-like conditions. South African law mandated that any black must perform any task for a white person who asked.

But Mandela faced even greater degradation as an alleged enemy of the state. As a prisoner there was little he could do when savage jailors beat him or others—no one prevented the crueler guards from urinating upon the inmates.

Black prisoners all ate the same tasteless "mealies" without variety, while "coloreds" (Indians and "middle races") ate slightly better food, and white prisoners ate an almost healthy menu. It is hard to say whether those who were deprived of meals, sometimes for days, were worse off than those who received a steady diet of "pap porridge."

Even during the cold of winter, the prisons had no warm or hot water. Often in solitary confinement, Nelson could talk only to the endless parade of insects with whom he shared residency. A sole light burned overhead day and night, making sleep difficult and irregular. Books were frequently forbidden unless one cooperated and informed on others.

Although Mandela protested wearing the prison uniform—shorts—which all black "boys" had to wear, and although he fought incessantly for jail reforms, he was frequently badgered by hostile guards like the one called "Suitcase," who wore a swastika tattoo, and by sadists like Warder Badenhorst. In an era when literally thousands of blacks were murdered and injured during the apartheid years in Soweto, Sharpeville, Natal, and beyond, hostile prison abuse was routine.

Such brutality was in fact a constant reminder of why Nelson Mandela had taken a strong, irrevocable stand to end apartheid. Violent bullies were the rule. Indeed, Alexander Kerr would foreshadow far more ruthless authorities in decades to come.

Beyond the abuses to his family, and the constant threat of death and dishonor, Madiba faced chicanery and betrayal. There were informers and cowards within his own organization, attempts to bribe him with the lure of greener pastures, offers of deals from state leaders who would have merely renamed apartheid, setups and traps staged by third parties, and acrimonious divisions within his own movement. Fighting for the greater good meant facing endless stinging insects while walking through minefields.

A GREATER DECISION

A five-year trial and over ten thousand days in prison, coupled with the death of key friends and family, would break most people. Even when he was not incarcerated, Madiba was often confined by his fugitive status to lead a hidden life in fear of capture. One would think he needed genuine rest and comfort after so much stress and confinement.

Yet, once he was released from prison, despite being seventy-one years old, the veteran activist did not find a path of escape. He had a much larger decision to face exactly fifty years after his confrontation at Fort Hare.

Mandela had every right to retire peacefully to his country home. No one deserved more rest and escape from politics than an abused, senior veteran prisoner. He was now a legendary folk hero, who would be honored in his latter years by his people and by future generations. Why not retire?

Mandela was being asked to negotiate, lead, and intercede between two peoples. Once again, the decision meant great sacrifice. Ultimately, despite his tired body and tormented spirit, he was willing to serve the African National Congress (ANC), engage in difficult and lengthy negotiations with a stubborn South African government, endure more tragic massacres and injustices to his supporters, face the hypocrisy and covert brutality of the corrupt South African police, and ultimately become both global diplomat and president of South Africa.

Not only did Nelson's integrity remain unbroken, but he became a role model of moral leadership for people worldwide. More than any other person alive, he had ensured a positive answer to the questions about unity and equality in South Africa.

IN HIS OWN WORDS

At Fort Hare, young Nelson had struggled to find the right words for Alexander Kerr. But with practice, over the years he became eloquent when publicly addressing Simon Legree. Facing a possible death penalty, Mandela later told the court: "These considerations do not sway me from the path that I have taken. Nor will they sway others like me. For to men, freedom in their own land is the pinnacle of their ambitions, from which nothing can turn men of conviction aside."

On another occasion, knowing that he was about to be sentenced to years in prison, he unflinchingly said to a court magistrate: "More powerful than my fear of the dreadful conditions to which I might be subjected in prison is my hatred of the dreadful conditions to which my people are subjected outside prison throughout this country…"

In the final analysis, Madiba would be driven by the values of justice, freedom, goodness and love. In *Long Walk to Freedom*, he wrote: "No one is born hating another person because of the color of his skin, or his background, or his religion. People must learn to hate, and if they can be taught to hate, they can be taught to love, for love comes more naturally to the human heart than its opposite. Even in the grimmest times in prison, when my comrades and I were pushed to our limits, I would see a glimmer of humanity in one of the guards, perhaps just for a second, but it was enough to reassure me and keep me going. Man's goodness is a flame that may be hidden but never extinguished."

Nor would he ever be forced to banish love from his repertoire of behavior. Despite the expectation that he would naturally hate the white authorities who had killed and persecuted so many of his colleagues, Mandela wrote: "I knew that people expected me to harbor anger toward whites. But I had none… I wanted South Africa to see that I loved even my enemies while I hated the system that turned us against one another."

A WORLD LEADER BUT NOT A SAINT

Madiba modeled reconciliation in broad brush strokes. In his later years, despite what seemed to him to be numerous cover-ups and betrayals by South Africa's President F.W. de Klerk, he worked relentlessly with de Klerk and his representatives to negotiate a new constitution, dismantle apartheid, and create a "new Africa" in which all races had equal rights.

Honoring the inter-racial teamwork, which was symbolized by Mandela's and de Klerk's civic partnership, the Nobel Committee awarded both men the Nobel Peace Prize, jointly, in 1993. Among those attending Mandela's inauguration were the very prison guards who had sequestered and emasculated him.

Of course, Madiba was not a perfect person. He was among the first to point out his own imperfections, such as stubbornness, defensiveness, deprioritizing family needs, and occasional overreaction. Despite his charm and social finesse, his relationships with his second wife, Winnie, with F.W. de Klerk, and with Zulu chief Buthelezi were among several plagued with chronic speedbumps.

Madiba frequently acknowledged his political and personal mistakes. Indeed, it was this honesty and humility that further endeared many to his genuineness. As an acclaimed British journalist concluded in Mandela's authorized biography: "It was his essential integrity more than his superhuman myth which gave his story its appeal across the world."

Once Mandela became an activist, his critics would argue that he was a terrorist, due to his violent means to cripple the state. Within the government's perspective, Mandela was not a man of integrity and not ethical, since these political authorities did not permit situational ethics, but only strict obedience to government rules.

Similarly, Fort Hare's administration would not view Mandela as a hero for standing firm, but rather as a rebel, ingrate, and even a rabble rouser. Some ethical systems that honor the rule of governments, owners, and administrations might deem Mandela unethical for being part of a boycott.

But most ethical systems would allow that being above the law is tolerated, if not venerated, as an act of self-defense. The lesser of two evils may sometimes be seen as the better, if not the virtuous, path. Being lawful or policy-driven is not the same as being ethical, especially in a corrupt or segregated society.

Indeed, ignoring one's conscience and refusing to help the systematically abused, demeaned, and raped may be seen as unethical, whatever the law of the land. Obeying the law of Nazi Germany or any other country practicing genocide may be legal within national law, but is illegal via international law, and only ethical within the self-created ethics of an inhumane regime.

THE TEN FACTORS:

1. **Notions of fairness and justice:** At Fort Hare, Madiba felt that students, not just administrators and faculty, should have basic human rights. Fairness dictated that each person in the school be treated with respect. Later in life, Nelson's foremost compulsion was for equal treatment before a just law. He knew that freedom fighters, militant protestors, and social activists are often seen as unethical when they hold themselves above the law. Like those labeled terrorists, religious extremists, and cultists, activists frequently hold the view that because the laws in police states are immoral, they may be broken in pursuit of a higher morality or greater law which is not man-made. In such cases, the ethical question becomes: who, if anyone, has a right to be above the law? To which other moral or natural law(s) are such people accountable?

   Mandela answered this difficult ethical question by claiming that South African law was "immoral, unjust, and intolerable." He argued that in such cases, men and women of conscience have a moral responsibility to challenge such laws. Later, he cited Bertrand Russell's willingness to violate British law as a protest against England's nuclear weapons policy as an example of virtuous, albeit illegal, behavior. Justice must be humane and universal, not just legal, especially within a corrupt regime.

2. **Impact or consequences:** At Fort Hare, Madiba faced the likely consequences of expulsion from school and stigma to family. Later, when violating South African law, Madiba and his colleagues constantly faced the likely consequences of violent reprisals to family, imprisonment, and death. Yet they strived for consequences of a different nature that could produce a humane society and unify South Africa. Mandela had to always weigh the pain and persecution of short-term consequences against the gain of long-term goals (see #9, "Implications," below). At Fort Hare, he was uncertain of the positive consequences of standing up for his classmates. Even if he stood firm, they might not gain the objectives of their boycott—but they would gain trust in each other and in their student leaders. They might also gain political power and momentum if Kerr backed down due to their strength in numbers.

3. **Ends and means:** The German philosopher Immanuel Kant wrote that people should never be used as only a means to an end, but rather also as an end of themselves. Unlike Kant, by supporting seemingly endless boycotts, strikes, slowdowns, acts of sabotage, and armed struggle, in his later years Mandela seemed to advocate using the enemy, and indeed innocent bystanders, as a means toward racial liberation. He also often used the press and third parties to pressure the South African government. Within his inner struggle, Mandela had to reconcile using other people, even his own "groundlings" within the ANC, without regard to their harm and comfort, to accomplish group goals.

Mandela struggled with these issues and eventually argued that the ANC should chose sabotage as their first and primary destructive act, because it was the least damaging to human life and welfare in comparison with other pressure-building options. But others who worked closely with Mandela sought to execute informers and sometimes unknowingly killed innocents. Did the ends justify these means? Madiba argued that harming others should be employed only as a last resort, and that "turnabout is fair play" against oppressors when more humane tactics prove impotent.

Prior to the Fort Hare standoff, Madiba was not yet thinking about ends vs. means. But, when he considered what to say to Principal Kerr, he had to consider if his ends (fair treatment to students) justified a means that could damage him, his family, and possibly other students.

4. **Tone and atmosphere:** Madiba wished to remain respectful and high-toned when addressing his principal, but he did not wish to become a sycophant. Later in life, although he greatly admired Mahatma Gandhi, he was committed to a non-violent tone only to the extent that it accomplished the goals of overcoming a corrupt state. Thus Madiba, debated with the Mahatma's son, Manilal Gandhi, a respected Indian in South Africa who advocated unconditional non-violence. Those supporting Manilal and opposing Mandela argued that non-violence was morally superior and modeled a civilized and humane approach to conflict resolution. Non-violence provided a higher tone and atmosphere.

   Non-violence could also protect protestors and victims from harsh recriminations. Mandela agreed with non-violence to the degree that it saved lives and effected change, but he argued that when non-violent actions proved impotent, it became necessary to change tactics. Although a high tone mattered, it could neither trump nor undermine the long-term goals of unity and universal justice.

5. **Motivation and higher law:** Just as eighteenth-century American and French revolutionaries argued that there were inalienable rights that could be restricted by neither the divine right of kings nor arbitrary human law, even so, Mandela thought such human rights are universal. The inherent rights of all South Africans to freely associate, marry, work, and elect and critique their government were non-negotiable and subject to a higher law than the law of white magistrates. In such higher law, one's inner voice meant more than South Africa's outer political authority and apartheid. Although Madiba could not yet articulate such a vision to Principal Kerr, he knew intuitively that all people have rights and that student votes and boycotts should not be ignored. Already he sensed that each voice mattered and that he should support democratic, rather than authoritarian, decision-making.

6. **Allegiance and loyalty:** Although Madiba felt allegiance to Fort Hare's administration and his family, he also felt a strong loyalty to his fellow students and to those who were unfairly and arbitrarily censored and potentially censured. The principal seemed to be censoring the voice of students. In the long run, Madiba's strongest loyalty would be to the voiceless and marginalized, although a loyalty to loved ones and financial supporters could never be dismissed. His allegiance to family, tribe, education, and personal growth made him reluctant to oppose Principal Kerr. Yet, his accountability to his constituents and conscience also carried potent moral force.

7. **Values and principles:** While Madiba knew that upholding principles is admirable, he also discovered that the absolute application of principle can be ethically problematic. For example, Immanuel Kant's absolute commitment to truth-telling may lead a truth-teller to be an accomplice to murder. For example, when answering this murderer's question of "where is your brother? I am going to kill him," a truthful answer can lead to homicide.

Madiba posed exactly this problem of "principles above all" when he struggled with how to respond to Fort Hare's principal. He asked himself: "Am I sabotaging my academic career over an abstract moral principle that, in the long run, may not be a high priority?" Many years later, despite the advice of many trusted attorneys, Mandela and others on trial decided they would not appeal their trial, even if they received the death penalty, as a matter of principle. In some cases, principle mattered above all else, but in others he was willing to sacrifice or dilute principles in order to save lives (including his own) or win tactical battles that strengthened his movement.

In such cases, his guiding principle was to "compromise wisely and live to fight another day." Yet, at this very early stage in his life, Madiba could not think of a compromise that would have appeased Principle Kerr. He had to make a concrete choice guided by principles such as "the greatest good for the greatest number" and "all people are created equal."

8. **Cultural context:** Madiba's tribal background upheld *Ubuntu*, and thus peaceful cooperation and community sharing was a desired goal. However, the *Überkultur* of the Dutch and British imposed upon indigenous Africans meant that cooperation was often closer to slavery. Mandela was caught between the culture of Madiba and the culture of Nelson. He felt more at home with being Madiba, but he would have to also be Nelson if he was going to succeed in South Africa. One culture promoted respect for all; the other supported both a class and a race hierarchy which afforded little respect for "lower" races and for the educational underclass called "students." Moreover, the students were black, and the educators were white in a culture that mandated that the educators would have both class and race privileges.

9. **Implications:** Madiba could not forecast the long-term implications of his decision. He knew that he would probably be expelled from college if he disobeyed his principal, and that he would be distrusted and disliked by his student colleagues if he submitted to Kerr. But there were larger, unseen implications. The stand that he took could inspire other students

to risk standing up to white authorities. Moreover, his decision could set a precedent for expressing integrity even in the face of great resistance, one which would establish a leadership trait he would demonstrate throughout life. Ultimately, multiple decisions of this nature would lead to the end of apartheid and a more liberated and democratic society.

10. **Proportion and balance:** Madiba's greatest sources of angst were in the realms of severe consequences and conflicting loyalties. Among his strongest motivating factors was a sense of justice propelled by a higher law than university fiat. Later in his life, he would often show a preference for higher law over immediate consequences, including backlash.

While ends and means, as well as tone, mattered, his strongest pull would be toward justice and accountability. Since the cultural context imposed a long-standing injustice, he realized he could not simply address injustice without also addressing and ultimately deposing the entire imperial culture.

THE LEGACY

Ironically, fifty years after he departed from Fort Hare, that university would honor Nelson Mandela as their most distinguished student. Indeed, his alma mater would be among over fifty universities and colleges (including Oxford, Harvard, Brown, Uppsala, Leiden, Havana, Howard, and Amherst) that awarded Madiba with honorary doctoral degrees.

Following Nelson's death in 2013, heads of state and their designees flew from six continents to attend his funeral. As portrayed by Morgan Freeman in the Hollywood film *Invictus*, President Mandela was depicted as the senior "healer of the nation" who strongly supported an almost all-white rugby match backed largely by the old-guard white supremacists. At that event and many others he reached out to demonstrate an ability to mend fences with all. Despite ongoing animosity between the white and black old guard, the nation's new president often reconciled factions. He placed some of his former enemies within key positions in his government.

In short, Madiba gave new currency and meaning to the world "ethical." Celebrated in his later years as "the pre-eminent statesman of his century," Mandela was also called the "testimony to forgiveness in the healing of the nation." Despite the ongoing politicking in South Africa following his presidency, he knew that his life had accomplished his primary goal—the unification of South Africa.

Moreover, he had modeled a path to world peace—he felt that if apartheid could be nullified, then leaders of good will could also temper global armed conflict. As his colleague and fellow Nobel laureate, Desmond Tutu, said about the end of apartheid: "If it can happen here, it can jolly well happen anywhere."

Perhaps no one person received as many distinguished statesmanship awards within recent history. His Nobel Peace Prize of 1993 was complemented by the Gandhi Peace Prize of 2001, the Presidential Medal of Freedom in 2002, the *TIME* Person of the Year in 1993, the Lenin Peace Prize of 1990, and top awards from the United Nations, Order of the Nile, Queen Elizabeth, the NAACP—not to mention prestigious honors dedicated to the memory of U Thant, Nehru, Gandhi, King, W.E.B. DuBois, Bolivar, and Sakharov.

Ironically, Alexander Kerr, who wondered if the disobedient Nelson was deserving of a college education, is barely remembered. Nelson is now the name most frequently associated with Fort Hare College, with world leadership, and frequently with the naming of African baby boys.

The Sanskrit term *mandala* (pronounced "man-della") is known as the "wheel of life." On that intense day in 1939, when facing Dr. Alexander Kerr, Madiba had chosen which place he would take on the great *mandala*.

From his own understanding of ethics, he had found it more compelling to do the right thing than to "gain the whole world and lose his soul." Leaving Kerr's office he might have said, just as he shouted following his circumcision ritual, "I am a man!"

The pattern of Madiba's decisions, beginning with the one taken at Fort Hare, would alter the course of history and uphold the dignity of humanity. Ultimately, the spirit behind the Kerr decision would lead both Madiba and Nelson to take an unflinching place on the great *mandala*... and become the great Mandela.

CHAPTER 12

MALALA YOUSAFZAI
(1997-)

FROM TWILIGHT TO DAWN

"Sometimes I think it's easier being a *Twilight* vampire
than a girl in Swat."

- Malala Yousafzai

TWILIGHT

How could she, at the age of fifteen, be in her twilight? Lying in a coma for days, Malala's hopes for survival seemed slim. Those on the medical team who were religious encouraged her father to pray, since this was no longer a strictly medical matter. Millions of people worldwide, including thousands of Malala's fellow Pakistani schoolgirls, joined him, holding vigils to pray for her recovery.

The images of Malala were from a horror story. She had left a trail of blood, resembled a ghoul, and would soon have a fragment of her skull removed. Loving hands found it easy to touch hers, but loving eyes found it heart-wrenching to meet hers inside their lopsided, discolored sockets after the surgery—and now both eyes were sealed and swollen.

As a Pakistani teen, Malala had managed to view the *Twilight* saga. Like many fans of Stephanie Meyer, she had been intrigued by the Hollywood romance between a mortal human and vampire that enlarged despite all odds. But unlike many of Meyer's fans, Malala had a direct corollary in her daily life to the creatures of *Twilight*—creatures who were the reason for her coma.

She had seen TV vampires who thrived by feasting, happily, on the blood of the innocent. They came out at night to destroy. So too, in Malala's world, did the Taliban, whom she likened to the blood-sucking night creatures.

The Taliban had already bombed over one hundred and fifty Pakistani girls' schools by night. They left the heads of decapitated policemen and gory bodies within public view. Blood and darkness seemed everywhere. Every night shadow seemed sinister.

Now her twilight was linked to theirs. As a marked target of the Taliban, she had received threat upon threat from the "vampires." Finally, on October 9, 2012, just one year prior to Nelson Mandela's (chapter 11) death, an unknown, bearded man stopped her school bus—which was actually a converted Toyota

241

truck—presumably to ask questions. While he talked to the driver, another Taliban assassin approached the back of the open truck and asked, "who is Malala?" Without hesitation, he shot at her face three times, and escaped into the bustling cityscape.

Fortunately, the bullet that hit Malala missed her brain—barely. But unfortunately, the shock of the bullet to her system caused potentially lethal swelling in her brain and sent bone fragments into highly sensitive parts of her head and ear. As the Taliban gunman slipped away, so too did a sizable trail of blood.

How could all of this happen to a fifteen-year-old schoolgirl who prayed for peace each night?

THE DECISIONS

In just fifteen years, Malala Yousafzai had faced a shocking number and variety of difficult ethical decisions. Before she faced the gunman in the converted Toyota truck, she encountered a series of harrowing moments and a number of related decisions. If at any point Malala had decided differently, she might have been able to prevent the crisis—to prevent her personal, morbidly altered twilight.

Well before the shooting on the truck, the police had asked if she would like bodyguard protection. And her father had asked if she would like to attend a boarding school with her brother, probably far away from danger. These were two important decisions that might have altered history. There was also, always, the possibility of backing down, of changing her actions so that the Taliban would no longer consider her a threat.

Such decisions, however, were not just pragmatic questions of survival for Malala. They were deeply moral and ethical questions she needed to weigh.

First, there was the bodyguard question. On the practical side, she had to ask herself if relocating or using bodyguards would necessarily be effective. On the one hand, the police had shown her father a file they kept about Malala that proved her death threats were not hoaxes. She watched his face turn ashen when he read the contents.

She knew as she watched him that she was in grave danger and that something had to be done. But on the other hand, she lived in a country where leaders with bodyguards had already been killed, some by the Taliban, and one leader even by his own bodyguard. Would bodyguards have been enough, even if she could trust them?

Hiring bodyguards would also have made her location and movements more obvious, and thus pointed her out as a larger target. Malala also knew that she would then endanger the lives of more people—her family, her friends, the bodyguards themselves, and even unknowing bystanders. Suicide bombers were a favorite weapon of the Taliban and they destroyed groups, not just individuals.

Although adding bodyguards might have increased the odds of survival, it certainly could not have guaranteed it. Guns have no respect for numbers. They can quickly eliminate targets and their bodyguards.

Would moving away to a boarding school have been a better option? At such a distance, the Taliban would have been met with more difficulty pursuing her. But she would still have been an easy mark if they prioritized her elimination, and outside the relatively protected zone of family and friends.

Malala's father, Ziauddin Yousafzai, was her primary influence in making such critical decisions. Faced with a similar choice, he had personally refused bodyguards in part because he liked to move discretely to different locations at night rather than endanger his family by sleeping at home.

But to him, his daughter was a different story. Indeed, he was the one who had suggested that she join her brother at a boarding school when he realized how menacing the Taliban had become.

The direct threats to Malala were of three kinds. First, she and other family members had received notes under the door warning of her pending death. Then, posts calling for her death appeared on Facebook. There were even ads published in newspapers.

There was also a legacy of more widespread warnings. Already, over one hundred and fifty schools for girls similar to hers had been demolished, since girls' education was seen as threatening to the old order. Photocopied notices had been circulated throughout the community calling for the termination of her own school, which was managed by her father. And over the years, many of her father's educator counterparts and activist friends had been killed, injured, or harassed by the Taliban. As recently as August 12, 2012, less than two months before the shooting on the bus, one of her father's friends, Zahid Kahn, had been shot in the face by a would-be assassin.

Many continued to warn her father: "Be careful. You are next." Her grandmother warned Malala to keep a low profile, and her mother kept imagining scenarios in which she would be accosted by Taliban intruders. A friend at her school experienced a horrific premonition, and Malala herself had recurring nightmares featuring Taliban treachery.

Malala's family were no strangers to adversity. Her father had been threatened so many times that the co-mingling of fear and courage had become a lifestyle. Bolting the back gate and fantasizing about how she would respond to a Taliban attack had become a normal practice in recent years. Her parents, who knew her to be outrageously brave, took note when even Malala felt the back gate needed to remain locked. Few days went by without word of another nearby flogging, murder, suicide bomb, rape, death threat, beheading, or school bombing.

But this time, the last line of defense had eroded. The police file made it clear that Malala's father was no longer the primary Taliban target in the family. His daughter was. For years, they had thought that a child would never be a mark, even for the Taliban. And yet the evidence presented by the police indicated that Malala had become a sitting duck.

Ziauddin Yousafzai had always carried himself as a proud father, gifted schoolmaster, and Malala's champion, hero, mentor, and role model all in one. He had spearheaded their campaign for universal education in the Swat Valley. Ziauddin had even added her name to the family tree, an honor reserved only for the men of his tradition. In times of fear and adversity, it was always her father who had sustained their momentum and refused to be intimidated.

And suddenly Ziauddin wished to retreat. If Malala left for boarding school, she would not only have been giving in to the Taliban, but it would have meant the end of their campaign, an end to their highly effective partnership.

Their mission was a critical one, one close to both Ziauddin's and Malala's hearts. They had stood up strongly for the rights of Pakistan's children to have universal education. In a country in which only seventy percent of the men and forty percent of the women were literate, their hope was that all children could have equal access to education beyond religious instruction.

In a climate in which many were being executed for dancing, wearing the wrong clothing, being raped (note: it was not the rapist but rather the victim who was stoned for rape), and owning televisions or DVDs, they were also taking a stand for human rights, choice, and dignity. She would hear—but never accept—that yet another Islamic woman had acid thrown into her face as a supposedly just punishment, or that another friend of the family had simply disappeared.

So, to Malala, their cause was crucial, and the deeper moral and ethical questions she faced went well beyond the matter of survival—what was the extent of her responsibility to unschooled children? To humanity? Would she be escaping duty or betraying others by relocating? What was her moral commitment to her father and family? To her school? To education? Would using armed bodyguards mean endorsing weapons? Abandoning non-violence?

What would backing down mean morally? Would she be conceding defeat to the Taliban? Letting fear replace courage? Abandoning the hundreds of young schoolgirls for whom she was becoming a role model? Violating her own integrity?

In short, could she live with her conscience if she conceded ground to the aggressor? Would she be tacitly supporting evil by protecting herself against it?

THE BACKSTORY: WHAT IS MINGORA?

Born on July 12, 1997, Malala grew up in Mingora, Pakistan, which is now described as a bustling, dirty city of 170,000. The city is located not far from the Afghan and Tajikistan borders. During Malala's childhood, Mingora was, to paraphrase Charles Dickens, the best of towns, and the worst of towns.

It was indeed a tale of two cities. The best Mingora was nestled in the beautiful Swat Valley, a land of waterfalls, emeralds, enchanted mountains, and trout-filled, clear lakes. Entering the Swat Valley, visitors read the idyllic sign, "Welcome to Paradise."

"Pakistan" can be translated as "land of the pure" in Urdu. It was born of the most ancient civilizations, and yet is one of the newest countries. This best Mingora blended a rich cultural heritage with the fresh possibilities of a new nation.

Malala also had much going for her. Her grandfather, an Iman (Islamic preacher), gave sermons so famous that worshippers would come from miles to listen. Her father received the nickname, "the falcon," when he became a master speaker as a child, one who could "soar above the others."

What made the falcon's speaking honors so notable was that Ziauddin suffered from a pronounced speech impediment. Against all odds, he had intensively practiced speaking, memorized entire monologues, and won the hearts of his peers and the judges.

Her mother was equally remarkable as the only girl in their region who, despite eventually dropping out, had attended a boys' school. Although out of necessity her mother performed the traditional maternal duties, she shared much knowledge of her father's world and work in a way that was rare among married couples in their area.

Despite the obstacles of time and tradition, her mother and father had been able to marry for love rather than through an arrangement by their families. Her father had also been able to fulfill his dream of opening a school. Eventually, he became a stable and respected principal.

Moreover, Malala, her brother, and her parents were never outsiders. They were instead among the ninety-six percent of the population in Pakistan who were Muslim. And within that religion, her family was also part of the Sunni majority. Malala was also of the Pashtun ethnic group, the second largest clan in Pakistan. Her family visited beloved relatives in the verdant countryside. Taking all of this into consideration, an argument could be made that Malala was born into relative privilege, freedom, beauty, and the best of times.

However, she was also raised in the worst of towns and times. The beauty of Swat was fading since many people were felling trees and poisoning the streams with garbage. Mingora also seemed out of touch with the larger world. No one she knew had ever visited the capital city, Islamabad.

During much of her short life, the people of Swat were caught between the warring Taliban and Pakistani army. Eventually, over half a million people were forced to evacuate Mingora, where the crumbling walls of bombed buildings were riddled with bullet holes.

Even prior to the Taliban invasion, Mingora faced widespread austerity. Pakistan was one of the poorest countries in the world. Even within her relative privilege, Malala recalled living in a small shack without a kitchen or bathroom. Her mother had to buy gas canisters from the bazaar in order to cook and then prepare the food on the ground. Clothes had to be washed under a tap from a sink at the school. Dirt and insects were a part of the family.

The disordered traffic included her neighbors who were crammed into rickshaws where they constantly inhaled diesel fumes. Malala was especially haunted by the rubbish mountain, where scavenging children competed with rats and crows for bites of decaying food and other salvageable garbage.

If this were not enough, the Yousafzai family also lived through a series of earthquakes in which up to 150,000 people were killed. Her family and friends also faced the worst flooding in Swat's recorded history. In her autobiography, Malala recalls mud filling their small home and covering the city. Thirty-four of Mingora's forty-two bridges were washed away. Mudslides did not bypass a single piece of their furniture. By the time she was sixteen, she had been forced to move seven times.

Dirty water contributed to the increase of cholera in a land where "obsolete diseases"—polio, typhoid fever, measles—were both common and lethal. And there were political diseases as well. Scandals surrounding CIA agents and the bombing of innocents by U.S. drones rendered the American government controversial for some, and the enemy for others. Later, the assassination of Osama bin Laden in Pakistan by Americans deepened the wounds, since the Pakistani government and police were never consulted.

All of this meant that it was never easy to tell who your friends were. Some of the secret intelligence and government seemed aligned with the Taliban, others with the West, and still others with Pakistan. And their loyalties could shift quickly under the influence of the dollar or a death threat.

Other so-called leaders were afraid to interfere. Bin Laden had been living close to a major military post, so many locals wondered why the Pakistani army had done nothing about him. Few had the courage to speak out, since anyone could be quickly and quietly reported to the Taliban or the police—or both. And social media were often used as anti-social media.

The combination of these factors presented a variety of daily challenges to all of Mingora, and threatened Malala and her family in a more immediate and personal way. Her father's dream school was a threat to traditionalists because it welcomed girls. Such a secular practice was seen as *haram* (i.e. sinful) by the more conservative *mullahs* (religious scholars). As the Taliban grew in power, the school and faculty would be seen as infidels and a symbol of secular Western values.

In short, despite her many advantages and liberties, Malala faced great adversity. Many of her former schoolmates had dropped out, died, disappeared, or relocated to tented refugee camps. Of the many obstacles they all had faced—floods, earthquakes, filth, disease, poverty, civil war, and much more—one terror stood above all others...

The Taliban.

TALIBAN AT TWILIGHT

Within the Islamic tradition, a *talib* is a student or seeker. The plural of *talib* is *taliban*. Thus, the name Taliban appeared in the 1990s when large numbers of students formed a burgeoning radical-fundamentalist Islamic group in Afghanistan. A decade later, Malala's family witnessed firsthand the Taliban spread into northern Pakistan.

To many, the "students of Islam" had initially seemed like a pro-social movement that would bring order and spiritual purpose to a chaotic Afghanistan. An insider within the movement would proudly point to the restoration of *sharia* (religious) law and wholesomeness as accomplishments of the early Taliban. However, it soon became obvious that the radical fundamentalism of the Taliban would be implemented with harsh, exacting, bloodstained penalties for non-conformity.

When the black-turbaned brigade arrived in Malala's Swat valley in 2007, one of her father's friends called them "the people deprived of baths and barbers" due to their unruly beards and smells. The people of Mingora became aware of Taliban philosophy when extremist Maulana Fazlullah began to broadcast from a neighboring FM radio station.

Initially, Fazlullah's messages seemed enticing. But it soon became known that he would harshly punish critics and those he labeled infidels. Seeking to impose the strictest interpretations of *sharia*, his followers began to execute and whip those deemed adulterers, thieves, and blasphemers. Throwing acid into the faces of girls, which disfigured them for life, was a popular penalty for young women who seemed unfaithful to Islam or were accused of being less than dutiful to their husbands.

The result was that by 2008—just a year after the arrival of the Taliban—over one thousand ordinary people had been killed within the Swat Valley. Why weren't they protected? Tragically, it was becoming commonplace for the bodies of police to be found after they had been beheaded.

Although the teachings of Islam protect the rights of women and support their education, Fazlullah's Taliban followed a strict, ultra-conservative interpretation of *sharia* law. They strongly opposed the schooling and public appearances of women.

Thus, the night bombing of girls' schools became business as usual to prevent *haram* education. The public flogging of women strictly reminded them to be seen only with men in their family, to fully cover their bodies, and in essence to remain invisible, asexual, and domestic.

One example of *sharia* law required that a woman who reported rape must produce four upright male witnesses, or she herself would be punished for the crime. Women were also stoned to death in "honor killings" for shaming their families, or as a remedy to a family quarrel.

So many extreme rules promoting such cruelty made even some moderate and conservative Muslims feel that the Taliban had gone too far. Thus, the community became polarized between pro-Taliban and pro-Pakistan forces. Taliban violence begat military violence and vice versa, such that the early signs of a Taliban-military civil war made ordinary citizens feel trapped between two fists.

But Malala felt far more than trapped. She felt personally frozen in her daily life and, most significantly to her, in her education. An edict came from Fazullah that all girls had to leave their schools in 2008. The same Taliban that had silenced Pakistan's only female prime leader, Benazir Bhutto, the year before would now ensure that there would be no more aspiring Bhuttos on the horizon.

WHY MALALA?

Among all the people who lived in the Swat Valley, some armed and treacherous, why would the Taliban target an unarmed fifteen-year-old girl? After all, she was deeply religious and prayed constantly, just like the most faithful of the Taliban. And she called herself "ordinary"—she enjoyed teasing her brothers and playing games like other teens.

It was not that Malala whom the Taliban detested, exactly. Rather, it was her alter ego, Gul Makai. Gul was a pseudonym Malala had adopted when interviewed by the BBC about the real conditions facing Swat residents. Repeatedly, Gul had talked about harsh realities using the Makai *nom de plume*.

Over time she was also speaking to other interviewers, blogging, and eventually reaching millions. In some cases, she had become more open about her real identity. It was this side of Malala that was so threatening—she had not only dared to voice her views internationally as Gul, but also in Mingora as Malala, without the Makai mask.

Indeed, by the time she was sixteen, Malala and her father had already spoken publicly together many times. The topic was often about promoting girls' education, and thus opposing the Taliban. Already a school had been named for her, and as a teenager she had won Pakistan's national peace prize.

So, it would be impossible to keep a low profile, and her visibility kept growing. She was contacted by a Stanford student who had seen her in the documentary *Class Dismissed*, and by others who guessed that they had figured out the real identity of Gul Makai.

NEVER ALONE

Gul knew she was speaking for millions of other girls, women, and children who were abused victims of stern patriarchy. Not only were many youths deprived of education, but she was also aware of those forced to marry someone they had never met. In some cases, young girls were sold to older men as brides, but those transactions seemed like prostitution under another name. Some preteen brides had children when they themselves were still almost children. There was no hope that they would experience freedom, privacy, education, autonomy, or, in some cases, even childhood.

Throughout the world, the perils of childhood were legion. Many children were forced into other forms of prostitution and extreme sexual practices. Others were sold into slavery and trafficked to distant lands. Still others were forced to be soldiers and to shoot other children and civilians before dying an early, violent death. Yet others worked in mines seven long days a week, where they inhaled the attendant fumes that destined them to very short lives.

While the Taliban were not responsible for all of these practices, they symbolized total disrespect for youth. Via various forms of bondage, bombing, and cruel punishments, they had adolescent blood on their hands.

Malala was especially concerned about the callous treatment of girls, many of whom could not laugh, sing, or be seen in public. And the women that these Taliban girls would later become faced onerous and often heartbreaking futures.

It almost seemed that the subservient women of the Taliban wore a thinly disguised garb of slavery. The "hot as ovens" full-length *burqas* they wore concealed everything except their eyes. Being anonymous, or literally faceless, appeared to be a defacing of human dignity and identity. Throwing acid in the faces of women as a punishment also totally eliminated identity and beauty, often for life. Cosmetics, beauty parlors, public speaking, and careers were totally forbidden in a world rigidly ruled by men.

Indeed, when Malala was born, no one congratulated her father. The neighbors commiserated with her mother. The birth of a boy was a reason to celebrate, but girls had little value. In the more traditional families, it was not unusual for a girl to be given to a rival family to resolve a feud. Other girls had been poisoned by their own families for flirting with men. Since the Taliban forbade women to work outside the home, thousands without husbands were forced to beg on the streets.

Data compiled by UNICEF was revealing. Twenty percent of Pakistani girls would be married by the time they were thirteen years old. Ninety percent of women had experienced some form of abuse—beatings, stonings, acid burnings, and domestic violence hidden from view. Up to one thousand women and girls were murdered in honor killings annually. And despite rare exceptions like Benizar Bhutto, who attended Harvard and Oxford, few attended secondary school, let alone college. Sixty percent of Pakistan's women were illiterate.

In the light of such darkness, Malala had felt especially privileged. Her father had refused to receive the traditional gifts of money honoring his son's ceremonies if the money were not also given for Malala's ceremonies. Unlike most Pakistani men, Malala's father consulted his wife, read to her, and had waited nine months for her hand in marriage. And, going against the grain of public approval, Ziauddin had insisted upon the education of his own daughter. He dreamed of extending that education to all the girls of Pakistan.

Such privilege, however, only heightened Malala's awareness of the plight of others. She realized that Taliban women could not vote, talk to men outside their family, or even laugh in some regions. Now, this lifestyle—or perhaps death-style—was being imposed upon all the women of Swat as it had been upon Afghan women.

Eventually, over four hundred schools would be bombed, and Malala often felt that hers could be next. From her perspective, this was misogyny, not religious freedom; it was cruelty, not cultural necessity; and it was an inhumane setback upon humanity, not just Pakistani girls.

SAVING FACES AND MORAL COURAGE

Imagine how the Taliban leaders must have felt about Malala and her father. The Taliban were not only being depicted as cruel and wrong, but this degrading image was being sent to the world. To add insult to injury, their message was proffered by a person who should have had no credibility or voice—an infidel girl.

They needed to save face. So she had to lose face.

But Malala was more concerned with saving other faces. Indeed, her own face was usually unobstructed. Although she wore a scarf over her head to show proper respect, Malala seldom hid her face behind clothing in the way that many Muslim women were forced to do.

So, on that fateful day when the gunman had asked, "who is Malala?" there were two clues to answer his question. First, although no one said a word, some of the other girls instinctively looked in her direction. More significantly, she was the only girl on the bus who did not cover her face. For many, this was a sign of bravery or independence. But for the gunman, it was blasphemy.

COURAGE ABOVE AND BEYOND

Malala had exhibited bravado in many other ways throughout her life. Despite parental warnings, she never closed her curtains in the evening. Just as her father had won speaking contests despite his stuttering, she had won great recognition despite her youth and gender.

She was a top student, often vying for first place in her class, and she didn't mince words, no matter her fear of the audience. By this point she was famous for her pointed public remark: "How dare the Taliban deprive me of an education."

Malala's courage was perhaps most powerfully evident on November 8, 2014, when she was photographed sitting up in bed for the first time after emerging from her coma. In her autobiography, Malala wrote: "Our fear was strong, but not as strong as our courage." She thought to herself, "if one man, Fazlullah, can destroy everything, why can't one girl change it?"

Every night she prayed to Allah for strength. Indeed, her faith brought a remarkable reservoir of courage. Later she wrote, "I love my God. I thank my Allah. I talk with him all day."

Neither her faith nor her resolve were ultimately shaken, even by an assassin's bullets. After her recovery, she would write that "the terrorists thought they could change our aims... but nothing changed in my life except this: fear and hopelessness died. Strength, power, and courage were born."

Adopting such an attitude had not been easy. Often, she faced an inner struggle. When fear sought to control, she had to say to herself: "Don't be afraid. If you are afraid, you can't move forward."

Much of the credit for her victory over fear and adversity had to be given to her parents. They had been shaken by the mud-filled, flooded homes, the aftershocks of earthquakes, massive evacuation during civil war, endless debt, disease, and death threats under the door. And yet the Yousafzai family emerged stronger and ultimately resilient.

What developed within her family was not only physical bravery but also moral courage. Nothing could subdue their integrity. No one could bully them into abandoning their purpose.

When Malala's voice was increasingly heard, she felt a greater sense of accountability to others. Later she wrote, "by giving me this height to reach all people, He (Allah) has given me great responsibilities... Peace in every home, every street, every village and country. That is my dream."

THE DECISION

Given her strong sense of purpose, Malala was sad, if not shocked, when even her father suggested abandoning their mission. He was now exceedingly concerned about her safety and his recommendation of boarding school was one measure of evidence. For the police to offer her, a young woman without title, expensive bodyguard protection was another omen to be taken seriously.

She understood her father's apprehension only too well. The police file, the "next-of-kin" murders of other activists, the endless school bombings, the multiple forms of public and private death threats, the brutal executions of those who had said far less than Malala—all added up to the warning given to her father by friends: "If you're not careful, you're next."

Then the pattern had shifted. In effect her father was giving her the same message: "If you're not careful, Malala, you are next."

What now?

She had thought the matter through and knew that vulnerable people of all kinds—schoolgirls, defaced women, educators, rape victims, Taliban children, even the nameless scavenger on the rubbish mountain—somehow depended upon someone to show moral leadership.

Malala's eyes met her father's as she declared: "You were the one who said if we believe in something greater than our lives, then our voices will multiply even if we are dead. We can't disown our campaign!"

There would be no escape to a boarding school and no need for bodyguards. Malala had spoken.

Although they may not have realized it at the time, the mantle of brave leadership had passed, but not from father to son. Symbolically, the focal point for courageous heroism would pass from father to daughter in an uncelebrated moment of unmarked transition. She had become not only the primary target and the most influential spokesperson, but also the family's spearhead of courage.

Although no one knew it at the time, this moment foreshadowed another when it was indeed Malala, not her father, who would face the bullets of a Colt .45. Penultimate courage in the face of penultimate darkness is not without consequence.

THE TEN FACTORS

1. **Notions of fairness and justice:** Although Malala was concerned about fairness of all kinds, three forms of discrimination—age, gender, and religion—most directly plagued her environment. Her stance was for equal access to education and career as well as freedom from religious oppression by extremists. In her later appeals to President Obama to cease the drone strikes, her plea for justice would be for the innocent victims of violence. All injustice was to be opposed, but it was especially the oppression of the muzzled and mistreated she wished to rectify. So great has her passion been for justice toward especially youth and women, that her life is now devoted to effecting equality for both groups.

2. **Impact or consequences:** Like her father, Malala aspired to universal access to education. She realized that one set of consequences for her decision would mean her own martyrdom, and possibly that of others. But, in a best-case scenario, the consequences could advance children's, women's, and ideally all people's rights and sovereignty. Concrete advances toward universal education and against discrimination toward

women, youth, and especially girls were desired consequences. In the short term, she wished to see a full stoppage of the bombing of schools and the beheading of policemen, but in the long-term she hoped for consequences that could lead to a fully educated populace without fear.

3. **Ends and means:** Arming herself, whether with guns or with bodyguards, would have been, in effect, a concession to violent means. If she desired a non-adversarial, non-violent outcome, would she not have to remain non-violent, even unarmed? But would not such an approach seem highly unrealistic, if not sacrificial? Her means needed to embody her goals and philosophy. From that perspective, it seemed that she needed to remain unarmed. No bodyguards should have been endangered as a means to protection, nor should family and friends have been placed in harm's way. Each person had to be respected as an end in and of herself and himself. So, the minimum number of people—one (Malala herself) would be put at risk rather than multiple people who were treated as a means to her safety, rather than as respected human beings out of the line of fire.

4. **Tone and atmosphere:** Although Malala could be a normal teenager in terms of boisterous quarrels with her brother and friends, her overall tone was one of a sacred, prayerful life of respect and peaceful tolerance. It was not only the horrid atmosphere of Taliban violence that concerned her, but the overall disrespectful tone toward the marginalized and toward life itself. She wished to be peaceful, not just to advocate peace. As a devout believer in Allah, Malala knew sacred tone to be an important consideration… but not as important as justice.

5. **Motivation and higher law:** Allah's law was a priority for Malala, but not as conceived by Islamic fundamentalists. Manmade interpretations of what seemed like greater universal laws had corrupted Allah's intention in Malala's eyes. A higher purpose called for honoring the sanctity of creation. Surely, an aspect of honoring human dignity was to provide each person with education and thus the tools for self-respect, prosperity, freedom, and the questioning of arbitrary authority. To her view, higher law did not call for violence and ignorance. She wished to surrender (a key concept within Islam) to a higher world order that would bring the passing of both ignorance and violence.

6. **Allegiance and loyalty:** While others profiled in previous chapters held allegiances to their constituents, spouses, or employers, Malala was a teen, so her primary environment contained family, friends, and school peers.

Her loyalties were initially minimal and local. However, as she dared to voice her views, she realized that she was a voice for a much larger environment of oppressed children and females far beyond .the Swat Valley. Although her initial allegiance was to the paternal order of Islam, and to her own father, she soon felt strong additional allegiances to oppressed women and children. Her primary allegiances were to her God, parents, aspirational vision, marginalized victims, and school peers.

7. **Values and principles:** One principle that seemed ignored by the Taliban was "let the penalty fit the crime." Another was "innocent until proven guilty." Everywhere, people were being executed for petty crimes based upon suspicions, hair-splitting interpretations of law, and hearsay. Malala stood for values that honored due process and reason, including the two named principles above. She valued the sanctity of life, education, and individual freedom. Traditions and principles that promoted authoritarian control were inherent to her heredity, but she wished to challenge them with principles of equity and universal access.

8. **Cultural context:** In a world in which only boys and men were valued, she advocated the worth of girls and women. Cultural mores held that a boy was worth several girls, and that leadership was inherently masculine. Tradition mandated that, in many situations, "might makes right." Literal interpretations of the Koran, coupled with arranged marriages, meant that Pakistani lives were micro-managed. While Malala's parents were liberal within this ultra-conservative milieu, she nevertheless fought an uphill battle against centuries of patriarchy, Islamic sect battles, *sharia* law, and rigid theocracy.

9. **Implications:** Malala's stated goal continues to be a world in which all children have access to open-minded and humane educational systems. The immediate implications of her activist actions were that a larger spotlight would be placed upon Taliban atrocities and her humanitarian goals, but the long-term implications could be that a far higher percentage of educated, successful, professional, and prosperous women and youth would appear. Already, both Pakistan and the United Nations have welcomed her voice and have taken tangible steps in that direction, such that one senses great potential in her vision becoming at least partially actualized worldwide.

10. **Proportion and balance:** When balancing the factors of her own personal safety against her goals of non-discrimination, non-violence, and universal education, Malala gave greater favor to others than to herself.

However much she honored the traditions of Islam, she gave greater merit to reforming the more inhibiting practices within her religion than to an unbending status quo. If the Taliban represented an extreme interpretation of the Prophet Mohammed, she favored a balanced, open-minded perspective including a symmetry between male and female rights and roles. Ultimately, the most important factors for Malala were justice, tone, and allegiances to deity and loved ones.

DAWN

Within a year of being shot, Malala miraculously recovered after multiple surgeries and remarkable medical care. She became the youngest person to be nominated for the Nobel Peace Prize, and was named runner-up for the award in 2013. She was also one of four runners-up in *TIME* magazine's "Person of the Year" award and the recipient of the prestigious Sakharov Prize for Human Rights awarded by the European Parliament. One year later in 2014, she became the youngest (co-) recipient of the Nobel Peace Prize.

Before Malala was shot, she had already been nominated by Desmond Tutu as one of five finalists for the International Children's Peace Prize, and also had won the national peace prize within Pakistan. By 2013 her awards had totaled over $100,000 in value, a sizable bounty for a teen in any country. Part of this money would be used to establish an education foundation for girls. Malala had survived twilight and a bright new day was dawning.

By March 2013, she had returned to school, albeit in England. After all, returning to Pakistan at that time could well have led to her martyrdom (in fact, the Taliban has repeatedly said that she remained a primary target), and residing in England would grant her far more freedom to build an international education campaign.

Only four months later, she became one of the youngest people ever to address the United Nations. There she called for universal schooling. Gordon Brown, the UN envoy for education and former prime minister of Great Britain, joined with Malala in creating a global campaign calling for every child to be in school by 2015. Her dream of global education received international backing and widespread media publicity.

No one could have been prouder of Malala than her parents, who had come to live with her in England. Her father was appointed education attaché to Pakistan's embassy in England, while her family moved to a new home in Birmingham. In the meantime, Pakistan has celebrated "Malala Day" and doubled its education commitment from two to four percent of the overall national budget.

In 2013, Dr. Yousafzai received an honorary degree from the University of Edinburgh and an honorary Ph.D. from King's College in Halifax—before being old enough to earn any college degrees. It is not surprising that *TIME* named her "one of the one hundred most influential people in the world."

Nevertheless, Malala's altered skull and face will never be the same, and she remains a marked exile from her homeland. When she met with President Obama, Afghan cynics said in effect: "You see, she is a spy for the West." Little did they know that she tried to persuade Obama to cease the drone strikes on Pakistan.

There is still opposition to universal education in Pakistan, although yet more schools have been named after Malala. While her world has become much brighter, she still recalls the neighbor girl who, amidst crows and rats, scavenged the garbage mountain. And whatever the fame of Malala, that rubbish-digger has probably met a harsh fate and been replaced by another girl just like her.

Nor has Malala escaped headaches. Those caused by the caustic threats of the Taliban have been replaced by the more pounding headaches of brain swelling, partial scalp removal, and follow-up surgery.

FULL CIRCLE

The question of how to save her people has haunted Malala just as much as it haunted Queen Esther. And thus, chronologically this book comes full circle from Esther to Malala. Despite thousands of years of alleged progress, has there been ethical advancement? It seems easier to posit that there has been technological and medical progress than to suggest that civil or humanitarian progress has transpired.

Has the millennium that produced the Holocaust and Truman's atom bomb evolved from the one in which Esther's husband enslaved hundreds of wives and quickly executed rivals? And many would claim that the most visible role models young people see on TV today—such as Putin, Trump, Johnson, and Kim—hardly point toward ethical progress in the twenty-first century.

So, it is not at all clear whether humanity has evolved or devolved. Justice in the face of the Third Reich, ISIS's mass beheadings, and the Taliban is no less important than justice in any other century.

Then there is the question of genuine tolerance and universal support. Has acceptance of difference evolved or devolved? While Malala is admired from afar, how many world citizens would positively answer this question: "Would I want my son to marry a Pakistani woman?" Depending upon where you live, you could substitute for the word "Pakistani" with words such as "Muslim," "African," "Hindu," "Jewish," "tattooed," "ultra-conservative," "radical," "gypsy," "Aboriginal," "transgender," "Turkish," "Catholic," "addict," "disabled," "African-American," "Protestant," "cult worshipper," "albino," "dwarf," "atheist," "honkey," "divorcee," "cougar," "senior," "Latina," "former prisoner," "swinger," "enlisted," "whitey," "debtor," "Asian," "obese," "fundamentalist," "space cadet," "immigrant," "gringo," "mentally ill," "disabled," "hippie," "mixed," "Polish," "biker," "diseased," "redneck," "activist"… The list continues. Everyone is on it.

How are we faring with genuine acceptance and human relationships? What lessons do Esther and Malala, Gandhi and Mandela, Wilberforce and Carson have for us today about inclusiveness and personal prejudice, whether against races, species, or our own hidden lists of untouchables?

Malala, Mahatma Gandhi, and Mandela, who each faced pronounced discrimination early in life, demonstrated that exceptional moral decision-making can come at any age within any culture from any gender. But while the books on Gandhi's and Madiba's lives are now closed, Malala continues a fresh chapter within the profiles of public whistle-blowing and ethical stature.

At the age of seventeen, she was the youngest recipient of the Nobel Peace Prize, and she shared the honor with Indian activist Kailash Satyarthi. Malala and Kailash decided to invite their prime ministers from Pakistan and India to attend the Nobel awards ceremony with them, a symbol of bridge-building between nuclear rivals and neighbors.

Like Esther, Malala's precocious actions against the odds have elevated her to become a beloved teen icon. She has received the Simone de Beauvoir Award, been granted honorary Canadian citizenship, honored by Harvard's Kennedy School, and labeled on CNN "the bravest girl in the world." She also uses part of the income from her awards to anchor the Malala Fund by which she initiates and supports education for those in greatest need.

Mullah Fazlullah, the cleric who ordered the attack on Yousafzai, was killed by a U.S.-Afghan air strike in June, 2018. Pakistani officials reported that the gang responsible for shooting Malala was arrested and would be brought to justice. However, most were freed due to a lack of evidence. Nevertheless in her recent return to Pakistan, Malala visited her hometown and expressed gratitude that she could do so without fear.

The precocious Pakistani scholar studies at Oxford University. Despite her honorary degrees, Malala wished to obtain one that she earned the hard way alongside her academic peers. At twenty-two, she is no less committed to "know thyself" than Socrates was at seventy.

Yousafzai's children's book, *Malala's Magic Pencil*, published in 2017, is an inspiration for youth worldwide while her earlier book, *I Am Malala*, remains such for the rest of us. Her most recent volume, *We Are Displaced: True Stories of Refugee Lives*, was published in 2019.

As she stares into the mirror and sees one eye that no longer quite matches the other, Malala also sees a face that was saved, and one that will save others from acid burns and acidic behavior. She sees the face of triumph and optimism against all odds, the face of a new dawn.

CHAPTER 13

ETHICAL DECISION-MAKING—WHAT IT TAKES

In the eyes of many people worldwide, several of the leaders discussed in this book could be called "ethics heroes," at least when considering the events portrayed here. Whatever their human shortcomings in other matters, when facing these critical decisions, they stood tall.

All faced and overcame an outer authority who challenged their inner authority or integrity. The outer authority was sometimes someone as close as a husband or colleague, or as potent as a president, principal, or king. Their inner authority came from their consciences or inner voices as informed by the ten factors, including their values, senses of justice, and cultural legacies.

In many cases they also faced additional, dangerous inner and outer adversaries who could invoke physical harm. Such outer adversaries might have been as formidable as Napoleon, the FBI, the Taliban, or powerful corporations, while the inner adversaries might have been serious illness, sustained doubt, the stress of conflicting allegiances, the pain of betrayal, or the fear of death.

These decisions frequently took much time, contemplation, consultation, and, in some instances, prayer. In each case, the decision-maker would be putting himself or herself, if not others, at risk.

In all situations, this risk might be called "physical to self," whether by illness, sleeplessness, death threats, looming war, or other potential violence. There was also often a risk that was "physical to inner circle," whether family, partner, colleagues, or close friends. For some, such as Socrates, Mandela, and Gandhi, these risks did not loom as large as for Murrow, Yousafzai, and Carson.

For most there was also a serious risk to career, although Socrates and Gandhi were too senior, independent, and committed to their self-sacrifice to be concerned about future employment. In worst-case scenarios these risks could have meant death to the careers, if not lives, of hundreds, thousands, and even millions of people... including an uncountable number of non-human species.

Despite these risks, each person emerged victorious in his or her own terms. Indeed, history has portrayed each as a moral victor, if not legend—although the reviews for all three American presidents (Adams, Truman, and Kennedy), if not others, are mixed. Most also felt personally fulfilled by their decisions, although for many the victory was bittersweet. Such victories were won at the cost of re-election, health, education, family bonds, or even life.

In several instances, the real opposition these people faced was the status quo. There was often a taxing inner struggle while opposing it. Each needed the courage not only to face a specific goliath, but also to counter civic norms and face some degree of social exile. In most cases, while each consulted outer voices, it was their inner voices that mattered most and ultimately outweighed both social and anti-social pressures.

Summarily, these individuals seemed to face formidable risks to health, life, family, and career in order to challenge the conventions of their country or culture. Each emerged historically victorious from their own perspective and to some degree personally fulfilled, whatever the casualties of their triumph.

CONCLUSIONS ABOUT THE TEN FACTORS

After reading and combining all of these profile cases, it is easy to review the ten factors in a new light. How do they configure in the aggregate?

1. **Notions of fairness and justice:** When comparing these cases, one discovers that Gandhi, Mandela, Esther, Wilberforce, and Malala, for example, all felt that there was a justice higher than that of the governing state in which they lived. The U.S. (Kennedy) and Soviet Union (Khrushchev) shared a vindictive mentality that involved an eye-for-an-eye, tit-for-tat notion of justice. Yet Gandhi observed that "an eye for an eye and the whole world goes blind." Indeed, Kennedy and Khrushchev, despite the reciprocity–fairness paradigm they inherited and practiced, realized that "a missile for a missile and the whole world perishes."

   Questions of "fairness" may be expanded to ask, "Fairness to whom?" What seemed fair to a superpower was unfair to humanity. What seemed acceptable to royalty appeared discriminatory and inhumane to Adams, Esther, and Wilberforce. For Carson, what seemed fair even to those who govern more democratically was not fair to most species.

   The great modern Harvard philosopher, John Rawls (1921-2002), argued that justice must ignore social distinctions such that race, gender, age, nationality, and so forth, cannot be reasons for disadvantage. Many of the dramatis personae in this book—Mandela, Gandhi, Yousafzai, Wilberforce, Esther, and Murrow—sought to be a voice for the voiceless to minimize, if not eradicate, such prejudice.

   In most justice paradigms, fairness implies the right use, rather than the abuse, of power; a theme which Murrow and Mandela, among others, championed. The junior senator from Wisconsin, Joseph McCarthy, no less than the Prime Minister of South Africa, used power to enforce two different types of apartheid—one racial, separating white people from black people, and the other political, separating patriotic Americans from alleged communists. Clearly, neither approach was a responsible use of power.

Whether an imposed separation of peoples was between Hindus and Muslims, as Gandhi witnessed, or between Persians and Jews, as Esther experienced, those opposing such prejudice were motivated by their own sense of justice. They were determined to ensure that leaders used power in more humane, if not democratic, ways.

2. **Impact or consequences:** In the Cuban Missile Crisis, except for the death of one spy plane pilot, all tragedy was averted. Some philosophers, such as the notable English thinker John Stuart Mill (1806-1873), articulated that harmonious outcomes or consequences are what matter most. In such cases, "all's well that ends well" is the desired goal. For Wilberforce, despite his parliamentary cheating, the outcome was the abolition of the British slave trade. For Adams, the outcome, despite losing his bid for re-election, was a peace policy that saved an untold number of lives. For Rachel Carson, despite her own pending death, the impact included greater protection of many species, including her own.

In his debates about tactics with colleagues, Nelson Mandela would often oppose an approach that, although well intentioned, would prove ineffective. Others, such as Mahatma Gandhi's son, argued with Mandela that unless goals were obtained legitimately and without violence, the outcomes were compromised. Thus, they would debate the relative value of ends and means (see #3 below). In each of the preceding ten cases, the hero strived for a pro-social consequence, but also struggled with whether such an outcome would have an anti-social price tag.

3. **Ends and means:** Some famous ethicists have argued that the consequences are not as important as the way in which they are obtained. Previously, I noted that the iconic German philosopher, Immanuel Kant (1724-1804), mandated that one ought never lie, even if deception might save a life. After all, to lie is to appear to condone chicanery and thus promote a world in which deception has both precedent and validity.

For several of the celebrated twelve leaders, differing degrees of deception were acceptable to attain greater social ends. Both Kennedy and Wilberforce used seemingly minor forms of deception relative to the customary practices of politics. Queen Esther, Adams, Truman, and Murrow kept important cards up their sleeves until it was the opportune time to play them. For some, withholding information in this way is a

263

form of deception. Gandhi, Mandela, Socrates, and Carson took a more direct approach to truth-telling—at least in the case studies at hand.

At key points in his life, Mandela advocated means that he might have ordinarily opposed, such as violence and deceit, to accomplish a greater purpose. Wilberforce consented to cheating when he realized all other paths to social equality were blocked. Kennedy feigned illness when the health of the nation was more important than the appearance of his own. Queen Esther felt it essential to engage in a cover-up of her heredity to obtain greater goals. And John Adams, like many presidents, knew that he could reveal his strategies to neither the enemy nor Congress prematurely without greatly increasing the odds of failure. While none advocated chronic prevarication, each felt that there were ends that justified deceptive means.

Like Kant, however, Socrates, Carson, and Gandhi felt a high affinity with pure truth since immoral means, no matter what the ends, inspire imitation and break trust. It is worth noting that both those who took the high road and those who rationalized prevarication achieved victorious outcomes. Their deception was not serious enough, or without justification, to affect the loss of reputation.

4. **Tone and atmosphere:** As previously noted, some moralists reason that it is ultimately what one models or demonstrates that matters most in an ethical decision. Thus, for some, the objectionable, inhumane tone of human torture is unacceptable no matter what the outcome. It becomes hard to tell one's children not to smoke while puffing on a cigarette within a smoke-filled room. Atmosphere, personal practice, and tone matter.

As noted earlier, for many indigenous nations or tribes, a tone of respect for all life was essential. A tree could not be cut down until there was a use for every part, including the bark and leaves. The pastures and water could not be soiled, let alone spoiled, as such a tone of action showed disrespect for future generations, for the creative spirits (cf. gods), and for Mother Earth. Clearly, Rachel Carson and her source of inspiration, Albert Schweitzer, agreed with this tone of respect and indeed reverence for all life.

For many world religions, this ultimate respect is for that which is "highest," such as Allah for Muslims, ancestors for Shintoists, God for Jews and Christians, or the Tao (the Way of Life) for Taoists. After all, if one should maintain a reverence for life itself, should not such reverence extend to the one(s) who created and sustained it?

As indicated earlier, feminist ethicists Carol Gilligan (born 1936) and Nel Noddings (born 1929) have advocated that the feminine voice and tone should be more central to ethical decision-making. Noddings advocates an ethics of care in which compassion and the quality of human relationships are as important as fulfilling more abstract notions of justice.

One rationale for tone being foremost is the sense that tone is the primary cause or essence of all action. Many world religions observe that one may not create a peaceful world if one is not personally at peace. Similarly, those who debated Lenin, Robespierre, Bolivar, and Washington asked them how a more peaceful world could be produced by violent revolution. This line of thinking maintains that to perform an ethical action, one must be ethical in spirit and atmosphere as well.

Certainly Gandhi epitomized this approach by advocating a non-violent tone no matter what the pain and penalty. Even when confronting those most violent, he, like Malala, maintained discipline and an atmosphere of daily prayer. Similarly, Esther directed Mordecai to engage in a season of prayer and fasting, a very sacred tone, while she prepared her special dinner for Haman and her husband. Mandela's tone to his college principal, and later to his warder in prison, remained respectful despite the action of non-compliance. Carson, albeit firm, never became belligerent. For almost all, tone mattered as an aspect of decision-making and action.

5. **Motivation and higher law:** In many ethical systems, making a moral choice that is self-serving is seen as less virtuous than if the same choice is motivated by service to others, to a higher law, or to the greater good. Many ethical systems posit that self-centeredness is the enemy of effective ethics. Thus, to serve society, family, country, deity, profession, life, or humanity, personal sacrifices are necessary.

In chapter three, Socrates sacrificed his own life not for family or friends, but for principles in which he believed, such as the laws and the truth. Similarly, in chapter two, Esther risked instant death to protect her people and to honor their god.

Although philosophers such as Nietzsche and Ayn Rand have made cases for an ethic that is self-serving, and although sometimes service to society includes service to the self, those profiled in this book obtained historical greatness by serving principles or other people ahead of themselves. In Kennedy's words, "Ask not what your country can do for you, but what you can do for your country." At a certain point in their developments, each person realized that what they could do for their country, cause, people, or planet often involved the downsizing of self-interest.

6. **Allegiance and loyalty:** Esther was torn between conflicting allegiances to husband and mentor, to state and religion, and to her people and her royal court. Many of these ethical decisions involved two or even multiple opposing allegiances to people who mattered to the actor. Socrates had a loyalty to his family and followers, but he argued that he had a higher loyalty to law and principle. Adams was pressured by a loyalty to his own political party and to the many endangered and captured U.S. sailors who counted upon him, their president, for protection from marauding French frigates—but he also felt a loyalty to conscience and to the thousands, if not millions, included within future generations who could be ravaged or eliminated by war.

All humans face potentially conflicting loyalties and sometimes must make agonizing choices. Many have claimed that their highest loyalty is what, for others, is an abstract. An ultimate allegiance to truth, conscience, principle, or a higher power such as God, Buddha, or Allah seems noblest to many. But, because belief systems differ, two people or groups may claim to give highest allegiance to the truth or to their belief system about their god(s), and still be at war with each other.

At times, those profiled named their ultimate loyalty with clarity. For Mandela, it was to South Africa and its people. For Wilberforce, it was to Christianity and those who had been mistreated in un-Christian ways, especially those who were enslaved. For Gandhi, it was to the victims of imperial discrimination and to an independent India. For Yousafzai, it was to Allah and the thousands of girls without a path to education.

Yet for each of these, and all the others, there were times when their ultimate loyalties stood in question. Their sleepless nights came when conflicting loyalties seemed to draw and quarter them in opposite directions. For example, both Murrow and Carson felt loyalty to their sons, one of whom (Murrow's) might be kidnapped or killed, and the other of whom (Carson's) had already lost a mother and could soon lose another. Yet both Carson and Murrow elected to honor a greater loyalty to a larger contingent of victims.

7. **Values and principles:** As noted in chapter one, values and principles can also come into conflict. For example, if I value both patriotism and my children's lives, I may feel torn about letting them enlist in the military. Similarly, if Edward R. Murrow equally valued truth and reputation, it

would have made it harder for him to broadcast a news story that told the truth but also tarnished the reputation of an American senator.

Principles may come into conflict when one considers that they are as different as "women and children first" and "all men (cf. people) are created equal." How could all be equal if women and children are given preferential treatment? Principles can also be as different as "to each according to his needs" and "what's good for the goose is good for the gander." Clearly, both cannot be true if the gander has greater needs than the goose.

Often a person of integrity sees herself as a person of principle. But, since many noble principles are at odds, the question then becomes, "Which principle?" In Mandela's childhood tribal culture, he was taught the important principle of respect for elders that certainly pertained to his college administrators. But he also honored the principle of accountability to constituency, and by means of this principle he felt accountable to honor a boycott supported by the vast majority of those who elected him, no matter how his elders felt about it. Ultimately, those in the hot seat must chose between conflicting principles and values as well as conflicting loyalties.

8. **Cultural context:** In modern China and in Esther's Persia, boys have been more highly valued than girls. Within John Adams' eighteenth century U.S. culture, free men were more highly valued than slaves, a value which was contested by William Wilberforce in England. Cultural context is important to the understanding of values. What is sacrosanct in one time and place may be verboten in another.

Elder euthanasia, harems, and human sacrifice are just a few cases in point. During France's Belle Époque period in which Curie lived, it was the cultural fashion of both national and male chauvinism that heaped mud upon her private indiscretion.

Religious cultures typically give greatest value to the unseen, while more scientific subcultures value visual evidence. The state (cf. the Party) highly values control and political leadership. Economic egalitarian principles are more valued in socialist states just as "first come first served," "survival of the (economically) fittest," and "money talks" principles matter more in capitalist states.

The host context is always at play as a factor in ethical decisions. For example, in Esther's story the king was supremely valued as both penultimate human leader and a deity on earth. But by the era of William Wilberforce, the divine right of kings was no longer accepted and thus parliamentary power was valued as much or more than a ruler. Not only was geography a significant factor in determining regal value, but also the era in which royalty lived.

The culture of Mohandas Gandhi's boyhood featured arranged marriages and honored the tradition of burning surviving widows with their deceased husbands. But the more cosmopolitan culture of Gandhi's elderly years was not as certain about these conventions. Two of the countries in which the Mahatma lived opposed such primitive practices. Gandhi himself had learned to reject the notion of untouchables and other time-honored traditional structures of Indian society. Time, location, inner compulsion, and cultural surround all influence ethical mores.

9. **Implications:** As explained in chapter one, Immanuel Kant's first categorical imperative asked that one should imagine a world in which everyone follows one's example when one makes ethical decisions. Although they could not fully foresee the complete impact of their actions, each case study made decisions caused potent repercussions. The ramifications of Carson's stand are still being felt by the Environmental Protection Agency and literally thousands of species. If the accounts of Esther's life are accurate, she changed the futures of millions of women, Jews, and Persians—and thus all generations to follow. Socrates inspired centuries of thinkers to ponder whether ideas are worth dying for. Wilberforce, with his supporters, prevented millions of Africans from being shackled, tortured, and killed.

Implications are often hidden. For example, it seems hard to think that Mandela's decision to stand up to his college principal had any great impact upon thousands of lives, let alone life-and-death consequences for his people. But in fact, the greatest consequence may have been upon the least likely suspect of all—Mandela himself. Once he had found the courage to counter arbitrary authority on a smaller scale, he had primed the pump to make future courageous decisions—decisions that changed history.

10. **Proportion and balance:** When many or all of the factors above— multiple loyalties, principles, values, risks, consequences, notions of fairness, ends, means, motivations, contexts, and implications—compete for attention, how does a decision-maker know how much weight to give each one? Aristotle's notion of finding a midpoint between excess and deficiency suggests that one might find the point of balance between any

two vectors or allegiances which seem at odds. Confucius and Lao-Tzu seem to have posthumously agreed.

But personal or cultural taste, or another notion of fairness, might call for an imbalanced decision. For example, if I have $3,000 to divide among my three children, should I divide it evenly among all three in a balanced way? Or should I instead give most or all of it to the disabled, bedridden child with unpaid medical bills, since the two healthy children are earning sizable incomes?

Facing difficult decisions, each of the profiled historical characters had to decide the relative significance of factors such as fairness vs. consequences or loyalty vs. values. In assessing such situations, is it wise to give the same proportion and consideration to each factor, or does one factor (such as the advent of genocide or nuclear war) outweigh all of the others?

Knowing the hidden implications, factors, values, etc., behind a situation is no more important than knowing how much weight to give each one upon the scales of justice. Each decision-maker had to weigh the factors on a different personal and cultural scale.

YET OTHER FACTORS

As has been seen, each case is unique and ultimately all decision-makers are to some degree subjective. Some may try to make extremely logical choices based upon the factors above. For example, Socrates presented a very reasoned case, supported by examples and logic, for his own choice to drink the hemlock.

But ultimately, other factors, including preference, previous experience, expectations, interpersonal history, and bias, also entered the picture, not just for Socrates, but for everyone. We are taught by both psychology and first-hand experience that no matter how reasonable we think we are, hidden motivations and subconscious compulsions influence our behavior.

In chapter one, it was noted that third parties and lobbying factions sometimes enter the plot. Soothsayers, priests, augurs, prophets, lawyers, partners, bookies, ministers, consultants, fortune-tellers, mistresses, rabbis, elders, advisors, shamans, and even dice have been consulted before some leaders have made difficult decisions. Nor was it always easy to tell if the advisors, even foreign policy experts or military strategists, were trustworthy or reliable.

As observed earlier, a myriad of other circumstances—illness, alcohol, limited vision, weather, nutrition, interpersonal chemistry, wild animals, heavy or mis-prescribed medication, insect infestation, addictions, and family tragedy—have been silent partners in decision-making. Such unseen factors were not initially noted, but later surfaced in journals and diaries, as catalysts to rushed, despondent, or impaired thinking.

As one case in point, John Adams' decision-making was especially plagued by 1) the betrayal of his vice president, cabinet, and party leaders; 2) the severe, prolonged, and eventually fatal illness of many of those closest to him; 3) an incessantly libelous press; 4) contradictory and possibly unreliable communications from leaders and envoys overseas; 5) endless lethal epidemics; 6) inflation and taxation dilemmas, and 7) much more. His health, family, re-election, political-party prominence, and especially world peace and thousands of lives were all at stake.

We can read about only some of these factors in journals, letters, biographies, and documents. How many other hidden influences, urges, incidents, mental aberrations, and relationships remain unknown? And in some cases, humans ultimately cannot explain, even to themselves, why a decision is made. So, humility is required when seeking to understand the past.

LESSONS LEARNED; EXAMPLES ESTABLISHED

When all is said and done, what may be observed and learned from these cases? Obviously, it cannot be assumed that these portraits are all representative of the millions of such decisions throughout history, or even that one could catalog all such cases since many were never recorded. Nevertheless, these are some of the lighthouses along the coast of human events.

Because these choices changed history and these heroes are admired by many, can we draw any conclusions? Although we cannot generalize fully from the observations that follow, they inspire thought and may well have implications for our own decision-making. Consider these common factors in almost all the case studies.

1) Many decisions became a tipping point in changing the social gridlock or the status quo by people who were ahead of their times. In fact, when historians looked back upon Murrow's famous broadcast, it was dubbed "the beginning of the end" for McCarthyism. Similarly, Gandhi's dramatic fast in Calcutta brought peacemaking attempts to an apex, and peace reigned for months after his fast concluded. Curie's stand opened the door for first dozens, then thousands, of female scientists to make a difference in medicine, universities, and society. And who can say how far the influence of Malala will have spread by the time she is mid-career?

The diaries, biographies, and autobiographies of decision-makers reveal that they are usually focused upon the decision itself and weighing the pros and cons of each specific action they might take. Decision-makers do not usually see these moments as milestones or turning points in history. They are too busy confronting and contemplating the opposition and lobbying forces facing them, and they are typically attempting to rally support, obtain cogent advice, postpone the decision with hopes of a simpler solution, or pondering alternatives.

Yet whether they realized it or not, their choices were often pivotal moments which turned the tides or set an example that others would later follow. It was only through hindsight that they were seen as the fulcrum for an entire shift or movement in social history.

As with key inventors, tipping-point change-makers may not realize that they are ahead of their time. Their primary sense may be that they must oppose something wrong, but, their persistence and vision allows something right to break through the old order and introduce a new wave of reform.

2) Those involved discovered that they were seldom acting alone. Such decisions may have seemed intensely private, and those encountering such dilemmas may seem isolated. Murrow anxiously walked the streets; Mandela experienced sleepless nights; Curie stared long into the ghastly mirror; yet others went through their individual, private agony.

Once a decision was made, however, virtually everyone—save Socrates—was backed in their decision by others. Organizations, appreciative letters, and volunteer supporters appeared to back up Carson, Wilberforce, Murrow, Truman, and others. Esther asked that the Jewish people privately pray and fast with her, and Gandhi received letters and telegrams from followers worldwide who supported his vigils, fasts, and actions. Once a decision was made and publicized, it became clear that others had already been contemplating the same dilemma or had already taken a stand in favor of the hero or her cause.

Wilberforce, for example stood on the shoulders of all abolitionists, freed slaves, leaders of slave rebellions, and allies in other countries when he seemingly opposed Parliament alone. Murrow and Carson received far more supportive letters and acknowledgements than they could ever answer.

When they struggled with a conundrum, these decision-makers tended to worry about all those opposed to what they would do, and yet there were usually people, sometimes in large numbers, waiting to support them.

3) It was usually in the enlightened self-interest of the person involved to make a decision benefitting others. Although it seemed like the decision-maker would be sacrificing himself—indeed, Socrates did—it was not typical that such a decision led to martyrdom. Whatever the sacrifices of time, health, and public disapproval, ultimately it was of benefit for the decision-maker to live in a more humane environment with a brighter future for family and friends. In Esther's case, her own life was saved, and in the case of Gandhi, Adams, Carson, Truman, and Murrow, they were saved from the ravages of war, chemical poisoning, an encroaching fascist government, and genocide.

At first glance, in ethical conundrums it can appear that the choice is between self-preservation and the preservation of others. Yet, when such cases are closely inspected, the decision-maker and those closest to him frequently benefit from the outcome. It is often in one's own, enlightened self-interest to serve the greater good, no matter what the appearance.

4) Rather than looking at these cases as the lesser of two evils, one may also look at them as the greater of two goods. For example, many might agree that it was good that Edward R. Murrow did not wish to use television as a bully pulpit, a home for one-sided presentations, or for the destruction of reputations as viewed by a national audience. His desire to use broadcasting as a positive tool for information, illumination, and inspiration seems commendable, yet his decision to stand up to McCarthy (who was indeed given equal time to make his own presentation) may be viewed as a far greater good for democratic society.

Similarly, many might claim that it was good that insect spray was utilized in the 1950s to eliminate pests, which carried disease. Thus, some pesticides saved many lives. Rachel Carson honored this good and did not call for the wholesale elimination of all pesticides and herbicides. However, by catalyzing regulation of the types and amounts of these chemicals, she advanced a greater good not only for Americans, but for all forms of life. While some cases may be construed as choosing between the lesser of two evils, there are often positive intentions and possible outcomes on both sides as well.

Had Socrates spared his own life, he might have made his family, friends, and advocates much happier, which would be seen as good by many. However, had he not abided by the laws of Athens and stood tall for what he believed, his influence upon history and philosophy would have been quite different.

5) The courageous or motivated decision-maker may sometimes be seen as a trim tab that changes the course of events. A trim tab is a small device that helps to steer a larger vessel, such as an airplane, boat, or elevator. When a ship's rudder has a trim tab, the tab functions as a mini rudder to the rudder itself. In an interview in 1972, Buckminster Fuller used the trim tab as a metaphor for leadership when he said:

> Think of the Queen Mary—the whole ship goes by and then comes the rudder. And there's a tiny thing at the edge of the rudder called a trim tab. It's a miniature rudder. Just moving the little trim tab builds a low pressure that pulls the rudder around... the little individual can be a trim tab.

Clearly, the metaphor can be expanded. The entire rudder is needed to turn the giant ship, not just the trim tab. In the case of Wilberforce, all the voices favoring abolition for centuries, all the slaves who resisted or ran away to tell their story, all those who supported Wilberforce's own efforts, were part of the rudder.

No one person can take all the credit or act fully alone to move the ship. Most would credit the forces behind them, be they invisible deities and social movements, or visible colleagues, partners, and mentors, as the rudder of change. And yet, these cases show that one person can serve as the tip of the arrow, the catalyst... the trim tab that directs the rudder and navigates change.

6) Hence, one cannot overestimate the importance and influence of the ethical individual. In that light, imagine the world without Carson, Adams, Curie, Truman, Wilberforce, Gandhi, Socrates, Mandela, Esther, Kennedy, Yousafzai, and Murrow. It would likely be vastly different. Would any of us be alive? Would our great-grandparents or parents have been born? Would we be breathing insecticide-ridden air, speaking a different language, or living as destitute survivors of a nuclear war?

If the decisions of only twelve people had this much impact, imagine how the world would be different if we chose to remove another dozen or a hundred similar decision-makers from the annals of history. No matter how cliché the idea may seem, one person can make a major difference.

We could just as easily note how the world would be different if those who made major unethical decisions—Hitler, Mussolini, Stalin, Jezebel, Attila—had never lived. Millions of people whom they slaughtered would have survived and sired millions of others. In many cases, a person has not only created a huge family tree over the centuries, but also a unique family legacy, whether of crime or creative arts or otherwise.

7) There are lessons for our own lives. Often, we face challenging decisions and believe that we are alone. We may also see the micro-version of our decision and think that it is only about a few people. And yet, sometimes, our choices—whether to become involved in environmental action or to question arbitrary authority at work, home, a civic meeting, or at school— become turning points that inspire others.

Recently, there has been an emphasis upon the issue of bullying among teens, with especial attention paid to cyber-bullying and its tragic consequences. The reports about bullying indicate that just one teen saying, "don't do that—that's not cool," when another was being bullied, has sometimes made all the difference. Without peer support or an atmosphere of indifference, a bully will often back down.

History has shown that just one respected voice calling for calm or reason among a lynch mob, or just one person of strong conscience on a jury, or just one journalist willing to mine for the truth, has turned the tide. If just one person can have so much impact, how do we each become that one person in our own fields of influence?

APPLYING THESE LESSONS TO BECOME DIFFERENCE-MAKERS

How exactly can we become difference-makers? Some students enter my ethics classes thinking that they can become great at ethics if they have a sharp mind. Certainly, good critical thinking skills are important, but for those who triumphed over ethical challenges outside the classroom, more than mental prowess was required. Although there are exceptions to every rule and case, on the whole, what was most required of these moral exemplars were specific qualities of character.

After studying these and many similar cases, here are the qualities which I sense have most frequently led to a moral victory. They are qualities I think we all need in facing ethical challenges, although each case is unique, and each remedy may favor a different mix from the list below.

Beyond inspired thinking about the ten factors, here are ten qualities of character which seem most important in ethical decision-making:

1) Courage

2) Persistence

3) Compassion

4) Integrity

5) Inner stillness

6) Self-discipline

7) Service to a higher cause or being

8) A longing for fairness

9) Uncompromising stamina under pressure

10) Love and respect for others no less than self

These ten qualities of character are different from, but overlap with, the ten factors.

Clearly, the qualities of character are important to express. It is not enough to think through any or all of the ten factors if one will nevertheless exploit an ethical dilemma strictly for personal gain. And it is of no value to think brilliantly about how to solve a conundrum if you will run from the situation when abusers or bullies breathe fire.

No amount of bright analysis will fully implement an ethical decision. The application and enforcement of the decision also requires a backbone and consistency in the face of pushback and criticism.

IS THIS APPROACH TOO COMPLEX? WHY NOT SIMPLIFY?

It might seem daunting to think that each of us must mentally consider the ten factors and then express ten qualities of character to make ethical decisions. After all, in some cases one must move quickly, and there is no time to scroll through a list of twenty considerations and then determine which ones seem paramount.

Essentially, both lists allow one to move quickly by scanning them and asking, "What am I missing? Where are my blind spots?" and similar questions. So the lists need not take immense time, nor is behaving ethically a matter of memorizing all twenty.

In fact, the twenty boil down to just three important imperatives—not twenty. Most of the ten factors are areas for mental consideration, while many of the ten traits of character involve emotional intelligence. Thus, when one must make a quick decision, the first list of factors may be reduced to, "Open your mind." The second list, in the aggregate, then implies the simple imperative, "Open your heart."

What do I mean? Let's say that my ethical decision is not just about the people who seem to be involved. As with second-hand smoke, my decision could influence many innocent bystanders who may not be visible upon first glance. If I do not open my mind and my frame of vision, I may not consider the possible consequences (factor #2) and implications (factor #9) of my action upon innocent bystanders. On the other hand, if I do not open my heart, I may not care enough to put myself in the shoes of these innocent people—I may not exhibit compassion (quality #3) and respect (quality #10) for them. So, I might give them little weight or ignore them completely when making my decision.

Therefore, I must open my mind to be aware of others and open my heart to be able to empathize with them and the impact my decisions might have upon them. It is hard to make an informed and wise decision if I cannot open my mental faculties to see all sides and open my emotional realm to empathize with all potential victims and parties, whether the abused or the accused.

The third and final imperative is, "Balance the first two imperatives." All thinking without the ability to care, as in Noddings' and Gilligan's ethic, leads to a purely abstract, dehumanized solution. But all emotion without thought may lead to a highly irrational, subjective, and possibly unjust decision. Many important details or pieces of evidence may be overlooked.

Wasn't it Edmund Burke, the great Anglo-Irish philosopher, who compared the pursuit of justice to a sailboat? The analogy likened the sail to passion and the centerboard to reason. Without a sail (passion), the boat goes nowhere. But without a centerboard (reason), the boat topples over, helplessly, in heavy wind.

Both reason and emotion are necessary—and when both are balanced, we can empathize with the parties involved in the case without losing our ability to think clearly. When there is balance, the decision-making process can sail forward in the wind. Reason grounds passion, and passion empowers reasonable ideas.

Hence, my bias is balance. Ultimately, a wise balance draws upon both the ten factors and the ten qualities of character. It calls for equal measures of an open mind and an open heart. The three imperatives are simple and prepare one to wisely handle almost any dilemma.

BEING THE DIFFERENCE

Whether or not our decisions visibly change history, they may deeply impact the lives of others. A bully may back down; a prejudice may be held in check; fairness or truth-telling may enter the picture. In the long-term, lives may be saved or injuries avoided. Even when something positive is already occurring, we may help to create or support the greater of two goods or avoid the greater of two evils.

As a professor of ethics for almost forty years, I am convinced that ethics instruction and thinking are helpful in our early adolescent and teen years. I am not simply advocating that parents train children to think about moral decision-making. They should also teach them how to anticipate, and thus temper, the impact of their actions upon other people, animals, and our planet.

Ethical decisions are so important to our society that it is wise to teach ethics at every stage of education. Although I teach at the college level, I am frequently impressed by the thinking of my students who already studied ethics as part of a philosophy class in a secondary school. It is never too early to consider what values, loyalties, principles, consequences, implications, ends, and means come into play when one is faced with a challenging conundrum.

In recent years, I have been involved in a United Nations project in which we developed an ethics curriculum that is available for worldwide use in primary, secondary, and tertiary levels of education. Although there are vastly different pedagogies and cultural histories involved when teaching ethics on a global scale, nevertheless, no culture, country, nor level of education should be excluded.

Some have argued that ethical training should be only the province of religion, or of the home, or of the philosopher's classroom. In the age of Enron, Madoff, Epstein, Wells Fargo, "fake news", cyber-bulling, steroid abuse, #MeToo, election hacking, and online scams, why not use every means available?

With ethics training, it should never be "either–or" rather than "all of the above." Although none of those profiled in this book had a Ph. D. in ethics, all received some form of instruction, whether in the classroom, synagogue, living room, church, temple, lab, tribal circle, Independence Hall, parliament, or prison.

Socrates recommended that thinking about our thinking and behavior should be an important component of our lives. It is a valued implication of his best-known command: "Know thyself."

It must be noted that training in ethics is sometimes insufficient. Human nature is a powerful force. Knowing what to do (or eat or drink or think) is no guarantee that one will do it. Serial killers may have received, and yet ignored, years of moral instruction. Even Enron had an ethics code. No one factor, code, or training is ever a guarantee that a world of virtue and justice will triumph.

Yet on the whole, ethical training has been shown not only to help expand awareness, but also to be valuable when genuinely challenging moral dilemmas arise. I have conducted studies involving eighty ethics faculty at leading institutions including Harvard, Oxford, Stanford, Cambridge, Yale, Princeton, and many others. While those professors were divided about the degree that ethics education can change human behavior at the university level (after all, college and university students are already at least seventeen years old), they were united in their affirmation of the value of learning to think about ethical issues and of teaching ethics.

Ethical thinking is invaluable when one must move beyond gridlock and take initiative. Ultimately, leaders must be decisive and move forward after weighing all of the costs, benefits, principles, people, and potential outcomes.

John and Caroline Kennedy were persuasive in their argument that the most important factor in decision-making is courage—courage to counter the status quo when it is immoral or intractable. There is the need for courage to risk political, if not personal, defeat; courage to be a lone voice for change in a chorus of entropy or indifference; courage to face opposition and rigidity; courage to be a whistle-blower whatever the cost; courage to be able to sleep with a clear conscience.

Ethical training, courage, initiative—all are important. And they are underscored and made more effective by wisdom. The wisdom derived from experience, contemplation, seeing the larger picture, and humility leads not only to making the right choice, but also to the right timing, tone, atmosphere, and teamwork.

In our own lives we not only have the benefit of possible role models, such as those in this book, but also others whom we trust to give us wise ethical advice and to ask us the right questions. We also have more workshops, courses, and special trainings in ethics than ever—although we still need more. It is important not only to seek ethical training, but also to advocate for and support it.

ONE AND THE TRUTH ARE A MAJORITY

What all those, from Esther to Malala, had in common was not only the longing to make the right choice, but ultimately the willingness and perseverance to be the difference. Being a trim tab, even in micro-societies such as families and committees, is not only possible, but essential to our forward motion.

Each of these profiles suggest that no matter what the pressure and potential danger, wise and influential ethical decision-making is both achievable and necessary. There is no "one size fits all" model regarding what a decision should be. Culture, timing, means, possible outcomes, dramatis personae, and available support are all variables. But what does not vary is the need for integrity and the willingness to step forward.

While it has been valuable to consider those who were willing to be the difference in the past, it is obvious that both the present and the future will need even more ethical leadership beyond Malala or whomever our current role models and inspirational leaders may be. Our challenge is to be the next generation of profiles, the voices of integrity, the trim tabs who effect a positive future no matter what the risks and odds.

In Gandhi's words, "we must be the change we wish to see in the world." And in Spike Lee's words, which inspired the title of this book, we must "do the right thing."

In the twenty-first century, the primary aggregate message we are told from the mass media, from cradle to grave, is the central theme of advertising: "There is something wrong with you. Buy something." And yet my own message is: "There is something right with you. Do something!"

Individually, we can do something to make a difference.

Collectively, we can do something to be the difference.

FOR FURTHER READING

PREFACE BIBLIOGRAPHY

Appiah, Kwame Anthony. *In My Father's House: Africa in the Philosophy of Culture.* New York: Oxford University Press, 1992.

Bauman, Zygmunt. *Liquid Life.* Cambridge: Polity Press, 2005.

Havel, Václav. "Post-modernism: The Search for Universal Laws." *Vital Speeches of the Day* 60, no. 2 (August 1, 1994): 613–615.

Küng, Hans. *Global Responsibility: In Search of a New World Ethic.* Translated by J. Bowden. London: SCM Press, 1981.

Nussbaum, Martha. *The Frontiers of Justice: Disability, Nationality, Species Membership.* Cambridge, MA: Harvard University Press, 2006.

Ward, Stephen J.A. *Disrupting Journalism Ethics: Radical Change on the Frontier of Digital Media.* Abingdon, Oxon: Routledge, 2019.

PRIMARY BIBLIOGRAPHY

Ackroyd, P.R. *Israel Under Babylon and Persia.* Oxford: Oxford University Press, 1970.

Adams, John. *Diary and Autobiography of John Adams,* edited by L. H. Butterfield, 4 volumes. Cambridge: Harvard University Press, 1961.

Alter, Jonathan. *The Defining Moment: FDR's Hundred Days and the Triumph of Hope.* New York: Simon and Schuster, 2006.

Aretha, David. *Malala Yousafzai and the Girls of Pakistan.* Greensboro, NC: Morgan Reynolds Publishing, 2014.

Aristophanes. *Aristophanes: Four Comedies,* edited by Dudley Fitts. New York: Harcourt, Brace, and World, 1962.

Belmonte, Kevin. *Hero for Humanity: A Biography of William Wilberforce.* Colorado Springs: NavPress Publishing Group, 2002.

Berlin, Adele. "The Book of Esther and Ancient Storytelling." *Journal of Biblical Literature* 120, no. 1 (Spring 2001): 3–14.

Beschloss, Michael R. *Kennedy and Roosevelt.* New York: W.W. Norton, 1980.

Bickerman, Elias. *Four Strange Books of the Bible.* New York: Schocken Books, 1967.

Brands. H.W. *Traitor to His Class: The Privileged Life and Radical Presidency of Franklin Delano Roosevelt.* New York: Doubleday, 2008.

Bronstein, Herbert & Albert Friedlander. *The Five Scrolls.* New York: Central Conference of American Rabbis Press, 1984.

Brown, Judith M. *Gandhi; Prisoner of Hope.* New Haven: Yale University Press, 1989.

Cafaro, Philip. "Rachel Carson's Environmental Ethics." *Rachel Carson: Legacy and Challenge*, edited by Lisa Sideris and Kathleen Dean Moore. Albany, NY: State University of New York, 2008.

Carson, Rachel. *Silent Spring*. Boston: Houghton Mifflin, 1962.

Cassidy, David C. *Oppenheimer and the American Century*. New York: Pi Press, 2005.

Coolidge, Olivia. *Gandhi*. Boston: Houghton Mifflin, 1971.

Cooper, John M., ed. *The Complete Works of Plato*. Indianapolis: Hackett Publishing, 1988.

Curie, Eve. *Madame Curie*. Translated by V. Sheean. New York: Da Capo, 1837, 1986.

Curie, Marie. *Pierre Curie*. Translated by C. and V. Kellogg. New York: MacMillan, 1932.

Dallek, Robert. *An Unfinished Life: John F. Kennedy*. New York: Little Brown & Company, 2003.

Dallek, Robert. *Harry S. Truman*. New York: Henry Holt and Company, 2008.

Dandamaev, Muhmmad A. and Vladimir G. Lukonin. *The Culture and Social Institutions of Ancient Iran*. Cambridge: Cambridge University Press, 1989.

Daryaee, Touraj, "To Learn and to Remember from Others: Persians Visiting the Dura-Europos Synagogue." *Scripta Judaica Cracoviensia* 8, (2010): 29–37. Krakow.

Davis, John H. *The Kennedys: Dynasty and Disaster*. New York: McGraw-Hill, 1984.

Doeden, Matt. *Malala Yousafzai: Shot by the Taliban, Still Fighting for Equal Education*. Minneapolis: Lerner Publishing Group, 2014.

Donald, Aida. *Citizen Soldier: A Life of Harry S. Truman*. New York: Basic Books, 2012.

Dweck, Nathan M. ed. *Purim Reader*. New York: Tebah Educational Services, 1985.

Edwards, Bob. *Edward R. Murrow and the Birth of Broadcast Journalism*. Hoboken, NJ: Wiley & Sons, 2004.

Edwards, Paul. *The Encyclopedia of Philosophy*, vol. 7. London: MacMillan, 1967.

Ferling, John. *John Adams: A Life*. Knoxville: The University of Tennessee Press, 1992.

Fischer, Louis. *The Life of Mahatma Gandhi*. New York: Harper & Row, 1950.

Friedel, Frank. *Franklin D. Roosevelt: A Rendezvous with Destiny*. Boston: Little, Brown, and Company, 1990.

Furneaux, Robin. *William Wilberforce*. London: Hamish Hamilton, 1974.

Gandhi, Mohandas. *Gandhi, An Autobiography: My Experiments with the Truth*. Boston: Beacon Press, 1957.

Goodwin, Doris Kearns. *The Fitzgeralds and the Kennedys*. New York: Simon and Schuster, 1987.

Goldsmith, Barbara. *Obsessive Genius: The Inner World of Marie Curie*. New York: W.W. Norton and Company, 2005.

Gordis, Robert, tr. *Megillat Esther*. New York: The Rabbinical Assembly, 1972.

Hague, William. *William Wilberforce: The Life of the Great Anti-Slave Trade Campaigner.* London: Harper Press, 2007.

Henrickson, John. *Rachel Carson: The Environmental Movement.* Brookfield: The Millbrook Press, 1972.

Hirsch, Emil G., with John Dyneley Prince and Solomon Schechter. "Esther," *Jewish Encyclopedia.* New York: Funk and Wagnall, 1906.

Holton, Woody. *Abigail Adams.* New York: Free Press, 2009.

Hromatko, Wesley. "John Adams," *Dictionary of Unitarian and Universalist Biography.* Scituate, MA: The Unitarian and Universalist Heritage and Historical Society, 2013.

Jezer, Marty. *Rachel Carson, Biologist and Author.* New York: Chelsea House Publishers, 1988.

Kelly, Cynthia C. *The Manhattan Project.* New York: Black Dog & Leventhal Publishers, 2007.

Kendrick, Alexander. *Prime Time: The Life of Edward R. Murrow.* Boston: Little, Brown, and Company, 1969.

Kennedy, Caroline, ed. *Profiles in Courage for Our Time.* New York: Hyperion, 2002.

Kennedy, John F. *Profiles in Courage.* New York: Harper & Row, 1956.

Klein, L.R. "Honor and Shame in Esther," *A Feminist Companion to Esther, Judith, and Susanna,* edited by A. Brenner. London: T&T Clark International, 1995.

Konstan, David, ed. *Xenophon's Apology of Socrates.* Bryn Mawr, PA: Bryn Mawr Commentaries, 1988.

Kovarick, Chiara. *Interviews with Muslim Women of Pakistan.* Minneapolis, MN: Syren Press, 2004.

Larsen, Rebecca. *Oppenheimer and the Atom Bomb.* New York: Franklin Watts, 1988.

Leeman, Barbara. *Jack Kennedy: The Education of a Statesman.* New York: Norton Publishing, 2006.

Leeman, Barbara. *Mrs. Kennedy: The Missing History of the Kennedy Years.* New York: The Free Press, 2001.

Levine, Ellen. *Up Close: Environmentalist Rachel Carson.* New York: Viking Press, 2007.

Levit-Tawil, D. "The Purim Panel in Dura in the Light of Parthian and Sasanian Art," *Journal of Near Eastern Studies* 38, (1979): 93–109.

Lincoln, Evelyn. *My Twelve Years with John. F. Kennedy.* New York: David MacKay, 1965.

List, Pater C. "Ethics on Land and at Sea: Rachel Carson's Environmental Ethics." *Rachel Carson: Legacy and Challenge,* edited by Lisa H. Sideris and Kathleen Dean Moore. Albany, NY: State University of New York, 2008.

Llewellyn-Jones, L. *King and Court in Ancient Persia.* Edinburgh: Edinburgh University Press, 2013.

McGrane, Sharon Bertsch. *Nobel Prize Women in Science: Their Lives, Struggles, and Momentous Discoveries.* New York: Carol Press, 1998.

Mandela, Nelson. *Conversations with Myself.* London: Macmillan, 2010.

Mandela, Nelson. *Long Walk to Freedom.* New York: Little, Brown & Company, 1994.

Mandela, Nelson. *The Authorized Portrait.* Kansas City: Andrews McMeel Publishing, 2006.

McCullough, David. *John Adams.* New York: Simon & Schuster, 2001.

McCullough, David. *Truman.* New York: Simon & Schuster, 1992.

Mehta, Ved. *Mahatma Gandhi and his Apostles.* New York: Viking Press, 1976.

Metaxas, Eric. *Amazing Grace: William Wilberforce and the Heroic Campaign to End Slavery.* New York: Harper, 2007.

Monk, Ray. *Robert Oppenheimer: A Life Inside the Center.* New York: Doubleday, 2012.

Pasachoff, Naomi. *Marie Curie and the Science of Radioactivity.* Oxford: Oxford University Press, 1996.

Payne, Robert. *The Life and Death of Mahatma Gandhi.* New York: E.P. Dutton, 1969.

Persico, Joseph E. *Edward R. Murrow: An American Original.* New York: McGraw-Hill, 1988.

Pflaum, Rosalind. *Grand Obsession: Madame Curie and Her World.* New York: Doubleday, 1989.

Quinn, Susan. *Marie Curie: A Life.* New York: Simon and Schuster, 1995.

Rayner-Canham, Marlene and Geoffrey. *A Devotion to Their Science. Pioneer Women of Radioactivity.* Montreal: McGill-Queen's University Press, 1997.

Reeves, Thomas. *A Question of Character: The Life of John F. Kennedy.* New York: The Free Press, 1991.

Reid, Robert William. *Marie Curie.* New York: New American Library, 1978.

Rowell, Rebecca. *Malala Yousafzai: Education Activist.* Minneapolis, MN: ABDO Publishing, 2014.

Salinger, Pierre. *With Kennedy.* Garden City, NY: Doubleday, 1966.

Sampson, Anthony. *Mandela: The Authorized Biography.* London: Harper Collins, 1991.

Schlesinger, Arthur M. *A Thousand Days, John F. Kennedy in the White House.* Boston: Houghton Mifflin, 1965.

Shirer, William L. *Gandhi, A Memoir.* New York: Simon and Schuster, 1979.

Sideris, Lisa and Kathleen Dean Moore. *Rachel Carson: Legacy and Challenge.* Albany, NY: State University of New York, 2008.

Sperber, A.M. *Murrow: His Life and Times.* New York: Freundlich Books, 1986.

Stone, I.F. *The Trial of Socrates.* Boston: Little Brown and Company, 1988.

Souder, William. *On a Farther Shore: The Life and Legacy of Rachel Carson.* New York: Crown Publishers, 2012.

Taylor, A.E. *Socrates: The Man and His Thought*. Garden City, NY: Doubleday, 1952.

Telushkin, Rabbi Joseph. *Biblical Literacy: The Most Important People, Events, and Ideas of the Hebrew Bible*. New York: William Morrow and Company, 1997.

Thayer, Mary Van Rensselaer. *Jacqueline Kennedy: The White House Years*. Boston: Little, Brown & Co.

Tomkins, Stephen. *William Wilberforce: A Biography*. Cambridge: Eerdmans Publishing Company, 2007.

Tenny, Tommy. *Hadassah: One Night with the King*. Minneapolis: Bethany House, 2004.

Truman, Margaret. *Harry S. Truman*. New York: William Morrow, 1973.

Vlastos, Gregory. *Socrates: Ironist and Moral Philosopher*. Cambridge: Cambridge University Press, 1991.

Walsh, Declan. "Taliban Gun Down Girl Who Spoke Up for Rights." *New York Times*, October 9, 2012. World: Asia Pacific, C1.

Weart, Spencer R. *Scientists in Power*. Cambridge, MA: Harvard University Press, 1979.

Woznicki, Robert. *Madame Curie: Daughter of Poland*. Miami: American Institute of Polish Culture, 1983.

Xenophon, *Memorabilia*. Cambridge, MA: Harvard University Press, 1923.

Yamauchi, Edwin. *Persia and the Bible*. Grand Rapids, MI: Baker Books, 1997.

Yousafzai, Malala, with Christina Lamb. *I Am Malala: The Story of the Girl Who Stood Up for Education and Was Shot by the Taliban*. New York: Little, Brown and Company, 2013.

The Holy Bible: 1611 King James Version. Nashville: Thomas Nelson Publishers, 1975.

FILMOGRAPHY

ABC News Productions. *Biography: Nelson Mandela, Journey to Freedom*. New York: A & E Productions, 1996.

Apted, Michael. *Amazing Grace*. Los Angeles: Bristol Bay Productions, 2006.

Attenborough, Richard. *Gandhi*. Los Angeles: Columbia Pictures, 1982.

August, Bille. *The Colour of Freedom*. London: Banana Films, 2007.

Bartel, Nick. *The Greeks Crucible of Civilization*, 3. New York: Public Broadcasting Society (PBS) and Atlantic Productions, 1999.

Birnbaum, Bernard. *McCarthy Years*. New York: CBS Inc., 1991.

Clooney, George. *Good Night and Good Luck*. Los Angeles: Warner Independent Pictures, 2005.

Eastwood, Clint. *Invictus*. Los Angeles: Warner Brothers, 2011.

Guggenheim, David. *He Named Me Malala*. Los Angeles: Fox Searchlight (and 15 other companies), 2015.

Hooper, Tom. *John Adams*. New York: HBO Films, 2008.

Roberts, Sam. *See It Now*. New York: CBS Inc., 1991.

Roos, Bram. "Queen Esther, Far Away and Long Ago," *The Mysteries of the Bible*. New York: A&E Productions and Multimedia Entertainment, 2007.

Vuillermet, Michel. *Marie Curie: Beyond the Myth*. Paris: Arte Frances and Les Films d'un Jour, 2011.

VisNews Productions. *Nelson Mandela: The History of a Struggle*. Princeton, NJ: Films for the Humanities (VisNews; Archives for the 20th

Century), 1990.

WEBLIOGRAPHY

Ahmed, Beenish. "The Making (and Breaking) of Malala Yousafzai." Washington, DC: Pulitzer Center on Crisis Reporting, December 30, 2012. Accessed June 4, 2014. http://pulitzercenter.org/reporting-pakistan-school-education-children-Taliban-economic-development-media-malala-yousafzhi.

Husain, Mishal. "Malala: The Girl Who Was Shot for Going to School."

London: BBC, Oct. 7, 2013. Accessed June 4, 2014.

http://www.bbb.co.uk/news/magazine-24379018.

The John F. Kennedy Library and Museum. "The World on the Brink: John F. Kennedy and the Cuban Missile Crisis." Accessed December 26, 2012. http://microsites.jfklibrary.org/cmc/oct28/

The John F. Kennedy Presidential Library and Museum. "The Cuban Missile Crisis." Accessed December 26, 2012. http://www.jfklibrary.org/JFK/JFK-in-History/Cuban-Missile-Crisis.aspx.

INTERVIEW

Frank Stanton. October 3, 2004. Boston: The Harvard Club.